LEARNING SKILLS
FOR COLLEGE
AND CAREER

LEARNING SKILLS
FOR COLLEGE
AND CAREER

SECOND EDITION

Paul Hettich
Barat College

Brooks/Cole Publishing Company

I(T)P® An International Thomson Publishing Company

Pacific Grove • Albany • Belmont • Bonn • Boston • Cincinnati • Detroit • Johannesburg • London
Madrid • Melbourne • Mexico City • New York • Paris • Singapore • Tokyo • Toronto • Washington

Sponsoring Editor: *Eileen Murphy*
Marketing Representative: *Tom Braden*
Marketing Team: *Jean Thompson, Romy Taormina, Deanne Brown*
Editorial Assistants: *Lisa Blanton, Susan Carlson*
Production Editor: *Karen Ralling*
Manuscript Editor: *Kathy Pruno*
Permissions Editor: *Cathleen C. Morrison*

Interior Design: *Scratchgravel Publishing Services*
Cover Design and Illustration: *Roy R. Neuhaus*
Art Editor: *Lisa Torri*
Illustrations: *Susan Horovitz Design*
Typesetting: *Scratchgravel Publishing Services*
Cover Printing: *Phoenix Color Corp.*
Printing and Binding: *R.R. Donnelley & Sons Company*

For more information, contact:

BROOKS/COLE PUBLISHING COMPANY
511 Forest Lodge Road
Pacific Grove, CA 93950
USA

International Thomson Publishing Europe
Berkshire House 168-173
High Holborn
London WC1V 7AA
England

Thomas Nelson Australia
102 Dodds Street
South Melbourne, 3205
Victoria, Australia

Nelson Canada
1120 Birchmount Road
Scarborough, Ontario
Canada M1K 5G4

International Thomson Editores
Seneca 53
Col. Polanco
11560 México, D. F., México

International Thomson Publishing GmbH
Königswinterer Strasse 418
53227 Bonn
Germany

International Thomson Publishing Asia
221 Henderson Road
#05-10 Henderson Building
Singapore 0315

International Thomson Publishing Japan
Hirakawacho Kyowa Building, 3F
2-2-1 Hirakawacho
Chiyoda-ku, Tokyo 102
Japan

Printed in the United States of America

10 9 8 7 6 5 4 3 2 1

Library of Congress Cataloging-in-Publication Data
Hettich, Paul I.
    Learning skills for college and career / Paul Hettich. — 2nd ed.
        p.   cm.
    Includes bibliographical references and index.
    ISBN 0-534-34878-5
    1. College student orientation—United States. 2. Study skills.
I. Title.
LB2343.32.H48   1998
378.1'98—dc21   97-17468
                                          CIP

To the students from PSY 100: Effective Study,
who encouraged me to write it;

to my family:
Mary Ann, Paul J., Phil, and Kristin;

and to my teachers
(you *did* have an impact!)

Contents

PART TWO
Essential Study Skills

PART THREE
Learning from Groups

Preface

College is one of life's most demanding investments; it requires thousands of dollars and several years of work. Yet, too many students begin unprepared. Even if they want to learn, they may not know *how* to learn. They lack critical skills and strategies for minimizing costs and maximizing the gains on their investment. *Learning Skills for College and Career* is a strategy for guaranteeing the student's investment of time and money. My objective is to show readers how to acquire the information, skills, and attitudes essential for learning *how* to learn—for surviving and thriving in college.

Learning Skills for College and Career was written for

- students of all ages, enrolled in college or college-bound

- students enrolled in liberal arts, transfer, and technical programs

- students enrolled in a study-skills or freshman orientation course

- individuals who want to read the material at their own pace without an instructor

The book makes one demand of its audience: the desire to become an *active* learner. Research has shown that learning is more permanent when we try to understand (rather than memorize) and apply (rather than passively store) the ideas and information we encounter. Long before there were educational researchers, the Dakota expressed this concept in similar words: "Tell me, and I'll listen. Show me, and I'll understand. Involve me, and I'll learn."

Organization

Learning Skills for College and Career is organized into three sections. Part One (Chapters 1 through 8) includes the "taking charge" concepts and skills needed to become a self-starting, active learner: motivation, goal setting, time and stress management, getting organized, and getting around. Part Two (Chapters 9 through 15) is devoted to traditional study skills such as listening, notetaking, reading, remembering, test taking, independent thinking, and public speaking. Although a few terms used in later chapters are defined earlier, the chapters in Parts One and Two can be read out of sequence with minimal loss of continuity.

Chapter 16, "A Primer on Interpersonal Skills," introduces Part Three and sets the stage conceptually for those insights and skills that students will develop in the group settings described in Chapters 17 and 18.

The chapters may be covered in sequence or separately. For example, sometimes I present time management (Chapter 5) immediately after the introductory chapter. Some teachers begin with Chapters 5, 9, 10, and 11 before returning to Chapters 2 through 4 and 6 through 8. Parts of chapters can be spliced to other chapters. For instance, I assign parts of Chapter 13 (test-taking skills) just before and after an exam. Some teachers begin a course with sections from Chapters 9 (listening), 10 (notetaking), and 11 (reading). This book has been written to be flexible, for you to use as you wish. Once again, we welcome your feedback.

Features

Learning Skills for College and Career is unique in emphasizing that study skills are also career and life-learning skills, not simply techniques for obtaining good grades. Most chapters end with a section that relates the topics discussed in the chapter to career and personal development. The book is also unique in its discussion and application of group concepts (Chapters 16 through 18) to the groups students belong to.

Student involvement is elicited in several ways, including

- Friendly Reminders at the beginning of each chapter that encourage students to practice techniques presented in previous chapters

- exercises incorporated into most chapters

- Action-Oriented Thought Starters at the end of each chapter

- examples based on actual student experiences (including my own)

- occasional words that require most readers to reach for their dictionaries

- journal writing and self-contracts, two feedback techniques introduced in Chapter 6

- a conceptual framework for each chapter topic rather than a do-it-yourself list of study-skill suggestions

- References and Recommended Readings for those who seek more information about a particular topic

- an informal style of writing, punctuated by humor, that engages the reader in conversation

- a glossary of key terms

A Personal Note

Although many ideas and recommendations in this book may be found in other texts, the attitudes and values expressed here reflect over 25 years of observing, teaching, advising, and listening to students. Several insights have been acquired from conversations with colleagues and alumni. Finally, as someone whose learning skills were learned through trial and error, I hope that this book lightens the burden of the reader's efforts.

Acknowledgments

Although my name appears on the cover, this book was a team effort. It could not have been completed without the assistance of several people whom I wish to acknowledge.

I am grateful to Brooks/Cole Publishing Company for supporting this second edition. I enjoyed being part of the team of professionals led by Eileen Murphy, Editor, who provided strong support, valuable suggestions, and perspective. I appreciate the talents and commitment of other Brooks/Cole staff and associates, including Tom Braden, Marketing Representative; Lisa Blanton and Susan Carlson, Editorial Assistants; Lisa Torri, Art Editor; Roy Neuhaus, Cover Designer; Cat Morrison, Permissions Editor; Karen Ralling, Production Editor; Anne and Greg Draus of Scratchgravel Publishing Services for interior design and typesetting; and Kathy Pruno, Manuscript Editor. For their diverse perspectives and thoughtful suggestions, I thank the reviewers: Gwen Crites, Northern Arizona University; Audrey Letteney Ennamorati, University of Southern Maine; Helen A. Jones, Houston Community College System; Maureen Reustle, Ocean County College; and Thomas K. Saville, Metropolitan State College of Denver.

I am grateful to six colleagues who committed their time, talents, and special knowledge as contributing authors: Pamela B. Adelman,

Jane S. Halonen, Camille Helkowski, Nancy F. Krippel, Merikay Kimball, and Sonia Powell. The Barat College Library staff who helped me obtain materials include Kathleen Lovelace, Joan Perlman, Ruth Prpich, and Zainab Saeed. Other colleagues who assisted in specific ways are Jerry Cleland, Maria Perez Laubhan, Robert Lemelin, Keith MacDonald, Yvonne Mitkos, Armand Policicchio, and Guadalupe Quintanilla. Finally, I thank the students who shared their time and experiences: Kerrie Boyd, Michelle Carreker, Annette Cronin, Betsy Gehlbach, Rita Gulrajani, Beverly Leigh, and Mark Tan.

Paul Hettich
May 13, 1997
Antioch, IL

PART ONE

Taking Charge

CHAPTER 1

A Guide to the Learning Skills

The *How* and *What* of Learning

What Lies Ahead: An Overview

Your Expectations

Action-Oriented Thought Starters

References and Recommended Readings

The only person who is educated is the person who has learned how to learn; the person who has learned how to adapt and change; the person who has realized that no knowledge is secure, that only the process of seeking knowledge gives a basis for security.

Adapted from Carl Rogers (1902–1987),
psychologist who created client-centered therapy

Would one be wise to hike through unfamiliar terrain without a map or a guide? Perhaps not. This chapter is your guide to the different themes and topics that you will encounter in the pages ahead. Knowing where you are going and what you will learn is part of the fun of getting there.

The *How* and *What* of Learning

Carl Rogers's words contain two ideas that are so important that they form the major theme of *Learning Skills for College and Career*. First, his belief that knowledge is not secure is supported by the explosion of information that has occurred during the past 30 years, especially in technical fields. Experts use the term *half-life* to describe the length of time after graduation in which the knowledge a person acquired during college becomes obsolete. For example, in some subspecialties of engineering, the half-life is approximately 5 years. This means that about 5 years after graduation approximately half of what the engineer learned has been replaced by new information. The length of a half-life depends on the field; a technical field will usually have a shorter half-life than one in the liberal arts. Further evidence that knowledge is not secure is painfully visible in the job market. Layoffs and downsizing force workers from all job levels to reevaluate what they know, retrain for other fields of employment, and adapt to a changing labor market.

Isn't it discouraging to spend so much time and money on an education and then have it become obsolete? Fortunately, knowledge and information are not the only *products* of your education, as the second part of Rogers's statement indicates. What counts is not only *what* you learn but also *how* you learn. The educated person is one who has learned *how* to learn, *how* to adapt to new conditions, and *how* to change when change becomes necessary.

For example, your success in dealing with many of life's most significant events—career, marriage, relocation, higher education, parenthood, retirement, divorce, death, personal tragedy, or triumph—is largely a matter of adapting to change, of knowing how to apply what you learned in similar circumstances. You have to learn to roll with the punches. Consequently, learning how to learn is an educational priority, even if it is not listed as a course in the school catalog.

According to educators Bette LaSere Erickson and Diane Weltner Strommer (1991), "The great challenge of the freshman year is learning to manage change, to adapt. While a student may say, 'I want to break out a little and expand my horizons,' adapting to something new virtually every day can be extremely stressful. In the space of a week, for instance, a new freshman may have to share a room for the first time in her life with one or two total strangers, write his first check, find her way around on an unfamiliar campus in an unfamiliar town, select his courses and prepare a schedule, learn a whole new set of policies, procedures, and rules, and decide whether to drink at the fraternity beer blast" (p. 31).

In addition, the new student must adapt to new ways of teaching, new classroom norms, and the necessity of allocating more time for study. Many students must adapt to the overwhelming "freedom" from supervision that becomes apparent during the first week of college. Clearly, the new student must learn how to learn in order to *survive*. When learning how to learn becomes a *priority,* the student learns to *thrive.*

Learning how to learn is the *process* of learning. Most courses teach you learning processes, but often the processes are hidden inside the content of the course. For instance, courses such as biology, economics, history, and humanities may appear to deal only with facts. However, good instructors are also teaching you how to think, analyze, and approach issues in that discipline. In courses such as logic, English rhetoric, and research methods, learning how to learn *is* the primary subject matter of the course.

In summary, what you learn in school contains two components: (1) the content, facts, and information (*products*), which someday may become obsolete; and (2) the learning-how-to-learn skills (*processes*) that provide the intellectual security needed to adapt and change.

What Lies Ahead: An Overview

Learning Skills for College and Career contains ideas that you will use throughout life even though they are presented in the context of college. In Chapters 2 through 8 of Part One, you'll learn the self-management skills that empower you to take charge of everyday behavior. Chapter 2, "Where Are You Going? Why? Motives for College," helps you examine your motives for attending college. Chapter 3, "Setting and Monitoring Goals," describes the steps for translating your motives into short-term, intermediate, and long-range goals. Together, motives and goals act as a compass that prevents you from drifting aimlessly in the sea of college life.

Today's pragmatic student wants to see a direct connection between course work and career. Sometimes the connection gets blurred in the abstractness or apparent irrelevance of an algebra, art history, or philosophy course. Chapter 4, "The Covert Curriculum: Connecting College to Career," proposes a unique perspective—that your routine activities help prepare you for the future.

Probably the most important "taking-charge" skill, especially for the freshman or inexperienced student, is time management. Chapter 5, "Take Charge of Your Time," describes four techniques that will enable you to reach your everyday goals and still have time for leisure. Chapter 6, "G.O.: Get Organized," argues that you improve learning and concentration by changing your physical environment and becoming more organized. The chapter also introduces you to journal writing and self-contracting as techniques for obtaining feedback about your activities.

Students new to the culture of college will discover in Chapter 7, "Getting Around," that a variety of resources exists on campus for improving their chances for success. College can be stressful, but Chapter 8, "Passing the Stress Test," will help you identify the things that push your stress buttons and the means for building resistance to stress. In summary, Chapters 2 through 8 present general concepts and recommendations that will enable you to take charge of your life.

Part Two covers the essential study skills you'll need to master. The first skill, covered in Chapter 9, is listening, the skill for which we have received the least training. Effective notetaking (Chapter 10) will enable you to summarize and integrate what you hear into a thoughtful, permanent record.

Chapter 11, "Getting Involved with Your Reading," explains the importance of being an active reader and presents strategies for increasing your reading comprehension. Remembering what we learn is a challenge for everyone. Chapter 12 summarizes the basic characteristics of memory and offers several suggestions and techniques for improving long-term memory. Like it or not, tests remain the most common method of evaluating what you have learned. Chapter 13, "Evaluation and Test-taking Tips," contains a rationale for evaluation along with concrete suggestions for improving test scores.

Chapter 14, "Becoming an Independent Thinker," describes the levels of thinking that we must master and emphasizes attitudes and skills needed to become an independent thinker. Chapter 15, "Improving Oral Communication Skills," will give you tips on speaking confidently and competently in front of a group.

Most study-skills textbooks give the impression that learning is an individual, solitary endeavor. In fact, one of the most powerful and permanent outcomes of higher education is your experience working in groups. Part Three proposes that the groups you belong to operate as informal *classrooms* for acquiring knowledge, attitudes, and skills in how to interact with others.

Chapter 16, "A Primer on Interpersonal Skills," introduces you to basic concepts and skills for communicating effectively in group settings. In Chapter 17, "Learning in Class and Study Groups," you will examine patterns of communication that operate in classrooms, reflect on your preferred mode of learning, and acquire techniques for studying effectively with peers in groups.

Chapter 18, "Learning from Campus Organizations, Residence Groups, the Workplace, and the College Climate," applies themes presented in Chapters 16 and 17 to four other groups that most students join. *Learning Skills for College and Career* closes with a brief epilogue. Think of it as a summary of key themes interwoven throughout the book, a snapshot of the journey you completed.

Your Expectations

Any journey should begin with expectations about the sights and activities you will experience. The previous section summarized the topics you can expect to encounter, but what should you expect from yourself?

1. Don't Expect a Miracle

After reading the description of what this book contains, some of you may have concluded that it is exactly what you've been looking for— *the answer* to *all* your questions! But don't forget that there are no easy solutions. This book won't do your learning for you. As writer H. L. Mencken once said, "There is always an easy solution to every human problem—neat, plausible, and wrong."

You will be introduced to the *basic* concepts of self-management, study skills, and learning from groups. If you sometimes feel overwhelmed by the information and suggestions offered, don't panic. You are not expected to use all the concepts and techniques each day in every course. It helps if you regard yourself as an apprentice in the "learning-to-learn" business. As you gradually gain experience with the tools of learning, you discover that your academic tasks often call for different skills and tools. With feedback from yourself and your teachers, you become more proficient with some tools than others. Finally, you realize that becoming a master student requires time, effort, the ability to tolerate frustration, and the ability to benefit from your mistakes. If you understand and apply the ideas presented in this book, you will gain the confidence and competence necessary for academic, career, and personal success. You should not expect miracles, but with patience and persistence you will probably achieve some significant victories.

2 . Expect to Work

The familiar saying "You get out of something what you put into it" definitely applies to learning skills for college and career. Be willing to *study* the ideas and *practice* regularly the advice offered if you truly wish to learn. Students who want to learn will be rewarded for their efforts. Students for whom W-O-R-K is an unpleasant four-letter word should realize that success in college and in life cannot occur without W-O-R-K. No one expects you to love the work required for your courses, although many students do. Yet the ability to persist, especially at tasks that do not excite you, is one of the most powerful skills that you can transfer to the marketplace. In 1996, Rear Admiral Marsha Evans was the highest ranking woman in the U.S. Navy. When asked to what she credited her success, she replied, "There's a popular saying, 'The harder I worked, the luckier I got.' Working hard overcomes a whole lot of other obstacles. You can have unbelievable intelligence, you can have connections, you can have opportunities fall out of the sky. But in the end, hard work is the true, enduring characteristic of successful people" (Picker, 1996). Similarly, when Abraham Lincoln was asked how to train to be a lawyer, he named the basic texts to study. But reading the texts was insufficient, for "work, work, work is the main thing" (Rhodehamel & Schwartz, 1993). *In short, view W-O-R-K not as an enemy but as your mentor on the road to success.*

Learning is not simply the passive receiving of information, even though earlier educational experiences may have created that impression. *To learn means to change your beliefs, attitudes, and behavior about the ideas you encounter.* And change requires W-O-R-K—your active involvement with the material you encounter. When students adopt a passive "tell-me-the-answer-so-I'll-remember-it-for-the-test" approach to education, hardly any learning occurs. What *does* occur is the waste of time and tuition money. Remember that education is *achieved* (active), *not received* (passive), and W-O-R-K is one of your best teachers. Box 1.1 describes a plan of action, a strategy that promotes active involvement with the material you encounter so that your W-O-R-K is efficient and meaningful.

Do you take primarily a Surface approach or a Deep approach to learning? Entwhistle discovered that students who used Deep strategies learned and remembered more than students who relied on Surface strategies. Changing from Surface to Deep strategies is a challenge, especially if you tend to memorize, learn passively, or ignore purpose, reflecting, and connecting.

Now is the time to begin developing Deep strategies for learning, and Action-Oriented Thought Starter 3 will help you begin. You can become a Deep learner if you work hard and accept gradual improvement. Some teachers and courses promote Surface strategies because some information must be memorized. However, the further you advance in your education the more likely your learning will be measured on your ability to use Deep strategies.

3. Expect to Succeed

As an apprentice learner who works hard and uses the learning tools covered in this book, you can expect to improve your study habits and grades. Some improvements may be seen immediately; others may not appear for months or after several terms. In time you will gain the confidence and competence that lead to academic, career, and personal success. Yes, basic learning skills are basic success skills.

Box 1.1

Surface versus Deep Strategies for Learning

Researcher Noel Entwistle (1987) observed that students tend to follow either a "Surface" or a "Deep" approach to their academic tasks. As you compare the two strategies for learning on the four dimensions below, determine which strategy you use more often.

Student's Role in the Learning Process

Surface Approach: Student accepts the material *passively* from teachers and texts.

Deep Approach: Student interacts with the material by taking notes, summarizing, asking questions, and reviewing. The student is proactive, not reactive, with the material being learned.

Student's Goal for Learning

Surface Approach: Student's primary goal is to *memorize* the material well enough to reproduce it on a test.

Deep Approach: Student's goals are to know and *understand* the material for use in the future, not simply to pass a test.

Student's Focus

Surface Approach: Student reads the information at hand and does not look for *patterns, guiding principles,* or *"the big picture."*

Deep Approach: Student reads the specific information *and* looks for *principles, patterns,* and the *"big picture."* Student searches for the *logic* behind an argument and evidence to support conclusions.

Connecting New to Prior Learning

Surface Approach: The student does not try to connect the material to prior course work or experiences.

Deep Approach: The student *tries* to connect new learning to prior learning, that is, to other courses and experiences. Sometimes, connections are made, sometimes not.

One way of becoming an active learner is to complete the Action-Oriented Thought Starters at the end of each chapter. These exercises are designed to get you to think and then act on issues presented in the chapter.

Action-Oriented Thought Starters

1. The major theme of this opening chapter is that learning *how* to learn (the process of learning) is as important as *what* one learns (the product of learning). To what extent does this theme agree with your experiences?

    a. Spend a few minutes reflecting on those two or three courses (high school or college) or nonacademic experiences (sports, hobbies, or clubs) from which you learned the most.

    b. Divide a sheet of paper into two vertical columns. For each of your favorite courses or nonacademic learning experiences, write down in the left column the most important *facts* and *information* you learned, and in the right column write the most important *skills* and *attitudes* you learned.

    c. Now, answer the following questions:

    - In general, did you acquire more facts and information or more skills and attitudes from those experiences?

    - In what ways are the two aspects of those experiences, facts/information and skills/attitudes, benefiting you now?

    - On the basis of what you wrote in each column, what can you conclude about Carl Rogers's concept of an educated person?

2. Chapter 1 has been a preview or survey of the remaining chapters. If you had skipped this chapter, you would not know what topics are covered in each of the following chapters or why the chapters are grouped into three parts. Previewing is an important study skill you can learn before you read the next chapter. Previewing is important because you gain a general understanding of (a) the author's purpose in writing the chapter, (b) major topics and subtopics, and (c) techniques used to present the material. Just as you test-drive a car before you purchase it, previewing fa-

miliarizes you with ideas that you will mentally "purchase." When you preview Chapter 2 and all subsequent chapters, use the following checklist.

_____ 1. Read the outline, title, and opening quotation. What could you learn from this chapter? Can you connect it with anything you have read or experienced before?

_____ 2. As you begin paging through the chapter slowly, read the paragraph headings and first sentence following each heading to get an overview of the material. Then ask yourself: "What does this [what you read] mean?" Asking questions about what you read starts the process of critical thinking.

_____ 3. Notice the techniques the author uses to promote your involvement in the material: checklists (complete them when you read the material), boxes (important topics that stand apart from the author's narrative), diagrams, clip-art in the margins, bulleted lists, numerical lists, and words printed in italics or boldface. These visuals are intended to help you identify, understand, and remember the material.

_____ 4. Read "Concluding Remarks," because that section brings together key ideas presented in the chapter.

_____ 5. The "Action-Oriented Thought Starters" section is designed to extend your involvement in the learning process. Why not complete one each chapter?

Previewing launches *you* into the chapter. Armed with a "big picture" view, the material is likely to be interesting. And you probably spent less than 10 minutes to perform the preview.

3. Taking a Deep approach to Chapter 1, see how well you can answer the items below.

a. What things did you do or could you have done to *interact* with the material when you read it? _____

b. To what extent was your major *goal* memorizing versus understanding the material? _____ What ideas do you understand best about the chapter? _____

_____

c. Page through Chapter 1 and then describe in your own words the overall *focus* or *"big picture"* of the chapter. _____

_____

d. Reflect on what you learned. In what ways can you *connect* what you learned with previous courses or past experiences?

_____

References and Recommended Readings

Entwhistle, N. (1987). A model of the teaching–learning process. In J. T. E. Richardson, M. W. Eysenck, and D. W. Piper (Eds.), *Research in education and cognitive psychology* (pp. 13–28). Milton Keynes, UK: Society for Research in Higher Education/Open University Press.

Erickson, B. L., & Strommer, D. W. (1991). *Teaching college freshmen,* San Francisco, CA: Jossey-Bass.

Picker, L. (1996, April 21). "The key to my success . . . ." *Chicago Tribune, Parade* section, pp. 4–5.

Rhodehamel, J. H., & Schwartz, T. F. (1993). *The Last Best Hope of Earth: Abraham Lincoln and the Promise of America.* San Marino, CA: Henry E. Huntington Library and Art Gallery.

CHAPTER 2

Where Are You Going? Why? Motives for College

Friendly Reminders

❏ Preview Chapter 2 using the Preview Checklist on page 11.

❏ Using Deep strategies improves retention. Reread Box 1.1 (page 9) to strengthen what you learn in Chapter 2.

"If you don't know the self you are looking for, how will you know when you've found it?"

Henry Holt (1840–1926),
American author and publisher

These words raise two crucial questions that students must begin to answer as soon as they start college: Why am I attending college? What are my goals?

If these questions make you a little nervous, don't worry. The fact that you are reading this page is a healthy sign of your interest in your motives and goals. Besides, you will probably change your answers, at least a little, each time you think about the questions. With so many career options available, many college students do not have clear goals when they graduate, much less begin college. Although it is not realistic to expect college freshmen and sophomores to know precisely where they are going and why, it is time for them to find preliminary answers to the questions asked above. The sooner you understand your motives and goals for attending college, the sooner you possess a compass that can guide your college experiences. This chapter will help you answer *why* you want to attend college. Chapter 3 describes a procedure for establishing and monitoring your goals.

Where Are You Going?

Recall Carl Rogers's belief that the educated person is one who has learned how to adapt and change. Change is such a continuous and powerful influence in life that you are likely to change considerably during one year of college. Psychoanalyst Erik Erikson observed that people go through eight stages of change and development in life. Each stage poses challenges and crises that must be met successfully before the individual can face the next stage effectively (Erikson, 1963).

The challenge for a student in Erikson's fifth stage, adolescence, is to become a good juggler. The adolescent must learn to develop a balanced and connected sense of identity (Who am I?) not only by responding to the intellectual, emotional, and physical changes being experienced, but also by adapting to the increasing demands of family and society. Eriksonian researcher James Marcia identified several *statuses* that adolescents can develop to resolve the identity crisis. Ideally, the adolescent wants to reach *identity achievement,* a status of maturity preceded by a period (usually years) of exploring, questioning, and clarifying one's values, career alternatives, and religious and political beliefs. For most college students, identity achievement is reached at the end of college and during the years immediately following college.

On the long, often difficult and twisting road to identity achievement, students may first be detoured (because of their prior experiences) to identity statuses that do not represent maturity. For example, many students experience a period of *identity diffusion.* Their sense of self seems incomplete, disjointed, or incoherent. They may experience disruptions in their sense of time (some events occur more quickly than they seem; other events take forever), feel excessively self-conscious, encounter problems in work- or achievement-related activities, and find it difficult to establish intimate relationships. Students in indentity diffusion do not have a good sense of who they are or why they are there. They are neither questioning nor exploring issues of identity, nor are they making commitments to specific beliefs or goals.

Many students may journey through the *foreclosure* status. "Foreclosed" students claim to be committed to certain beliefs and goals even though they have not carefully explored them. For example, a student's plans for entering a particular occupation may reflect childhood hopes or parental expectations, not a careful study of the occupation. By failing to examine other careers, the student has foreclosed on other vocational options, a decision that may cause regret later in life. In contrast, some students adopt a *negative identity* status and make choices that operate against early beliefs or parental expectations. Examples of negative identity include the daughter of a college professor who does not want to attend college, the son of a politically conservative family who joins liberal causes, or the member of a strongly religious family who stops attending religious services.

Most adolescents reach a *moratorium* status during which they question their beliefs and experiment with alternative ideas, yet do not commit to them. Erikson views the moratorium as a normal "time-out" from society's demands in which adolescents have freedom to interact with other people and explore ideas, attitudes, and beliefs that differ from their own (Steinberg, 1993). College can be an excellent, although expensive, opportunity to experience the diversity of beliefs and choices that are found in the formal and informal activities of a campus.

Many educators maintain that the essence of college is for students to be challenged by, and respond thoughtfully to, the diversity of ideas and people that energize the environment. Work settings can provide opportunities to explore new ideas and develop skills, but the options for intellectual, social, and emotional growth are, generally, not as broad as the college environment. Together, educational and work settings contribute immensely to one's identity achievement. Because much more can be said about identity (e.g., the complexity of ethnic and gender identity), students are encouraged to enroll in courses on life-span development or adolescent psychology. In the meantime, try to locate and direct your position on the road to identity achievement.

Adolescence does not last forever, but the challenges continue! According to Erikson, the major challenge facing young adults in the sixth stage of development is to establish intimate relationships. To the extent that individuals resolve identity issues successfully, they are likely to develop healthy relationships in a variety of settings. College is an excellent opportunity to explore and establish many kinds of relationships that have a major impact on the total college experience. Young adults are also challenged to establish personal and financial independence as well as career goals.

Look around campus and you will notice that many students are in their thirties or older, an age that reflects Erikson's mature adult (seventh) stage of development. The "returning student" seeks a college education for several reasons, which may include preparing for, maintaining, or advancing in a particular job; supporting a family; preparing for an advanced degree; enriching oneself; or completing an education that was interrupted years earlier. The returning middle adult student usually faces multiple responsibilities and challenges, including a challenge that Erikson calls *generativity*. Generativity is a general concern for guiding the next generation. Adults express their generativity when they share their values, beliefs, experiences, and expertise in various forms of support to family, friends, fellow students, employers, and community. College can be an opportunity to extend and expand generativity (McAdams, 1994).

Some students find Erikson's ideas on psychosocial development fascinating and plan to learn more. However, a few students may protest, "I thought I was going to learn study skills! How will Erikson's ideas teach me to manage time and pass tests?" Your impatience is noted, but your concern is legitimate! Research shows that the mastery of specific study skills (e.g., the material covered in Chapters 10 through 15) is *not* sufficient for becoming an effective student. In addition, you must also become more aware of yourself: your self-concept, your motives and goals, how you regulate (or don't regulate) your behavior effectively, the ways that stress influences your beliefs and actions, and how you reflect on your thinking. The remainder of this chapter addresses your motives for college. Motivation for college is the engine that drives your efforts. What do you know about that engine? Will it have the power to move you forward when the road gets rough (e.g., those tough or boring courses)? Or does the engine operate only on smooth, flat surfaces? To be a *committed* time manager, an *alert* listener, an *active* notetaker, a *persistent* reader, an *efficient* retriever of information, and an *effective* test taker, you should understand the values that motivate your learning behaviors. To understand your values and motives, it helps to know the identity status that you are currently experiencing. In short, what you learn from your teachers and others you encounter in college is influenced by the self you are and the self you are looking for. As Henry Holt asserted, "If you don't know the self you are looking for, how will you know when you've found it?"

Why Do You Want to Attend College?

Psychologists believe that our behavior is motivated. A *motive* is a process that energizes our behavior and directs it toward a particular goal. So, motives and goals go together. Numerous motives direct our everyday behavior. For example, we are born "pre-wired" to satisfy our physiological motives or needs for food, warmth, shelter, and safety. As we develop, we *learn* a variety of motives from our culture, such as the motives to achieve, to please others, and to gain power.

Identifying our motives for attending college is a complex process, one that should go well beyond such answers as "because I want to go," "because my family wants me to go," "so I can get ahead in life," or "because I want to make money." To identify your specific motives, you need to keep asking why.

- Why do I want to go?

- Why does my family want me to go?

- Why do I want to succeed in life?

- Why do I want to make money?

- Why this . . . ?
- Why that . . . ?

Whether your answers to all these questions enlighten or cloud your thinking, you will discover that there are many motives for attending college. Many of them overlap, and some motives reflect more maturity than others. At any rate, these are tough questions to answer. However, identifying, specifying, and monitoring your motives is another learning-how-to-learn skill that marks the educated person Carl Rogers described.

So, what *are* your motives?

To identify your current motives for attending college, mark all statements on the following checklist that describe why you want an education. The additional spaces at the bottom are for you to add other motives the checklist omitted. As you complete this and all subsequent exercises in the book, be completely honest with yourself. Do not mark answers just because they are socially desirable; no one but you will evaluate them. There are no right or wrong answers on this checklist, just *your* answers. You may want to complete this checklist periodically, so use a pencil or cover your first set of responses before subsequent use.

Motive Checklist

My motives for attending college are (check *all* statements that apply to you):

_____ 1. To prepare for a personally satisfying, well-paying career.

_____ 2. Because my family wants me to go.

_____ 3. To gain information and learn more about the world.

_____ 4. To have the some status as friends who attend college.

_____ 5. To meet the personal challenges that college provides.

_____ 6. To avoid getting a job at this time in my life.

_____ 7. To learn to know myself better and mature.

_____ 8. To gain respect from the people I know.

_____ 9. To develop my intellectual and social skills.

_____ 10. To meet other people.

____ 11. To satisfy my curiosity about things.

____ 12. To meet my future spouse.

____ 13. To learn how to plan and manage my future.

____ 14. I really don't know why I want to go to college.

____ Other motive: _____

____ Other motive: _____

____ Other motive: _____

Now count your responses to the even-numbered and odd-numbered items separately.

Did you check mainly the even-numbered or the odd-numbered items? Younger students often check some even-numbered items. Why? Because at this age you are accustomed to being supervised by parents and teachers, and attending college can be a form of compliance with their wishes. Also, younger students often experience pressure from peers to attend school. Some students fear, or are not interested in, working full-time after high school. As you mature, so should your motives.

Extrinsic and Intrinsic Motives for College

If you checked more even-numbered than odd-numbered items, you may be *extrinsically motivated*. That is, the major influences on the processes that energize your behavior (our definition of *motive*) for attending college originate outside of yourself. They come primarily from other people such as family or friends, or they lie in external conditions such as the job market.

If you checked more odd-numbered than even-numbered items, you may be *intrinsically motivated*. You want a college education because *you* want to learn more about yourself and the world, because *you* seek challenge and the chance to develop your abilities, and because *you* want a satisfying and well-paying career.

If you waited several years before beginning or finishing college, chances are that you are intrinsically motivated. Motivation is not your problem. Your concerns probably focus on establishing and managing your priorities and on trying to find enough time each day to accomplish everything that needs to be done.

Does being intrinsically motivated appeal to you? If you are not intrinsically motivated, should you try to be? Definitely! The process of maturing occurs gradually, including the change from primarily extrinsic motivation to primarily intrinsic motivation, from always complying with others' wishes to acting on your own initiative, and from dependence to independence. These dimensions operate on a continuum, not as "yes–no," "have–don't have" categories. On the continuum illustrated below, motivational maturity is represented by moving from the left side to the right.

Motivational Maturity Continuum

Growth proceeds
from: *to:*
Extrinsic _____ Intrinsic
What others want _____ What I want
Dependence _____ Independence
Less mature _____ More mature

This shift occurs at different times for each person, usually from adolescence through the mid-twenties. There are no pat answers or quick tricks for making the transition. But facing these issues honestly while applying the concepts contained in this book is a step in the right direction. As Box 2.1 indicates, each extreme can be a problem.

Your Locus of Control

An aspect of behavior related to motivation is *locus of control.* Psychologist Julian Rotter (1971) coined the term *locus of control* to refer to the extent to which people believe that their actions are determined primarily by their own behavior or by factors outside of their control. Persons who operate with an *internal* locus or source of control believe that, in most situations, their own actions determine what happens to them. They accept responsibility for the consequences of their behavior (Greenberg & Baron, 1993). For instance, their locus of control and their reasons for attending college originate primarily within themselves. They feel and act empowered to exert considerable (but not total) control over their destiny.

Persons who operate with an *external* locus of control believe that much of what happens to them is caused by forces and events beyond their control. Often, they hold fate or other people responsible for the good and bad things that happen to them. For example, people with an external locus of control might think: "It was mainly through good luck that I received the high grade on the exam, got promoted,

Box
2.1

Intrinsic Motivation:
Too Little and Too Much

Too Little

Becoming intrinsically motivated about college is difficult if you experienced educational failure or strongly disliked school. Failure generates low self-esteem, the feeling that you are not smart enough or can't succeed even when you try. Similarly, if school was boring, or if you were not mature at the time, you may approach college with psychological baggage that hinders the development of intrinsic motivation. If these remarks describe you, discuss your intrinsic motivation with a college counselor; most are experts on this subject. In addition, construct your environment to contribute to your success. For example, take courses that you like and can succeed in, but do not try to do too much. For now, be satisfied with C or B grades, favorable remarks from teachers and peers, and the personal insights that you gain from your learning. Intrinsic motivation increases when you see yourself succeeding at small tasks. And small successes usually lead to large successes.

Too Much

Although intrinsic motivation is an essential goal, avoid becoming a "super-intrinsic," someone who attempts to thrive totally on his or her own psychological and physical resources to control his or her destiny. No matter how intrinsically motivated we become, each of us is strongly influenced by external factors throughout life, including our relationships, jobs, abilities, and limitations. To the extent that we value our commitments to others, we may not obtain all the independence we want.

or won the award. I failed the exam because it was too hard. I lost the promotion because my boss is unfair. I didn't win the award because I don't have any contacts. I can't help it." Their locus of control exists beyond, not within, their control. Fortunately, we can shift our source of control from outside to inside ourselves as we learn to accept responsibility for our behavior.

Because many of life's events are not under our control, fate sometimes operates for and against us. Sometimes luck *is* a factor. However, students who operate from an internal locus of control know when to take credit for their accomplishments and when to assume responsibility for their mistakes. Research suggests that people with an internal locus of control recognize the direct link between their efforts and their performance, and between their performance and the rewards that follow. Such people are likely to be more successful and satisfied in their careers and more able to manage stress than individuals with an external locus of control (Greenberg & Baron, 1993).

"But What If I'm Not Motivated?"

Did you check item 14 on the motive checklist, "I really don't know why I want to go to college"? If you did, and it's true, pat yourself on the back for being perceptive and honest. The socially desirable response was to not mark that statement. Perhaps one of the following situations describes you.

- You have little or no motivation to be in college, at least not at this time in your life.

- You may feel somewhat motivated, but you are unclear or confused about your motives and goals.

- You may want to be motivated but aren't.

If any of these statements describes you, don't feel alone and don't feel guilty. Many college students feel the same way. However, if you do not have some intrinsic reasons for pursuing an education, or if your motives are vague or primarily extrinsic, your first term at college is likely to be more difficult than if you were intrinsically motivated. Why? Chances are that you will encounter at least one of these challenges when you begin college.

- It is your first time living away from home. You are responsible for your personal needs and belongings. You no longer experience the daily support of your parents. You're on your own.

- As a commuter student, you get frustrated by transportation problems, bad weather, the time spent commuting, living with your family, and feeling left out of campus activities.

- You live in a residence hall or in other group living arrangements, so you share a room with a stranger.

- You are a returning student whose family or job responsibilities leave little time for studying and no time for yourself. In addition, you lack confidence in your ability to succeed.

- As a recent high school graduate, you discover that you have more unstructured and unsupervised time in college than you ever experienced before.

- You have to work to remain in college. Your job pays a low salary, has inconvenient hours, or requires considerable travel time (or all of the above).

- Courses are more demanding, teachers less directive, and good grades more difficult to achieve than they were in high school.

- The size of your college may overwhelm you, especially if it is a large state university and you graduated from a small high school.

- You have personal issues that consume a lot of your time and emotional energy.

It may be the impossible roommate, the demanding course, the feeling of being overwhelmed, the fear of insufficient finances, or *all* of these obstacles and more that confront and intimidate you during your first term of college. If you must face such obstacles, who would you rather be?

1. the unmotivated or confused student who does not know why she is there

2. the extrinsically motivated student who is in college mainly to please family and friends

3. the intrinsically motivated student with a "take-charge" attitude who is there to learn, to develop intellectually, and to prepare for a particular career

If you chose 3, you are correct!

Intrinsically motivated, you have a much better chance of successfully dealing with the unruly roommate, the Ancient-History professor (or ancient History professor!), the huge campus, and the frustrations at home. The difficult classes, the low-paying job, and the hassle of daily living are manageable when you operate under your own power (intrinsic motives), not someone else's power (extrinsic motives), or no power at all (no motivation). Intrinsic motivation generates confidence and competence, unbeatable resources for learning how to survive and thrive in college. Intrinsic motivation *empowers* you. Extrinsic motivation can *enslave* you.

Review Your Options

For some students, motivation is not a problem. For others, the ideas discussed above may lead to anxiety. The goal of this book is to make you think, not worry. Don't panic. Thousands of students in college are unsure of their motives, and they manage to survive and develop intrinsic motivation. If you are among those who wonder whether you should be in college, carefully examine the options that are open to you.

❏ 1. Get a Job Now. Attend College Later.

If you're uncertain about college, discuss your concerns and options with family, teachers, counselors, and others whom you respect. Examine the pros and cons of each option. Carefully consider others' opinions. Actively analyze your motives for attending or not attending college at this time in your life. Many people succeed in life without a college education. However, studies show that many individuals who do not pursue a college degree lose future educational advantages, do not earn as much, and find it more difficult to advance in their occupations. According to a 1995 report from the U.S. Department of Labor that studied 1992 college graduates, "most college graduates were employed in college-level jobs, earned substantially more than the average of all workers, and experienced lower than average unemployment rates. This provides clear evidence that, on average, 'college pays'" (Hecker, 1995). The differences in pay between workers with a high school degree and those with college education can translate into hundreds of thousands of dollars in a lifetime. However, the report also indicates that having a college degree does not guarantee either a high-paying or a college-level job. Still, jobs requiring an associate's degree or higher are projected to grow substantially in the next decade.

Nowadays, thousands of men and women first start college in their twenties, thirties, or forties, after they've matured and experienced life. Most are intrinsically motivated; they know where they're going. However, college places special demands on returning adult students, such as managing jobs and family *and* finding the time and money to attend college. Ultimately, *you* must evaluate the advantages and disadvantages of working now and attending college later.

❏ 2. Try College Now. "Stop Out" if It Doesn't Work.

Each year thousands of students try college for a semester or two and then stop out (leave with the intention of returning sometime) because of insufficient funds, poor grades, low motivation, or personal circumstances. They work for a year or two, mature, then return to college. The stop-out option has certain advantages:

- It can prevent a bad first college experience and the loss of self-confidence that accompanies failure.

- It may save money in the short run.

- It provides a break from formal education.

- It lets you experience the world of work (although the wages may be low and the work unchallenging).

- It can provide the time for your interests to mature.

But stopping out has its drawbacks:

- You may become trapped into spending too much of your earnings on attractive consumer goods purchased on credit, leaving little savings for tuition.

- You may be lulled into believing that you can advance in your job without additional education.

- You may never return to college.

If you think that college is too expensive, remember the words of former Harvard president Derek Bok: "If you think education is expensive—try ignorance."

❏ 3. Attend College Full-time and Grow as You Go.

The journey from extrinsic to intrinsic motivation, from dependence to independence, can follow many roads. You may get a job immediately after high school and experience the benefits and drawbacks mentioned above. Or you can explore the potentially stimulating but formidable (to the extrinsically motivated or unmotivated student) terrain of college. On either road you can discover yourself, have fun, and achieve the maturity you seek. However, the journey through college offers a unique opportunity for growth that the marketplace does not provide. College offers self-discovery through course work, relationships, student activities, and cultural events in a setting *designed* to foster your intellectual, psychological, and social growth.

If you are neither motivated in your courses nor willing to stop out of college, inquire at your campus Career Planning/Placement or Student Activities offices about the following options.

- paid or unpaid internships that afford an opportunity to learn by doing

- volunteer work or service learning in educational or social service settings

- cooperative education programs, available in some academic majors, in which students alternate between course work and job settings

These activities can vary considerably in the opportunities they offer for growth and the time required to participate. As concrete, hands-on learning experiences, they can provide the connections, meaning, and motivation needed to succeed in the classroom. Finding meaning in your sociology, biology, or history courses may not be so difficult after you perform a few hours of community service in a homeless shelter, recycling center, or museum.

❏ 4. Attend College Part-time *and* Work (College = Work + Course Work).

If the first three options leave you confused, consider a fourth: working and attending college, either full- or part-time. For students who cannot afford college full-time, working is the only option. The advantages of work plus course work are:

- You can test your academic interests and abilities without a costly full-time commitment.

- You can test your job skills and career interests before choosing an academic major.

- Under some circumstances you may be able to integrate the two activities.

- You can acquire skills on a job that can strenghten your study skills

For example, a woman named Carmen accepted a clerical job immediately after high school to earn her living. The work stimulated her interest in office management to the point where she enrolled in a business course at a community college. Her course work and experiences became so intertwined that she continued her studies and completed her associate's degree four years later. In the interim Carmen received two promotions for her outstanding work. She transferred to a four-year college, where she completed her business degree six years later while working full-time. She was justifiably proud of her accomplishments.

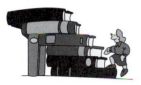

Carmen obtained her bachelor's degree while working full-time, but she needed ten years to complete her education. Ten years will seem too long for many people who seek a four-year degree. Some students work part-time and attend college part-time for several years. Then they borrow money to go full-time and "get it over with."

Contained in the four options identified above are other issues that influence a decision to attend or remain in school. Should you attend a community college or a four-year institution? Should you commute or become a resident student? Each choice can have serious implications for finances, work, and relationships. Students' situations, backgrounds, and goals are so complex that only a few examples were sketched above. However, carefully examine these and other options by talking with family, friends, counselors, and teachers. Search the shelves of bookstores and libraries for materials about college and careers. Remember that changing your mind is all right when new information warrants it, but don't get trapped by the confusion of endless, ever-changing information.

Concluding Remarks

This chapter has focused on your motivation to attend college, but motivation to *remain* in college is also important. After the novelty of college fades, you may face stressful situations that drain energy, even if you are an intrinsically motivated student: discomfort with the new environment or new relationships, outside commitments, finances, work, difficult or unchallenging courses, peer pressure, routine, and personal problems. There are no quick fixes. However, a relentless determination to work toward your goals one day at a time and use the ideas and activities recommended in this book will help *sustain* your motivation. What does it take to *sustain* your motivation? Box 2.2 provides one person's answer.

Box 2.2

Three Steps to Success: You Want, You Plan, You Persist

Having recently moved to the United States from Mexico, Guadalupe Quintanilla spoke only Spanish. However, the IQ test that she was required to complete prior to entering first grade was administered in English. Predictably, the test scores were so low that she was classified as mentally challenged. As there were no classes for the mentally challenged at her school, she was placed in first grade with English-speaking students. Those most difficult days of her life were filled with sadness, loneliness, confusion, and desperation because she could not understand anything going on. Still, she reported to school faithfully until an incident with her teacher and principal caused her to drop out of the first grade.

She lived with her grandmother and she learned to cook, sew, keep house, and read and write in Spanish. She married young and had three children, who entered a school system where children were placed in tracks according to their ability to learn. Because of her children's lack of familiarity with English, they were placed in a track for slow learners called "yellow birds." Guadalupe knew that her children were bright. She was determined to learn English and teach it to her children so that they would not endure the frustration she experienced. Because she lacked a high school diploma, she was rejected from several schools where English was taught. But through her remarkable *persistence,* the first-grade dropout finally gained entry to an English course taught in a community college.

In her own words, Guadalupe describes her first semester in college as ". . . a tremendous ordeal. I was very frightened and confused, but I followed instructions and studied and studied and studied. After classes I would get home, clean, wash, cook, feed my family, help my children with their school work, put them to bed, and then study until almost morning. At the end of the first semester I had a wonderful revelation. I could learn! So I enrolled for subsequent semesters and then there was no stopping me. After I earned my associate of Arts degree in my home-

If you accept responsibility for the things that you can control in your life while developing learning skills for college and career, you dramatically increase your chances for personal and professional success. Some researchers call this kind of behavior *positive self-control* (McCombs, 1982).

The motive checklist at the beginning of this chapter is designed to trigger your thinking. Try to complete it two or three times each

---

town, I learned to drive in order to pursue my bachelor's [degree] at a town 140 miles away. We then moved to a bigger city to pursue my master's and my doctorate.

"It was a long and difficult journey but definitely worth it. I learned a lot during that journey. I learned that success is personal and that we must have our own definition of it in order to accomplish it. I realized that my formula to success can be described in three steps: you want, you plan, and you persist. The challenge in step one is to know the difference between wanting and wishing. I wanted to learn to help my children in school; wishing would not have been enough. Step two, planning or goal setting, simply means: Where do you want to go with your life? If you do not know, you are never going to get there. Step three, persistence, is in my opinion the best antidote to failure. One has not failed until one stops trying.

"I also realized during my journey that I am, as the poet Amado Nervo said, 'the architect of my own destiny.' I also learned two very important lessons: one, that I can do anything that I really want to do; two, that it is a privilege to have the opportunity to learn. Furthermore, I realized that it is okay to have limitations, e.g., I speak with an accent, but that we must not turn those limitations into excuses.

"As for my three 'yellow birds,' two are attorneys, one is a medical doctor; all three graduated with honors from their respective institutions, and I am very proud of them! When somebody calls my house and asks for Dr. Q, 'Which one?' is my reply. 'There are four of us.'"

These remarks were abstracted from "Almost a Failure," a keynote address by Dr. Guadalupe Quintanilla to the National Association of Developmental Education, February 29, 1996, in Little Rock, Arkansas. Dr. Quintanilla is Assistant Vice-President for Academic Affairs at the University of Houston. She has received numerous honors, including several presidential nominations and appointments. See Blane (1984) and Wade (1995) in References and Recommended Readings at the end of this chapter for publications about her life and accomplishments.

year. It is a useful tool for remaining in touch with your thoughts and feelings about your future. If you monitor your motives regularly, you will, as Henry Holt suggests, know when you have found the self that you are searching for.

To summarize, motivation is one of the toughest issues to face during your first year of college. Ideally, when you begin, you should be more intrinsically than extrinsically motivated. The absence of intrinsic motivation should not necessarily deny or delay your education, though it will make major obstacles more difficult to overcome. One tool that helps you focus your motives is goal setting, the subject of Chapter 3.

Action-Oriented Thought Starters

1. During the next several weeks, try to interview at least two people who fit the following categories:

   a. entered college immediately after high school and completed an associate's or bachelor's degree

   b. entered college immediately after high school but withdrew before completing a degree

   c. entered college immediately after high school, withdrew, then returned years later to complete a degree or program

   d. did not begin college until after age 25

   e. works full-time, attends college part-time (or vice versa)

   f. never attended college or vocational school

   Some of these people (except f) may be sitting next to you in class, so inquire. When you conduct your interviews ask people about the importance of their motivation for education at various stages of life. What advice does each person offer? What insights have you gained from this exercise?

   Note: If you completed this thought starter, you engaged in another learning-how-to-learn skill—using other people as resources. By interviewing others about their motivation for college, you acquired useful information you did not have before the interviews. Knowing how to identify and benefit from the expertise of others is an important lifelong skill.

2. Does Julian Rotter's concept of locus of control interest you? The following items are adapted from questions contained in Rotter's I–E (Internal–External) scale.* Check the item in each horizontal pair that best describes you.

I more strongly believe that:	or
Promotions are earned largely through hard work and persistence.	Making a lot of money is largely a matter of getting the right breaks.
In my experience I have noticed that there is usually a direct connection between how hard I study and the grades I get.	Many times the reactions of teachers seem haphazard to me.
In our society a person's future earning power is dependent upon his or her ability.	Getting promoted is really a matter of being a little luckier than the next guy.
Getting along with people is a skill that must be practiced.	It is almost impossible to figure out how to please some people.

The choices in the left column reflect a stronger tendency toward internal control, whereas those on the right reflect external control. These statements may cause you to think about your motives, behaviors, and attitudes in other aspects of your life.

3. Reread Box 2.2. Dr. Guadalupe Quintanilla's experiences have much to teach us about life.

   a. What specific events in her life are examples of her three steps to success (wanting, planning, persisting)?

   b. What can you apply from her experiences to your life?

   c. Many people have overcome serious obstacles of one type or another on their road to success. Think of one or two persons and compare their experiences with Guadalupe Quintanilla's.

   d. The Mexican poet Amado Nervo remarked in his poem "At Peace" that ". . . I realize at the end of this long journey that I have been the architect of my own destiny" (1962, p. 1732). What does this statement mean to you? How do Nervo's thoughts relate to locus of control?

*Rotter, 1971.

References and Recommended Readings

Blane, J. P. (1984, June). The triumph of Guadalupe Quintanilla. *Reader's Digest,* 77–89.

Erikson, E. H. (1963). *Childhood and society* (2nd ed.). New York: Norton.

Greenberg, J., and Baron, R. A. (1993). *Behavior in organizations* (4th ed.). Boston: Allyn & Bacon.

Hecker, D. E. (1995, February). Further analyses of the labor market for college graduates. *Monthly Labor Review,* 39–41.

McAdams, D. P.(1994). *The person: An introduction to personality psychology* (2nd ed.). New York: Harcourt Brace.

McCombs, B. L. (1982). Learner satisfaction, motivation and performance: Capitalizing on strategies for positive self-control. *NSPI Journal, 21*(4), 3–6.

Nervo, A. (1962). *Obras completas* (Tomo II). Madrid: Aguilar.

Rotter, J. B. (1971). External control and internal control. *Psychology Today, 5*(1), 37–42.

Steinberg, L. (1993). *Adolescence* (3rd ed.). New York: McGraw Hill

Wade, M. D. (1995). *Guadalupe Quintanilla: Leader of the Hispanic Community.* Springfield, N.J.: Enslow Publishers.

Setting and Monitoring Goals

Principles of Goal Setting

1. State Specific Goals

2. Set Difficult but Realistic Goals

3. Obtain Feedback about Your Goals

Preparing Your Goals Statement:
Goal Setting for Fun and Future

Concluding Remarks

Action-Oriented Thought Starters

References and Recommended Readings

Friendly Reminders

❏ Preview Chapter 3 using the Preview Checklist on page 11.

❏ Use the Deep strategies of learning on page 9 to improve retention.

❏ Check your motivation to learn this material. Is it primarily intrinsic or extrinsic?

"The person who makes a success of living is the one who sees his goal steadily and aims for it unswervingly."

Cecil B. DeMille (1881–1959),
American film producer and director

Lou Holtz, the renowned football coach, was once fired from an assistant coaching position at age 28. His wife was eight months' pregnant, he had little money saved, and he was feeling down. At a crossroads in his life, he wrote a list of 107 goals for himself. By 1996 he had achieved approximately 90 of his goals, including eating at the White House, rafting the Snake River, seeing the Pope, recording a hole-in-one, landing on an aircraft carrier, and learning magic tricks. Holtz advises, "Experience those things. Don't be a spectator in life, be a participant" (Sherman, 1988).

Do you recall Henry Holt's quotation in Chapter 2 about the importance of knowing the self you are looking for? At a low point in his life, Lou Holtz searched for the self he wanted to become. By 1996 he had accomplished over 80% of the 107 goals on his list, including many that were exotic and difficult to achieve.

Goals are the results or milestones that a motivated person strives to reach. Goal setting is the *process* of identifying specific milestones and the means of reaching them. It is a valuable technique for planning and it can be applied to many aspects of life. Families set goals for major household purchases and vacations. Some corporations set one-, five-, and ten-year goals to accomplish their objectives. Successful college students establish goals and periodically review them.

Principles of Goal Setting

Jerald Greenberg and Robert Baron (1995) have identified three principles for successful goal setting in business and industry:

- State specific goals.
- State difficult but acceptable (realistic) goals.
- Provide feedback about goals.

You can apply these principles to your academic and personal objectives and, simultaneously, develop an important lifelong learning-how-to-learn skill.

1. State Specific Goals

If your academic objective is "to work *harder* this semester," you are not being specific. What do you mean "to work harder"? Study and additional hour each day? Study at least five hours on weekends? Take notes in class? Avoid studying with the television on? All of the above? If your academic objective is "to do *better* this semester," you are not being specific. What do you mean "to do better"? To go from a C to an A, or from a C to a C+? "Better" in what subjects? All of them? Your easiest subject? How do you know when you are doing better? Will you accept your own opinion or an objective measure such as a test or course grade? In short, specific goals are *measurable* goals.

You are being specific when you say "My goal is to earn at least one A, at least three Bs, and no more than one C this semester." But if you reviewed your strengths, limitations, and environmental constraints (for example, job and family commitments), you could be more specific: "I'll work for an A– in English, Bs in Math, Economics, and Humanities, and at least a C in Physics." That goal statement is specific and measurable; it leaves no opportunity for self-deception.

A goal should not only be measurable, but also express a specific *action* you plan to take, such as *study* five hours on weekends, *seek tutoring* three hours a week for math, *complete the optional assignments* to earn a B, *reduce* television viewing by one hour a day, and *practice* two new study skills each week. In short, a specific goal should be stated as a measurable action.

You can also establish goals for your personal and social activities:

- exercising a half hour three times a week

- writing a friend or relative each week

- saying thanks when someone shows consideration

- attending at least one concert, lecture, or cultural event during the term

- attending at least one workshop sponsored by the college health center

- starting to look for a summer job in February instead of May

2. Set Difficult but Realistic Goals

Students find it easier to set specific goals than *realistic* goals, the second step in the goal-setting process. Realistic goals are challenging objectives that are attainable. If your goal is to study six hours on weekends, a weekend job and family responsibilities could create a major conflict. Perhaps three or four hours is a more realistic goal. If your goal is to receive a C in English when you normally perform at the B level, your goal is unrealistically low. The challenge is minimal, and there is little or no payoff for performing below your ability. Weak goals promote laziness and apathy.

Box 3.1

Reaching Goals Gradually, Realistically, Actively

Unrealistically high goals can switch you from the fast track to the self-destruct track as they did to a student named Ken his first semester of college. Ken dreamed of becoming a clinical psychologist, a profession that requires high grades for entry into graduate school. In spite of his borderline reading and writing skills, Ken insisted on making A his goal for his first psychology course. He also set high goals in his other courses.

Although he appeared strongly motivated, Ken behaved as if *wanting* the goal was sufficient for reaching it. He "blew off" the Ds he received on early tests, refused to seek help from teachers and tutors, and remained convinced that he would still get his A. Ken received a D in the course, performed poorly in other courses, and was dismissed after his second semester.

Ken's case exemplifies two common mistakes made in setting goals. First, his goal of receiving an A in a difficult course was unrealistically high, given his borderline skills. Ken should have been content with a C or a B his first semester in college and should have sought help to improve his basic skills. Second, Ken thought that *wanting* and *talking about* his goals were the same as *reaching* them. It takes more than desire and feeling motivated to reach goals.

As race car driver Mario Andretti remarked, "Desire is the key to motivation, but it's the determination and commitment to an unrelenting pursuit of your goal—a commitment to excellence—that will enable you to attain the success you seek."

Conversely, expecting an A if your best efforts in the past yielded a B– is unrealistic. Instead, make B or B+ your new goal (even if you read *Learning Skills for College and Career* from cover to cover in the interim!). If you set goals unrealistically high, chances are you will not achieve them. Failure may produce frustration, guilt, anxiety, and low self-esteem. These are psychologically deadening ingredients that can start a self-perpetuating, self-destructive cycle of behavior.

Finally, failure to reach unrealistically high goals can tempt you to attribute your failures to external forces, a trap that promotes extrinsic motivation. For instance, if your expectation of an A is unrealistic, you might blame a B grade on unfair tests, a rigid teacher, or the D.A.R. (Darn Average Raiser) sitting next to you.

❏ How to Determine What Is Realistic

How can you tell whether your goal is realistic? Follow these steps:

1. Evaluate your past accomplishments and failures in relation to the goal. You should not expect an A in English if you had to work hard to receive C+ in earlier courses. If a course was difficult for you in high school, chances are that it will be difficult for you in college. If you achieved excellent history grades in high school, you may be able to earn similar grades in college history courses, allowing for stronger competition and more difficult assignments. Although past experience is not always an accurate predictor (maturity, teachers, and other factors may have contributed to earlier experiences), it is an important factor to consider.

2. Advance one step at a time. Create many small steps for your most difficult courses, fewer and larger steps for your easier courses. If English is your toughest subject, perhaps you should be content to move from a C+ to a B– or B, rather than from a C+ to a B+. Consider enrolling in prerequisite courses or seek tutoring to strengthen skills needed for a particular course.

As an example of the one-step-at-a-time principle, several academic majors require a course in statistics. Many students are apprehensive about statistics because of past negative experiences in math or stories they hear about course demands. They can reduce their fears first by determining their level of proficiency in mathematics, then enrolling in courses that build skills needed for statistics. For some, but not all, students, that may mean beginning at the bottom, enrolling in a fundamental math course, and being content with a grade of C. The next step is to complete the next higher prerequisite course and work toward a slightly higher grade. Each prerequisite course gradually builds confidence and competence that, along with a positive mental attitude and hard work, enables students to succeed in a course that they perceived as a major obstacle to completing a major. Achieving a difficult goal requires awareness of and commitment to mastering each of its component steps. Athletes do not win Olympic medals by running one or two races.

3. Create an action plan to meet your needs. If you want to improve from a C+ to a B in English, determine *how* you will do it. How much more study time will you allocate to English? Will you seek tutorial assistance to improve your basic skills? What activity do you have to give up to earn the B? Without a realistic action plan for improving your grade, you are like Ken in Box 3.1, who thought that *wanting* the goal was sufficient for achieving it. The often-heard resolution, "I'm turning a new page in my life this semester," means nothing unless it is accompanied by hard work and a plan that shows exactly how you will turn the page. Practicing the recommendations described in this book can be part of your action plan. Box 3.2 illustrates some environmental constraints that should cause students to carefully evaluate their academic goals.

3. Obtain Feedback about Your Goals

Can you imagine becoming a good skier or an accomplished musician without receiving feedback about your performance? How would you feel about spending four months on a new job or completing a college course without an evaluation? Greenberg and Baron's third principle of goal setting is derived from research that demonstrates that goal attainment is made easier by systematic feedback. In other words, practice can make perfect *if* you get feedback. In the next section you will complete a goal-setting exercise designed to identify and provide feedback about your goals. Two techniques of obtaining feedback, journal writing and self-contracts, will be described in Chapter 6, "G.O.: Get Organized."

Obtaining feedback is not simply a technique. It is an attitude, an orientation that is crucial for growth and development. The feedback attitude helps you ask yourself, "How am I doing?" or "What can I do to improve?" The feedback attitude generates self-awareness of who you are as you interact with other people and with your environment. Self-awareness and motivation are prerequisites for change and the attainment of goals.

Goals and Their Constraints

Box 3.2

When outside constraints and commitments conflict with your academic goals, you must face the reality of your situation and examine your priorities. For example, a student named Dorothy was the class valedictorian in nursing school. When she returned years later to complete her bachelor's degree, she expected to continue her A average. Consequently, she was angered and frustrated with the C she received on her first test.

When she discussed the grade with her instructor, she found the differences between her nursing school experience and her current situation difficult to accept. As a returning student she was 20 years older, married, the mother of three active children, and a supervisor in a stressful full-time position. Furthermore she was enrolled in two required courses, neither of which she liked.

Was it realistic for Dorothy to expect an A on her first test given these constraints? Perhaps not. Dorothy thought about her roles as supervisor, wife, and mother and weighed the impact that working for an A would have on her health and her commitments. She decided to be content to work at the B level for the rest of the course. Students who add high academic expectations to an already stressful life often place themselves in a rat race. When you find yourself in a rat race remember the words of comedienne Lily Tomlin: "The trouble with the rat race is that even if you win, you're still a rat."

Preparing Your Goals Statement: Goal Setting for Fun and Future

How can you establish objectives for yourself using the three principles of goal setting? This exercise demonstrates a five-step procedure for developing your goals and connecting them to potential career paths. You may feel apprehensive about this exercise if you have never completed a goals statement, but chances are you will be pleased with the outcome. Allow yourself at least a half hour to respond thoughtfully to the items below.

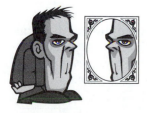

❑ Step 1. Reflect on Your Past Experiences

You should begin your goals statement with the process of reflection, so that your past experiences help you perform an honest and realistic appraisal of your beliefs and goals. Use a sheet of paper or the space below to record your responses.

Now spend a few minutes reflecting and taking notes on the following dimensions of your life. Be honest with yourself. No one but you can evaluate what you write.

- Your strengths—those skills, attitudes, personal characteristics, interests, and past achievements that give you a sense of identity, confidence, competence, and self-esteem

  _____

  _____

  _____

- Your limitations—those deficiencies, attitudes, and characteristics as well as external conditions that have been obstacles to your achievement

  _____

  _____

  _____

- Your role models—those characteristics of persons whom you most admire and seek to imitate

  _____

  _____

  _____

- Your core values—those central values (e.g., concern for others' welfare, honesty, hard work), beliefs, and attitudes that you regard as essential to your identity (self-concept) and functioning, now and in the future

  _____

  _____

  _____

The next three steps in your goals statement require you to begin with the future and work back to the present. Don't worry about today or this week because the time-management techniques presented in Chapter 5 will show you how to achieve your daily goals.

❏ Step 2. Identify Your Long-range Goals

Look five to ten years into the future. Ten years may seem too far to imagine, but if you are an action-oriented person, ten years passes quickly. What type of work do you want to be doing in five to ten years? Dream a little. If you are aware of your strengths, limitations, values, and role models, chances are that you will dream realistically. Ensure that the goals you formulate are yours, not someone else's. Recall from Chapter 2 that students in the *foreclosure* status of identity have quickly committed themselves to goals they have not carefully examined. If you have never actively created *your* goals, now is a good time to begin. Yes, it's all right to change them.

Long-range goals are realistic objectives that you work to achieve in a five- to ten-year period. For example, in ten years you may want to be a certified public accountant and the department head in a large accounting firm. To accomplish this objective you must have sufficient training and considerable experience as well as supervisory potential. A CPA needs a four-year college degree in accounting plus other requirements.

Perhaps your goal in five to ten years is to have completed a successful tour in the Peace Corps and subsequently serve in an administrative position. You must contact a Peace Corps representative, discuss the educational and personal criteria for acceptance, and evaluate the options that simultaneously interest you and match the needs of the Peace Corps.

If you have *no* idea what you want to be doing in five to ten years, choose something that you have always wanted to do and continue to complete the second and third steps of this goal-setting exercise. The exercise may prompt you to visit your college career counselor, a good idea even for first-semester freshmen.

In addition to a specific career goal, include long-range personal goals such as marriage, home ownership, travel, or community involvement. Write your long-range career and personal goals below or on a sheet of paper.

_____

_____

_____

_____

_____

Box 3.3

Is Survival a Goal?

Some of you may have read the section on goal setting and thought: "That's all fine and good for students who have time to think about the future. But I don't! I just want to survive!"

Survival *is* a realistic goal for many college students, especially those with tremendous responsibilities and limited financial resources. That includes single parents, full-time students working full-time jobs, parent students with full-time jobs, anyone who is barely subsisting on a limited income, persons with profound personal problems, students on terminal academic probation, anyone with very low self-esteem, and others who are trying to get an education while "barely hanging in there."

Summarizing key points from Christina Maslach's 1982 book *Burnout: The Cost of Caring,* Joannis Flatley and Cindy Turner (1991) believe that burnout is a problem for many college students. Burnout includes physical and emotional exhaustion, depleted energy, depersonalization, feelings of low personal accomplishment, and displaced anger. Burnout, which can strike people in any occupation, occurs when there are too many demands and too little time to accomplish them, when too much is asked of a person and too little is returned. It is a response to ongoing stress.

Students experiencing genuine burnout should work with campus resources such as the financial assistance office, the placement office, counselors, academic advisors, support groups on or off campus, and others. These students may or may not gain relief from stress and frustration. But they must seek help. Your tuition entitles you to several on-campus services, so take advantage of them. Also, do not feel that you are the only one in need of help. You are not alone: There is someone to assist you, and there are others who need assistance.

Sometimes the best option is to remain in school, living one day at a time. A student named Chris, a single mother diagnosed with depression, works part-time

❏ **Step 3. Plan Your Intermediate Goals**

To reach your long-range goals, you must establish and achieve intermediate objectives. *Intermediate goals* are specific and realistic objectives required for your long-range goals that you can accomplish within one to four years. For example, the accounting student must complete an accounting major and a four-year degree program.

and enrolls in one or two courses per term on the advice of her therapist. She knows that it will be years before she graduates. However, Chris is satisfied with her progress toward a degree, and she obtains average or higher grades. She finds that the courses challenge her intellect and prevent her personal problems from dominating her daily life.

Sometimes the best solution is to take a break for a year or two. Jay was a full-time student who worked two part-time jobs and borrowed heavily to finance his education. His goal was to obtain a master's degree, but his grades were not as high as they should have been. Because of an abusive father, Jay and his mother lived together with Jay's older sister. Soon after his mother was diagnosed with terminal cancer, his attention to school diminished, causing his grades to drop. After consulting a counselor and his faculty advisor, Jay took a leave of absence to obtain a full-time job and spend more time with his mother. Two years later he returned to school part-time, using his savings to pay tuition. Jay's part-time job helps him get by financially and his grades are improving.

There are many students like Chris and Jay who struggle every day and reach their goals slowly. Seldom do they experience the pleasurable aspects of college (e.g., travel, social events) available to others. For them, survival is the goal. But survival is also a skill they develop and use when they encounter subsequent crises. Most important, they are satisfied with their steady progress toward their goals.

In spite of their situations, students experiencing burnout still need to develop short-term, intermediate, and long-range goals. Specific, realistic goals can point the way out of some difficult situations, like the well-known light at the end of a tunnel. Goals reflect options, offer flexibility, and lead to involvement in activities designed to reduce stress and feelings of helplessness. Charles Nobel expressed it this way: "You must have long-range goals to keep yourself from being frustrated by short-term failures."

Community-college students could obtain an associate's degree, then transfer to a four-year program. The Peace Corps-bound student would need to pursue a specialty area that he or she can use as a Peace Corps volunteer.

Your intermediate goals are going to include completing the general education requirements of your institution and the course work required for your major. In addition, there are other academically re-lated activities. For instance, have you considered an internship dur-ing your junior or senior year? Most institutions offer internship op-portunities for advanced students to work in real-world settings where students apply knowledge acquired in the classroom. Internships are good skill-building and career-planning experiences. They can lead to jobs and favorable evaluations on graduate school applications. Simi-larly, consider research opportunities with faculty, resident-assistant positions, service learning, a semester abroad, and campus leadership among your intermediate goals. Some of your most significant educa-tional experiences will occur outside the classroom or off campus! Write your intermediate goals below or on a sheet of paper.

_____

_____

_____

_____

_____

❑ Step 4. Plan Your Short-term Goals

Goals

To reach your intermediate goals, you must establish and achieve short-term goals. *Short-term goals* are specific and realistic objectives that you can accomplish within a year, usually in two or three aca-demic terms plus a summer break. The exact length and nature of the terms vary according to the system used at your school—semester, tri-mester, or quarter.

Short-term goals are specific and measurable realistic statements of what you hope to accomplish academically each term. Typically, they are the courses you plan with your academic advisor. Short-term goals could also include related activities such as visiting a career counselor, reading career-related magazines, searching for jobs, or performing volunteer work in career-related activities. The accounting student could talk to a tax accountant during the break. The Peace Corps-bound student would look for returning Peace Corps volunteers and for news about the country of choice.

Try to list some of the courses you are likely to take (for your aca-demic major and for general education requirements) and other im-portant activities (e.g., job, volunteer work) that you are likely to pur-sue. Consult the college catalog and schedules to complete this section.

_____ Term (semester, quarter)

_____

_____

_____ Term (semester, quarter)

_____

_____

_____ Term (semester, quarter) or Summer period

_____

_____

❑ **Step 5. Give Yourself Feedback**

Try to complete this exercise about twice a year, preferably before the fall and spring terms or in January and July. By reviewing your goals periodically, you develop the habit of using feedback. For instance, as you compare past and current goal statements, look for evidence that your motives are becoming intrinsic and focused. Courses related to your goals should be meaningful; motivation should increase. To your surprise, general education courses you disliked before may now seem useful after you discover how many careers call for strength in writing, speaking, and cultural awareness. Connecting your goals to your courses strengthens your resolve to overcome the obstacles discussed in Chapter 2.

Concluding Remarks

Goal setting is not a panacea for planning your future. By completing this exercise you have learned that setting goals takes time and thought. However, goal statements become a yardstick for comparing your plans with your current activities. Along with motives, goals are the compass that directs your energy. When you master time-management techniques presented in Chapter 5, you will have developed a plan that links your present to your future, your daily activities to your tentative ten-year plan, and college to career.

The chart below illustrates the linkage of time to the tools that can help you reach your goals.

Time Frame:	Daily	School year	College	Beyond
Tool:	Time management	Short-term goals	Intermediate goals	Long-range goals

Because education is achieved—not received—you can nurture your goals in these additional ways:

- Take advantage of your school's career counseling services to explore and obtain feedback about your goals. Set a goal to meet with a career counselor. Visit the center regularly to review materials.

- Listen to the wisdom of individuals whose experience and expertise you respect. They probably faced similar issues when they were maturing and deciding what to do with their lives.

- Use a technique popular with corporate motivation trainers. Write your short-term, intermediate, and long-range goals on 3×5 cards and think about them daily.

- Read the biographies of people you admire. Look for the key factors that enabled them to mature and deal with adversity.

Heed the advice of wise people such as:

- movie producer Cecil B. DeMille—aim for your goal unswervingly.

- coach Lou Holtz—be a participant, not a spectator, in life.

- philosopher Albert Camus—"to know oneself, one should assert oneself."

Action-Oriented Thought Starters

1. Write down what you think were the most significant insights you gained from reading this chapter. How difficult is it to write specific, realistic, short-term goals? Is it difficult to write long-range goals? Why?

2. This chapter focused on career goals, but personal and social goals are also important. Develop a few short-term goals for ac-

tivities that will enrich your experiences. Consider the following specific goals as examples. You may want to make some of them your goals.

- to learn how to use a word-processing program before the beginning of the next term so that I can prepare papers on a computer

- to relax a half-hour each day

- to learn by the end of the next term how to change the oil and perform a minor tune-up on my car (some colleges offer auto tune-up courses)

- to learn how to control my temper

- to take an aerobics class this term, or swim or walk for a half-hour three times each week

- to volunteer in a shelter for the homeless once a month

- to seek a significant relationship with a member of the opposite sex

- to play in one intramural sport each semester

- to bring my spouse and children to at least one campus event

- to join and participate in an outreach group

- to put aside a certain amount of money each week for a trip during spring break

- to attend at least two social and cultural events on campus this term

- to correct certain speech habits, such as "ya know"

- to take charge of buying and caring for my clothes

- to join a campus organization

- to begin appreciating the music of Bach, Beethoven, Berlioz, Bizet, or Brahms

- to take lessons in cross-country skiing

Your short-term goals could, if you enjoyed them, become intermediate goals:

- to save enough money for a trip to London
- to become an officer in a campus organization
- to learn another intramural sport
- to develop a database on the computer
- to learn to meditate while I relax
- to work twice a month in the shelter for the homeless
- to replace the brakes on my car
- to attend a performance of the symphony
- to cross-country ski in at least three areas I've never before tried

If you find them fulfilling, your intermediate goals could grow into long-range goals:

- to buy and rebuild an old car
- to become coordinator of our county's shelters for the homeless
- to learn and practice several methods of relaxation
- to bicycle through England
- to serve my alma mater as class liaison
- to upgrade my computer skills regularly
- to hold a season subscription to the symphony
- to ski in Wisconsin's Birkebeiner cross-country marathon race

Do some of these sound exciting? If you want to enjoy the benefits, start setting some short-term goals.

3. Chapters 2 and 3 require students to reflect on their self-concept, motives, and goals. One technique that promotes self-learning is to keep a journal. Each day or several times each week, find a quiet time and a quiet place to reflect and write. You do not have to write much—a few sentences can be sufficient. When you express your thoughts and feelings in a journal, you become more aware of yourself and the ways you interact with other people and your environment. Turn to pages 98–99 in Chapter 6, where journal writing is discussed as a source of feedback about your study

habits, and to page 150 in Chapter 8, where journal writing is used to recognize stress patterns. Many students keep journals. For example, Donna began "journaling" in her study-skills course to record her study habits. Now she writes in her journal several times a week to help her understand and deal with matters pertaining to school, work, family, and future plans. She enjoys journal writing and so do some of her friends. Why not search your room for a notebook, or purchase a blank book from a stationery store, or open a new file on your computer and discover some things about the most influential person you will ever meet—yourself!

References and Recommended Readings

Flatley, J. K., & Turner, C. C. (1991). Student burnout—Strategies for decreasing exhaustion and increasing success. Paper presented at the meeting of the National Association of Developmental Education, Nashville, TN.

Greenberg, J., & Baron, R. A. (1995). *Behavior in organizations: Understanding and managing the human side of work* (5th ed.). Boston: Allyn & Bacon.

Sherman, E. (1988, December 25). " 'Average guy' Holtz still reaching for sky." *Chicago Tribune,* Section 3, pp. 1, 6.

CHAPTER 4

The Covert Curriculum: Connecting College to Career

Friendly Reminders

❏ Preview Chapter 4 using the Preview Checklist on page 11.

❏ Is your motivation to read Chapter 4 mainly intrinsic or extrinsic?

❏ As you read Chapter 4, ask yourself how the material is related to your short-term, intermediate, and long-range goals.

❏ Is the previous question an example of a Deep or Surface learning strategy?

"Personally I am always ready to learn, although I do not always like being taught."

Winston Churchill (1874–1965),
English statesman and writer

After you proudly announced to family and friends that you were going to college, someone probably asked, "What are you going to study?" Depending on your motives and goals, you could have been vague ("I'm not sure.") or specific ("I will major in biology and minor in economics and management so I can operate a biotechnology company in ten years."). Or perhaps you replied, "I'm not sure, but English and math are required and I want to take sociology, biology, and history because I like them."

The Overt versus the Covert Curriculum

The subjects you take are part of the institution's *curriculum,* the specific courses or programs of study. Unless you enroll in a technical program, most subjects you complete during the first two years of college are required general education (liberal arts) courses. Although some requirements are unpopular with many students, the courses constitute the core of your education. They add breadth and depth to your experience, teach critical-thinking skills, and expose you to potential academic majors. As a consumer of learning you can view the required liberal-arts courses as an educational shopping center with something for everyone. Students in four-year programs spend their last two years completing required and elective courses in their academic major. The courses that you complete for a degree may be viewed as your *overt curriculum* because they are part of the official educational offerings published in the catalog and listed on your transcript.

However, as you learn the content of courses contained in the overt curriculum, you are simultaneously acquiring important experiences that comprise the *covert curriculum.* The experiences are called *covert* because students are generally unaware of their educational significance. The covert curriculum may be defined as those numerous, routine skill-related activities, behaviors, and attitudes that are transacted inside *and* outside of classrooms. Collectively, they reflect a student's overall work orientation and habits. Sometimes these experiences are called life/learning or lifelong skills. The overt curriculum focuses primarily on the communication of *content* such as facts, concepts, and theory. The covert curriculum focuses primarily on the *processes* involved in learning skill-related behaviors and attitudes.

Here are some examples of the covert curriculum.

1. submitting an assignment on the day it is due

2. taking organized and legible notes

3. listening attentively in class

4. increasing your reading speed and comprehension

5. maintaining an appointment book that lists dates of tests, assignments, and special events

6. periodically examining your goals and values (does this sound familiar?)

7. analyzing the attitudes and behaviors of role models (for example, student leaders, teachers, administrators, peers)

8. learning how to cope with stress

9. changing the physical environment to strengthen your concentration

10. practicing techniques to improve your memory

11. accepting responsibility for your behavior and attitudes

12. seeking and using feedback about your behavior

Each example is a familiar part of the college experience. Each reflects an activity that we often ignore or take for granted. *Think of the covert curriculum as a collection of unscheduled, self-taught, non-credit minicourses that helps you succeed in the overt curriculum and in your non-academic experiences.* They are not listed in the catalog or on the schedule, nor are they *directly* reflected on your transcript. Yet these minicourses are learned behaviors and attitudes that exert a powerful educational effect on you during and after college.

Box 4.1

Education and Training: What's the Difference?

During a discussion of the covert and overt curricula and their connection to jobs, occupations, and careers, students sometimes ask about the difference between education and training. This is the distinction that many educators make.

Education exposes students to a variety of liberal-arts disciplines (the sciences, arts, social sciences, humanities) for the purpose of developing general knowledge of one's world, values, and a variety of thinking skills. Education prepares students broadly for various occupations where communication, interpersonal, reasoning, and problem-solving skills are required.

Training provides specific information and skills in a particular occupational field for the purpose of using the knowledge and skills in a job or cluster of jobs.

The contrast between training and education is apparent in the degree offerings of two-year colleges. Students working for an associate of arts or associate of science degree for transfer to a four-year baccalaureate institution complete most of their credit hours in liberal-arts courses. In contrast, students working for an associate of applied science degree complete most of their credits (30 credit hours or fewer for certificate programs) in a specialty such as business, health services and sciences, social and personal services, trades, or technologies.

Training prepares students for specific entry-level jobs in technical fields, whereas liberal-arts education prepares students generally for a variety of less-technical jobs. The distinction between trained and educated individuals sparks controversy at two ends of the work spectrum. Who is better prepared to obtain available entry-level jobs? Who is better prepared to move into executive positions years later? Some college programs are designed to train *and* educate students. In a combination of training and education, the covert and the overt curricula operate simultaneously to prepare you to succeed in a variety of situations that you are likely to face. Remember the words of psychologist Abraham Maslow: "If the only tool you have is a hammer, you tend to treat everything as if it were a nail."

marketplace and to our personal lives. Contrary to some students' expectations, these skills are not automatically conferred with the degree when you graduate. Rather, they are achieved only after years of self-awareness and effort. Very few courses in the overt curriculum provide direct instruction in these skills, yet the achievement of academic excellence often requires their mastery.

Confirming the Connection between College and Career

Chances are that you are skeptical about the covert curriculum. How can the ordinary activities of student life prepare you for a career? How can we talk about career preparation without thinking about accounting, business, engineering, health studies, or other occupations?

The American Society for Training and Development identified 16 skills that employers report are essential for success in the workplace (Carnevale, Gainer, & Meltzer, 1990). The skills are grouped as follows:

- learning to learn: the foundation skill on which all others are based

- reading, writing, and computation: technical skills that employers consider basic for entry and advancement

- oral communication and listening: skills that enable people to communicate in their jobs

- problem solving and creative thinking: skills that enable employees to think and act flexibly

- self-esteem, motivation/goal setting, and employability/career development: developmental skills that help people maintain their job and advance

- interpersonal skills, teamwork, and negotiation: skills that enable people to work together in groups

- organizational effectiveness and leadership: the "influencing" skills that help individuals navigate through the organization

Some students might be frightened by this list, but you're not, because you have read the contents pages of this book and its first three chapters. You already know the importance of learning to learn, career development, motivation, and goal setting. Subsequent chapters will cover at length or briefly the topics of reading, listening, oral communication, self-esteem, interpersonal skills, leadership, and organizational effectiveness. The overt and covert curricula will provide opportunities to develop the remaining skills in depth. So feel confident that college is preparing you for your future, regardless of the academic major you choose.

Just in case you're still a little skeptical, consider other evidence that what you learn in college will prepare you for careers. According to a survey conducted by the National Association of Colleges and

Employers (NACE), employers are looking for the following skills in job candidates (Collins, 1996):

- oral communication skills

- interpersonal skills

- teamwork skills

- analytical skills

- flexibility

- written communication skills

- proficiency in the field of study (your academic major)

- leadership skills

Collins advises freshmen and sophomores to take the following steps to ensure that they enter the job market with an edge.

- Gain work-related experience through part-time jobs that are relevant to your field, internships, or cooperative education programs.

- Get actively involved in campus organizations and/or extracurricular activities by seeking leadership roles.

- Keep your grades up as best as you can, especially during the last two years of college.

- Acquire and develop computer skills, regardless of your career plans. Computer skills are no longer "nice to have," they are a necessity!

These and similar studies confirm the basic proposition of this chapter, that *the covert curriculum consists of marketable skills, including the learning skills described in this book.*

The Covert Curriculum: Good News for Students

Your transcript may not directly reflect your mastery of the covert curriculum. But mastery of those skills and attitudes is good news for students.

1. It's *good news for students whose motivation is unclear or mainly extrinsic.* Even though your motivation may be shaky, you still seek happiness and success. Recall Winston Churchill's remarks at the beginning of this chapter: "Personally I am always ready to learn, although I do not always like being taught." His words reflect the attitude of many college students who have the ability and desire to learn but are unhappy with or not ready for demands imposed by the overt curriculum.

Just as goal setting was shown in Chapter 3 to link your present and future, so too the covert curriculum can serve to link, *if you work at it,* the present with the future. Why is this so? When you practice the covert curriculum you *are* preparing for your future. Your future *will* use those skills, as any career counselor can testify.

Finally, proficiency in the covert curriculum can be intrinsically motivating and, consequently, a sound basis for establishing your goals. In the absence of intrinsic motivation, let the covert curriculum guide you. If you want to think about these ideas further, write the following statement on a 3 × 5 card and read it at least once a day: *The covert curriculum connects college to career.*

2. The *covert curriculum* is *good news for students who do not like some of their courses.* Are you one of those students

- who sees no earthly use for algebra?

- who believes that psychology is common sense obfuscated? (If you do not know the definition of *obfuscated,* look it up in the dictionary. That's the "take charge" approach to learning!)

- who finds science too complex to be worth understanding?

- who knows that the humanities are irrelevant to making money?

Even if you do not yet like a required course, remember that the reading, notetaking, listening, and critical-thinking skills that you engage in will pay off some day when you seek advancement. *In other words, if you do not like learning for the sake of learning at this point in your life, then work hard to develop job-related skills and attitudes for the sake of your future.* Perhaps someday the memories of your psychology, French, and chemistry courses will merge to influence your promotion to sales manager for the French-owned chemical company you work for.

3. The *covert curriculum* is *good news for students enrolled in technical programs.* If you have chosen data processing, electronics, nursing,

engineering, human services, health technology, or another of the several technical programs offered in two-year and four-year schools, you have the advantage of knowing what you want to do. If you are currently working in a career-related job, you have the opportunity to *integrate* technical knowledge and skills with the skill-based behaviors and attitudes of the covert curriculum. There is a mutually reinforcing connection between the classroom and the office. For instance, the promptness, precision, flexibility, and responsibility you must demonstrate in your job can readily transfer to the requirements of your course work.

4. The *covert curriculum* is *good news for adults returning to college.* Students over 25 years old beginning or returning to college often lack confidence. Study skills are rusty, commitments to job and family reduce study time, and younger students seem sharper and more energetic. Against these possible constraints, returning students have advantages. Matured by life experiences, they are motivated and goal oriented. Their specific career goals may not be clear yet, but they will examine different options, seek career counseling, and talk to friends. They probably have more skills than they know, especially if they have been homemakers, employed, or cared for others; performed community service; or held other positions of responsibility. The returning students' skills may be classified as technical, communication, problem-solving, organizational, interpersonal, time-management, stress-management, and others that employers report as essential for success in the workplace. In short, having completed most minicourses of the covert curriculum, most returning students can concentrate on the overt curriculum.

5. The *covert curriculum* is *good news for students whose prior work and educational experiences have been limited or unsuccessful.* Knowing the distinction between the overt and the covert curriculum can help you establish goals. For example, if you want to work in a social-service agency or in retailing, the communication skills you develop by writing reports, speaking in class, and reading about current events are important. Try to attend skill-building workshops conducted by your college's counseling or student affairs offices that help you catch up in other skill areas.

6. The *covert curriculum* is *good news for the recent high school graduate who developed sound learning skills in school.* If you learned how to maintain an appointment book, complete homework assignments on time, develop initiative, take good notes, study in a quiet place, read with good comprehension, and if you practiced other minicourses in the covert curriculum, your task is to *refine* those skills in college.

Coffee, Capitalism, and the Covert Curriculum

Warren was a full-time Economics major with a B average who worked part-time at a large bookstore where he performed all the tasks associated with serving gourmet coffee drinks. The connections between the covert curriculum and his job were obvious to Warren when he wrote the following in his journal: "From the intellectual standpoint, there is no real connection between studying in the classroom and working in the bookstore, but I take the same attitude and responsibility at school and work. I show up at work on time, and I take my job seriously even if it's a meaningless task of taking the garbage out or sweeping the floor. I strongly believe that what I learned through the years in school has helped me to develop a better overall understanding of dealing with the workplace."

During a semester-long internship, he also spent one day a week at a branch office of a large brokerage firm where he served as the assistant to the Financial Consultant. Again, he practiced skills of the covert curriculum but at a higher level than in his part-time job. For example, the listening, attending, and note-taking skills he casually used in his college classrooms were quickly sharpened when he learned the importance of carefully writing his supervisor's instructions regarding client names and portfolio information. His reading and research skills improved because he was often assigned to investigate investment options for clients. He became more organized and methodical in his approach to work. He learned to pay greater attention to details because it was easy to make serious mistakes. He was aware that his oral, written, and interpersonal communication skills were continually tested in each setting and that they improved as a result. Finally, the work ethic that he practiced in his schoolwork and job helped him succeed in his internship.

The skills of the covert curriculum work in both directions. The skills that Warren developed throughout his earlier education helped him in his part-time job and in his internship. Conversely, the tasks he performed in the job and internship settings further strengthened his motivation and skills as a student. In short, the covert curriculum connects college to career, *and* it connects the workplace back to the classroom.

Box 4.2 describes one student who recognized the importance of the covert curriculum.

Concluding Remarks

Taking charge of yourself in college includes knowing your motives and goals. Just as goals enable you to link your present with your future, the covert curriculum enables you to connect your college experience to your future, whatever it may be. In the next chapter you will be introduced to the most important minicourse of the covert curriculum: *time management,* the technique that empowers you to accomplish your goals daily.

The relation between the covert curriculum and your career is so important that each subsequent chapter will conclude with a section entitled "Connecting (the chapter topic) to Your Career." The remarks will forge additional links between your daily activities and your future.

Action-Oriented Thought Starters

1. Show the four lists of covert curriculum skills (the text's on page 52, yours, the NACE list on page 57, and the one below) to someone who holds a responsible position.

   - striving to improve relationships with your roommate, family, and friends

   - interacting effectively in study groups

   - accepting a leadership role in a student organization

   - trying to find the similarities between student jobs and a "real" job

   - analyzing the social dynamics of your classes

   - learning to use the college's resources

   - learning to make the best of a boring situation, whether it is a job or a course

   - being prompt for appointments; calling ahead when you know you will be late or unable to keep the appointment

   - learning to understand and get along with persons from other racial and ethnic groups

- learning to cooperate with others when it's needed, especially when you don't want to

a. Ask the person to discuss how important some of these behaviors are in his or her job.

b. Ask the person to add to your list.

2. For those of you who work (include homemaking), what are the most important three to five skills you practice in your job? Do they help you in your course work? How?

3. Create a career plan.

a. Go to your library or career planning center and search for *Chronicle of Occupational Briefs* or other sources that describe occupations and careers.

b. Read about the occupation or career that you identified in the Chapter 3 goal-setting exercise.

c. Describe the occupation or career of your choice. Also note the type of training required and the major benefits and drawbacks of that occupation.

d. Explain your reasons for entering this occupation. Are your reasons based on direct knowledge of the career, on your images and perceptions gained from the media or casual information, or on the expectations of others?

e. What else can you do to learn more about that occupation or career?

f. What skills and attitudes of the covert curriculum will be important for success?

g. After you complete this exercise, write at the top of the page with a colored marker in bold letters: Review this each semester!

References and Recommended Readings

Carnevale, A. P., Gainer, L. J., & Meltzer, A. S. (1990). *Workplace basics: The essential skills employers want.* San Francisco: Jossey-Bass.

Collins, M. (1996). The job outlook for '96 grads. *Journal of Career Planning & Employment,* LVI (2), 51–54.

CHAPTER 5

Take Charge of Your Time

Friendly Reminders

❏ To what extent does your ability to manage time originate in you (internal locus of control) or in outside forces (external locus of control)?

❏ As you read Chapter 5, ask how the concepts you learn can help you reach your intermediate goals.

❏ As you read, consider how each time-management technique relates to the covert curriculum.

"Dost thou love life, then do not squander time, for that's the stuff life is made of."

Benjamin Franklin (1706–1790),
American printer, author, inventor, and diplomat

"Perhaps the most valuable result of all education is the ability to make yourself do the thing you have to do, when it ought to be done, whether you like it or not."

Thomas Huxley (1825–1895),
British biologist and educator

The upbeat advice of Ben Franklin joins the stern observation of Thomas Huxley to form the central principle of time management: If you want freedom to enjoy life (Franklin), first learn self-discipline (Huxley). This chapter provides you with principles and techniques for taking charge of your time so that you can gain freedom to enjoy life.

When you master time, you gain the power to reach your daily and weekly goals and increase the chances for achieving your short-term, intermediate, and long-range goals. In other words (Thomas Huxley's words), time-management skills enable you to do the thing you have to do, when it ought to be done, whether you like it or not. For many students, time management is the "make or break" skill to be mastered during the freshman year. Time management is a problem for many students for several reasons.

1. Some students are not aware of the large blocks of "disposable" time—the overwhelming freedom—that characterizes college life. Beyond the 12 to 18 hours students are required to be in class or lab each week, the remaining time is theirs to use, or abuse, as they choose.

2. Some students are not aware that success in college requires a strong commitment of time. When a sample of college freshmen were asked about the number of hours they studied each week as high school seniors, they reported an average of 6 hours. Depending on your academic goals (grades, major), you can expect to spend from 15 to 50 hours per week (as a full-time student) with your course assignments, excluding your job.

3. Some students do not realize that college is intended to prepare them for the world of jobs—not merely with a body of knowledge, but also with a variety of skills, attitudes, and physical and emotional stamina. Although a student can "slide" through college performing at the minimal level (C) and still graduate, an employee who works at minimal performance standards may be fired, given today's competition for jobs.

Most challenging full-time jobs require at least a 40-hour workweek; many require 50 to 60 hours in entry-level positions. If you spend 40 to 50 hours a week with your course work, you should have the physical and mental stamina needed to handle a challenging position. *When you treat college as a full-time job, you prepare yourself for the reality of life after college.*

4. Although most people have at times put off work that should be performed, procrastination is a serious problem for some students. The time-management techniques and principles presented in this chapter may be of limited assistance to true procrastinators unless they simultaneously seek assistance from a professional counselor who can help reveal and treat this complex problem.

5. Some students have problems managing their time because they lead very active lives filled with many responsibilities and little spare time. Chances are such students use time-management methods well; they want to become optimally efficient.

6. Some students do not control time effectively because they do not recognize or accept their priorities. Students who possess, and remain aware of, their long-range goals are willing to forgo the favorite television program, the hour conversation with an acquaintance, the alluring weekend with a friend, the 2-hour workout, and excessive cocurricular activities. To manage time productively, a student must constantly ask: How important is this activity in reaching my short-term and long-range goals? Students with job or family responsibilities must constantly determine what task is most important at the time. For an in-depth discussion of the distinction between tasks that are urgent and those that are important, consult Covey, Merrill, and Merrill's *First Things First.*

The rest of this chapter will teach you how to use four methods for managing time in college. They include the term schedule, the weekly work list, the daily DO-list, and the appointment book.

If you already have strong time-management skills, you're probably using these techniques, individually or in combination.

THINK before You Register!

Some time-management problems are affected by course selection. Commitments to work, family, and cocurricular activities often limit your choice of courses, but when you have the option to choose, consider the following factors.

Box 5.1

1. *Be realistic about the number of credit hours you can handle successfully.* If you have a full-time job and/or family responsibilities, how many courses can you take and still succeed in all of your commitments? If you must work hard to earn a grade of C, should you enroll for 18 or 21 credits? If you plan to attend graduate or professional school, where high entrance grades are required, what maximum number of credit hours can you take on during a term and earn A's, given your other commitments? It may be better to extend college an extra semester or year and earn the high grades needed for graduate school than to finish sooner with a less desirable grade point average. Certainly you want to complete your education quickly, with minimal costs, and get on with your career, but carefully consider the consequences of being unrealistically ambitious.

2. *Spread out your courses when possible.* Spreading out your courses through the week gives you sufficient time between classes to complete your many assignments. Allowing time between classes held on the same day enables you to have breaks, review your notes from previous classes, and prepare for subsequent classes. You will appreciate those breaks on days when exams or major assignments are scheduled.

3. *Listen to your body talk.* If you are a late sleeper, avoid early classes. If you get drowsy after lunch, avoid afternoon classes (or have a light lunch). If your energy is highest during the morning, try to take your most difficult courses then. If you work before you attend class, consider your mental and physical state during that class, and during the following class.

4. *Balance your schedule with courses that differ.* The adage that "variety is the spice of life" holds true for college courses. Students completing general education requirements can create balance in their course work by complementing demanding reading courses with a studio arts course, or mostly social science courses with a humanities course. Avoid taking more than two or three courses in your academic major during the term, to avoid boredom or exhaustion.

Consult your academic advisor about these and similar issues involving course scheduling and time management.

However, if you are a poor time manager or a very busy student, you should make it your goal to practice all four techniques simultaneously until you are in firm control of your daily activities. With proficiency you can select or modify techniques to best fit your personal needs and lifestyle. If you have access to a computer, check your library or counseling center for one of the computerized scheduling programs on the market.

The Term Schedule: Your Academic Term at a Glance

College is a unique time in the life of many students. If you work less than 20 hours weekly and have few or no family responsibilities, you have far more "free" and unsupervised time than in high school or in most occupations. Students who have substantial amounts of unstructured time available are in greatest need of a term schedule to ensure that they reach their short-term goals. They are most vulnerable to wasting time because they can experience the illusion that there is plenty of time to complete assignments. Students who carry heavy course loads, hold jobs, and/or have family responsibilities also require a term schedule to ensure that their scarce unstructured time is used productively.

Whether you follow a semester, trimester, or quarter system, each week usually repeats the schedule of the previous week. Consequently, you can construct a term schedule like the one shown in Figure 5.1. To save time, draw a master copy of a blank schedule using 30- or 60-minute intervals and make several copies, or ask your instructor for a copy.

Although circumstances may not permit you to incorporate all of the guidelines discussed next into your schedule, follow as many as possible to achieve optimal efficiency.

Constructing the Term Schedule

❏ The Tentative Term Schedule: Identifying Your Highest Priorities

Before your first class, construct a tentative version of your term schedule.

	Sunday	Monday	Tuesday	Wednesday	Thursday	Friday	Saturday
7:00 AM	←			WAKE-UP Breakfast Commute		→	
8:00							
9:00		Hum. 227	Gym	Hum. 227	Gym	Hum. 227	WORK
10:00		BIO. 104	study Math	BIO. 104	BIO. 104	BIO. 104	
11:00		Review Notes	↓	Review Notes	Lab	Review Notes	
12:00 PM	←			LUNCH		→	
1:00	Exercise	Campus Club	Math 152		Math 152		
2:00	plan week	study Soc.	↓ review Eng.	Study Soc.	↓ review Eng.	Study Soc.	↓
3:00	Study	SOC. 101	ENG.	Soc. 101	ENG.	Soc. 101	Relax
4:00	↓	WORK	115 review notes	WORK	115 review notes	WORK	review Notes
5:00	↓		Dinner	↓	Dinner		Dinner
6:00	Dinner	↓	Relax	↓	Relax	↓	OUT
7:00	T.V.	Commute dinner	study - library	Commute dinner	study- library	commute dinner	
8:00	↓	Relax		Relax		OUT	
9:00	↓	Study	↓	study	↓		
10:00	Study		↓	↓	↓		
11:00	Study	↓	relax	↓	relax		
12:00 AM	←			BED	→	↓	↓

Figure 5.1 The Term Schedule

1. Account for *all* your waking hours, from the time you arise to the time you shut off the lights, and from Sunday through Saturday. Accounting for all your hours is important because considerable time can be easily wasted during the first and last hours of the day. Similarly, weekends should be scheduled with your basic activities, including blocks of time for study. Students who believe that weekends are "free" of course assignments may be in for a surprise after their first series of exams.

2. Schedule your highest priorities (i.e., your fixed commitments): class meeting times, work, family tasks, meals, travel times, and necessary chores. These times are "written in stone," and they reflect the most important activities you perform each day. Then, mark out *blocks* of time for course assignments but do not specify them in detail on the tentative term schedule to allow flexibility (see Box 5.2). To the extent that you are honest and realistic about your highest priorities on your tentative term schedule, you can reduce the likelihood of frustrations later in the term.

3. Sometimes distinguishing a high-level priority from a second-level priority is difficult. For example, is your daily exercise a first-level or second-level priority? Only you can answer that question, but you should be guided by this principle: What is the consequence to my physical and psychological health if I miss one day of exercise? If I miss three days of exercise? Can I reduce exercising from 60 to 45 minutes per day? If exercise is a high priority, what lower-level priorities must I change to accommodate my exercise? Can I do without an hour of television? Can I save time when I get up in the morning? Recognize that on some days, one high priority (eating lunch) may be displaced by a higher priority (e.g., taking a sick child or roommate to the doctor, filling in for someone else at work). Pay close attention to the consequences of your choices. *Always be willing to reevaluate your priorities in relation to your short-range and long-term goals.*

❏ **The Revised Term Schedule: Fine-tuning and Filling Out the Spaces**

After one or two weeks of school *and* a careful examination of each course syllabus, most students should have a good idea about the work requirements of their courses and the time needed to complete them. Revise your term schedule following the steps below.

1. Schedule *realistic* amounts of time needed to complete each of the fixed commitments (your highest priorities) you wrote on your tentative schedule.

2. One of your highest priorities is preparation time or study time, the hours required to complete all assignments in each course. How much time should you allocate to preparation? The answer depends on the importance (its priority) of the course to you. A popular rule of thumb stating that students should spend 2 hours outside of class for each hour in class means that if you enroll for 15 credit hours, you would spend an additional 30 hours per week preparing for courses. A weekly commitment of 45 hours (15 in class, 30 outside of class) to full-time course work is equivalent to a full-time job. Are the grades you want worth the time required? Only *you* can determine *your* priorities. If all you want is a C, you may get by with a few hours per week in each course. If your long-range goals require high levels of knowledge and skills, then view your courses as a full-time job, one that may involve unpaid "overtime" on a regular basis.

A student named Tom deceived himself semester after semester into thinking he could get good grades with little study time. His tendency to blame outside forces (hard courses, tough teachers, sports commitments, friends, etc.) for his mediocre grades continued through his sophomore year. In the beginning of his junior year when his goals were becoming clear, he realized that he must double or triple his study time each week to earn the grades he needed to enter a graduate program. He regretted his mistakes, became discouraged by his low grade point average, and felt frustrated by his circumstances. Learn from Tom: Make an early commitment to working hard in your courses. Then compare the output (grades, learning) to your input (hours) and decide whether you want to spend more or less time preparing for courses. Don't wait until it's too late, like Tom did, to increase your study time.

After you block out the study periods on your final term schedule, how much time is left to do other things? What are the likely consequences of your decisions to do or not do these other things at the level you wish to do them? What is most and least important to you? When you keep such questions in mind, you are better able to match your actions with your priorities, whatever your priorities may be.

3. Keep track of your preparation time using the Weekly Work List described in the next section. Subsequently, compare your actual preparation time with the grades you receive. Prepare to adjust your term schedule to match your priorities.

4. As you construct your final term schedule, follow the suggestions contained in Box 5.2 for achieving the greatest efficiency and productivity from your study times.

Box 5.2

The Tentative Term Schedule: Flexibility without Guilt

Be flexible during your first few weeks of school and avoid this student's mistake. Mike created a term schedule on the first day of class with noble intentions of turning a new page. Unfortunately, he felt compelled to treat the schedule as if it were a law. When he broke his schedule a few days later, he felt guilty, frustrated, and angry with himself. He created a new schedule with a stronger resolve to stick to it no matter what. Within a week he broke it again and felt very discouraged. The guilt and discouragement led to self-admonishment, which lowered Mike's self-confidence. Finally, he realized that it was unrealistic to accurately predict the use of each hour of each day for the whole term, based on the first two weeks of classes. Having revised his schedule and his attitude toward schedules, Mike felt more comfortable managing his time.

With these recommendations in mind, return to the term schedule in Figure 5.1. This full-time student is enrolled in five courses and works 12 hours a week. Preparation time is almost double that of class time and includes review sessions and study periods immediately before a class. Still, there is time for regular exercise and relaxation.

Returning adult students, or students in special circumstances, may follow a schedule very different from the one depicted in Figure 5.1.

- Anita is married with four children and enrolls for two courses each term. Her days begin at 6:00 A.M. and end at 11:00 P.M. They are centered on her children and their many activities, preparing meals and keeping house, and family life in general. An A-level student, Anita schedules seven 2-hour study blocks each week, which include one on Saturday and two on Sunday. When necessary, she adjusts her schedule on a priority basis, with exercise and housecleaning as the first activities to be eliminated. Sometimes she can study while exercising on the stationary bike. She tries to remain flexible. Never knowing when an emergency will arise, she completes all projects in advance. Everything is written on a calendar.

Box 5.3

Optimal Scheduling: Making the Most of Your Study Periods

To derive the most from your study time, practice the following recommendations.

1. Schedule study time to match your circadian (24-hour) body rhythms. Try to study your most difficult subjects when you are most alert. Avoid heavy meals before class so that your brain does not compete with your stomach for your blood supply. Try to determine whether you are a morning, afternoon, or evening student.

2. Schedule review times as soon as possible after each class. A 5- to 10-minute review per class hour (a) strengthens your understanding of the material; (b) enables you to fill in gaps in your notes while the material is fresh; (c) builds self-confidence that you are on top of your work; and (d) ensures that you won't be staring with glazed eyes the night before an exam trying to decipher old notes.

3. Analyze how best to use your long and short study periods. Blocks of 2 to 3 hours are ideal for preparing term papers, projects, or long reading assignments. Hour-long periods are good for shorter reading and homework assignments. "Time pockets" (the 10- to 45-minute periods between classes, eating, waiting in line, or commuting) are good for reviewing, thinking, or doing short assignments. The important point is to constantly remain aware of your time and devise ways of using it properly, if you want to learn and earn high grades.

- Kelly is a single person who rises at 5:30 A.M. and commutes one hour to a full-time job that begins at 8:00 A.M. and ends at 4:30 P.M. He studies during lunch and for an hour after work in preparation for his two night classes that meet from 6:30 to 9:30 P.M. He is in bed by midnight each night. To maintain his high grade point average, he also studies during a 5-hour period on Saturdays and for 1 hour on Sundays.

- Ellie is a single resident full-time student with a B average and a part-time job who has been diagnosed with attention deficit hyperactivity disorder (ADHD). The greatest challenge for her is to find enough time in the day to perform her class assignments. Because she spends much more time studying than most students, she has difficulty juggling her daily activities. She studies 3 to 4

4. Avoid studying similar subjects in tandem (go ahead, look up tandem in your dictionary if you don't know what it means) to prevent memory interference. For example, studying psychology and sociology in sequence may lead to confusion of concepts from disciplines that overlap.

5. Schedule an hour or two of leisure in such nonacademic activities as sports, family time, quiet time by yourself, exercise, leisure reading, calling friends, or socializing. The most energetic and dedicated student will burn out if leisure is not part of the routine. For most students, however, the challenge is to control leisure time: Doing the things you have to do, when they ought to be done, even if you don't want to do them. Or, in the words of a popular beer commercial: "Know when to say when."

6. Occasionally, a student's job schedule requires different hours each week or a rotation of the schedule. If a term schedule does not accurately reflect inconsistent work hours, simply note the inconsistent schedules in dashed lines or in color on the schedule.

Be flexible, but follow this advice as much as you can and as often as you are able. Be sure to reward yourself when you succeed.

hours per class each day and up to 7 hours a day to complete her homework. This leaves her with little or no free time and the tendency to experience burnout. Although she keeps daily time sheets, she still has difficulty managing her time.

Regardless of your particular circumstances, try to follow those guidelines that maximize your gains and minimize your personal costs. Strive for balance: balance between excessive flexibility (no schedule) and rigidity and a balance among your highest priorities. After you receive the results of your first exam, or your first major project, review your priorities and prepare to adjust your schedule. Your term schedule is a valuable visual representation of your weekly commitments. Carry it with you during the first month of the term or until you have it memorized.

The Weekly Work List

Some people don't like to make lists; they resist all attempts to order and categorize their daily lives. If you are such an individual, *and you earn high grades*, you may not need to construct a weekly work list. However, most college students benefit from this kind of list. Your term schedule may show you where you should be each period every day, but it may not indicate specifically what you should be doing. The weekly work list is a second time-management technique that enables you to control your time by identifying in advance the tasks to be completed and the time and resources needed. Like a production manager who calculates the time, labor, and materials needed for a job, or the agency director who allocates the resources required to serve clients, students should plan for the time and resources needed in their work.

The weekly work list is an overview of the time and resources needed to complete each assignment by its due date. Thomas Huxley would have recommended this time-management device because it shows at a glance what must be done by when.

Constructing a Weekly Work List

1. Early in the weekend, take time to review the next week's assignments and develop a work list like the one shown in Figure 5.2. It represents the type of assignments faced by the student whose schedule is shown in Figure 5.1.

2. As you prepare the list, cross-check it with your appointment book (see "The Appointment Book/Weekly Planner") and term schedule to verify times that are available for completing the assignments. For example, if your humanities test is on Friday and a visitor is staying overnight on Thursday, you must plan for those events in advance.

3. Account for *all* class assignments, *all* due dates, and the resources needed including labs, computers, group projects, library reserve readings, and materials.

4. Estimate the amount of time required to complete the assignment. Note that the "Time Needed" column is divided into the time you *estimate* is needed and the *actual time* you spent to complete the

WEEK OF APRIL 16-20:

Course	Assignment	Due Date	Resources Needed	Time Needed: Estimated	Actual
BIO. 104	Read Ch. 14	M-W-F 4/18-4/20	text pp. 312-340	1 1/2	2
BIO. 104	Lab Report	Wed 4/18	notes, manual	1 1/4	1 1/4
ENG. 115	Read Ch. 9 PP 272-290	Tue 4/17	text	1	1 1/4
ENG. 115	Prepare Persuasive Speech	Thurs 4/19	notes, text TIME mag.	1 1/2	2
MTH. 152	Read Ch. 13	Tues 4/17	text	1	1
MTH. 152	Do problems #17-25	Thurs 4/19	text math lab?	1 1/4	2 1/2
HUM. 227	Finish Ch. 9	Wed 4/18	text library reading	1 1/2	1 3/4
HUM. 227	Test: Ch. 7, 8, 9	Fri 4/20	text, notes	3	3 3/4
SOC. 101	Read Ch. 17	M-W-F 4/18 - 4/20	text	1 3/4	1 1/2
			HOURS:	13 3/4	17

Figure 5.2 The Weekly Work List

task. Discrepancies between estimated and actual times are bound to occur because the demands of assignments vary, sometimes in unpredictable ways. When you estimate time, remember the law of time management: *things take longer than you think they will!* It is better to overestimate than underestimate, better to rejoice afterward in having saved time than to be discouraged about insufficient time.

5. Enter the amount of time you actually spent on an assignment. Then try to assess *why* there was a discrepancy between the estimated and actual times. Why was the assignment more difficult than you expected? Is there anything you can do to reduce the discrepancy the next time you have a similar assignment? Were there interruptions?

At the end of the week, total the estimated hours and compare that number to the total actual hours spent. Do you need to adjust your term schedule?

Learning to pinpoint the discrepancies between estimated and actual times develops another learning-how-to-learn skill useful for college and career: feedback. Feedback sharpens your capacity for accurately estimating subsequent assignments.

6. After you finish an assignment, cross it off the list and experience the pleasure and relief that accompanies a task well done.

The weekly work list is an invaluable time-management tool. It puts you in charge of each assignment for the week ahead. It zooms in on your academic priorities. You can adjust your coming week's schedule in advance (for example, spend another two hours on math), which in turn empowers you to be proactive, not reactive, to unforeseen changes. The weekly work list helps you gain confidence in your ability to complete assignments during the most demanding of weeks.

Daily DO-List

It's Tuesday morning. Your term schedule lists the times for your classes, study periods, and job. Your weekly work list shows that a two-page essay due for English on Wednesday will require about two hours to write. With two time-management techniques operating, you should feel completely covered. But from the depths of your consciousness comes an uneasy feeling that you're supposed to do something else today. It's not something you do every day, and it wasn't important enough to place on your activities calendar. *But what was it?*

If you kept a daily DO-list, you'd know immediately what that something was that you don't do every day. The DO-list is a small sheet of paper or a space in your appointment book used before bedtime to list special, often last-minute, tasks that must be completed the next day: cashing a check, phoning a friend, doing laundry, shopping. To use the daily DO-list, either write the tasks in the order of their priority or use a "star rating" system to designate priority. After you complete a task, don't forget to cross it off the list.

The Appointment Book/Weekly Planner

Some students combine the functions of the weekly work list and the daily DO-list with a weekly planner or appointment book. Peruse the shelves of an office supply store for an appointment book or weekly planner (there are many brands and styles available) that is small enough to be carried conveniently, but large enough to contain the information you would record on your weekly work list and daily DO-list.

During the first week of class enter all test and homework assignment due dates from each course syllabus in your appointment book. Next, enter the dates of special activities such as visits, concerts, sporting events, club meetings, and similar activities of interest. Leave space for assignment details and DO-list kinds of items. Consider color-coding the information by course or by event so that important items are readily identified.

The appointment book/weekly planner has the advantage of allowing you to incorporate both kinds of information into one convenient source, but it may not be large enough to record the detailed information desired in the weekly work list. In addition, mark your wall or desk calendar with the major academic and nonacademic events of the month for quick reference.

In summary, you have learned time-management techniques that enable you to organize your weekly commitments for each term (term schedule), identify weekly the time and materials required for each assignment (weekly work list), list miscellaneous tasks to be performed daily (daily DO-list), and combine in an abbreviated manner the functions of weekly work lists and daily DO-lists (appointment book or weekly planner).

Time Out!

"STOP! STOP!" you exclaim. "I'm suffering from Time Trauma," you claim. "When am I going to do my work when I'm spending so much time keeping track of it on a term schedule, a weekly work list, a daily DO-list, and now an appointment book?"

Your patience is admirable, your frustration understandable. However, consider these points.

Box
5.4

A Scenario of Savvy and Success

If the previous remarks didn't convince you of the importance of time management, consider Sarah's experiences. Sarah began her freshman year at a large university fearful of the competition and lacking confidence in her academic and social skills. She knew that she needed to manage her time wisely, so she bought a large appointment book that contained several blank lines for each day of the week, one week fitting on two pages. Using the course syllabi, she recorded each assignment for each course in her appointment book. In addition to noting test dates, she wrote "study for _____ test" at the beginning of the full week before an exam. Similarly, after recording term paper due dates, she worked backward on her calendar and wrote "do library research" and "complete rough draft" weeks in advance. Sarah developed the habit of completing a whole week's reading assignments during the weekend before to gain confidence in her readiness for those classes. By dividing her major tasks into smaller and more manageable tasks, she accomplished each one and developed confidence from her many small successes. Sarah's disciplined approach to time management helped her attain a high grade point average in her freshman year, and it instilled competence as well as confidence. By carefully controlling her schedule, she had more free time for leisure, exercise, and social activities, which in turn strengthened her social skills.

Sarah transferred to a small college at the beginning of her sophomore year, where she continued to develop and refine her time-management techniques. By the end of her sophomore year, she had obtained a cumulative 3.90 grade point

1. If *you* don't take complete charge of your time, who will? You have only one or two academic terms to develop this crucial skill. You may need all the help you can get.

2. Less than one hour per week is required to practice these techniques. It takes an hour each term to construct and revise a term schedule, about 20 minutes a week to construct the weekly work list, about 2 minutes a day to use a daily DO-list, and a few minutes to mark an appointment book. You spend less than one hour a week to keep track of the other 167 hours (111 hours if you deduct eight hours of sleep per night). Isn't *one* hour a week a worthy investment to protect the remaining 167 hours?

average (on a scale of 4), served as a club officer, and was selected as a dormitory resident assistant.

Her intelligence and other personal characteristics contributed to Sarah's successes. Yet she believed strongly that the disciplined approach to time management that she developed her freshman year was a major factor. She viewed her appointment book as a self-contract for reaching her short-term (semester) goals. Sarah also used her appointment book for reaching her long-range goals. For example, she scheduled time during her junior year to prepare for the Graduate Record Examination, which she took before her senior year and prior to applying for graduate school.

Her approach to time management included combining the appointment book and the weekly work list approaches, except she did not include time estimates. Furthermore, Sarah kept a term schedule for the first few weeks of class and a daily DO-list.

In addition to her resident assistant responsibilities, she worked about ten hours each week on a college work-study program. Sarah believed that having a part-time job and a full-time course load taught her to be continually aware of her time. And yes, there usually was time left over for fun. Isn't that what Benjamin Franklin would want?

Sarah's time-management habits were rewarded. Recently, she achieved her doctorate in clinical psychology.

3. Remember, when you manage time well you "buy" freedom to pursue other activities: leisure, exercise, sports, socializing, or more work if you must.

4. With practice you'll learn to fine-tune, combine, and reduce the four techniques into two or three.

5. Time management is a highly marketable skill. Ask any executive.

We introduced four techniques for controlling your time: the term schedule, the weekly work list, the daily DO-list, and the appointment book. If you have difficulty managing time, the small amount of time each week that you will spend using these techniques will pay high dividends. As you increase your ability to take charge of time, you may refine or combine these tools. Time management is a tool that develops the self-discipline to create free time.

Connecting Time Management to Your Career

Taking charge of your time is one of the best habits you can establish for your career. For example, if your career goals include graduate or professional school, time management is a true survival skill in an intensive and rigorous postgraduate program. Talented persons move into leadership positions in their organizations partly because they use their time and plan their work effectively. They control time spent with coworkers, on the telephone, at lunch, on low-priority tasks, and on breaks. They have the self-discipline to say no at work to a social conversation that could go on and on, no at home to their favorite television show when priorities beckon, and no to paging aimlessly through their reading matter.

Business and professional associations often sponsor workshops at conventions devoted to fine-tuning a manager's skills. The most efficient managers acknowledge their need for continually sharpening their time-management skills, even though they are expert organizers. Learning how to organize your resources and environment is the next minicourse of the covert curriculum. It's called "Getting Organized."

Action-Oriented Thought Starters

1. Reread the case of Sarah.

    a. Name the specific time-management techniques she used individually and in combination.

    b. What skills described in previous chapters was Sarah practicing?

2. Do you ever wonder how you actually spend your time? Most of us tend to overestimate our ability to control it. Laziness, low mo-

tivation, vague goals, and boring tasks are the major reasons we waste time. Hardcore procrastinators usually have no idea where their time goes. If these remarks describe you, do what time-management experts recommend: conduct a time inventory.

Follow yourself around with a notebook during a typical week and note how you spend your time. You may be amazed at what you learn. Follow these steps.

a. Divide the top of several notebook sheets into the following vertical columns:

Begin   End   Total Time   Activity   Category

b. Record every activity you perform from getting up to bedtime, using units of 15 minutes minimum. For each activity that lasts 15 minutes or longer, note the Begin and End times and name it in the Activity column.

c. At the end of each day, spend a few minutes entering the total time spent on each activity in the Total Time column. Then classify each activity into essential categories such as meals, sleep or rest, transportation, class, job, family, study/assignments, leisure, rising/retiring, domestic chores, socializing, and other major categories if necessary. Reduce your activities to 15 or fewer categories.

d. At the end of the week, take your seven days of data and count the total number of hours you spent in each of the categories. The total time should approximate 168 hours (7×24).

e. Calculate the percent of time you spent in each of the activity categories by dividing the hours in a particular category by 168. If you prefer to calculate your activities based on waking hours only, divide by the total number of waking hours in the week.

Yes, this *is* a time-consuming activity! However, if you are one of those individuals who has tried but failed at time management, a time inventory may be an insightful experience. Find someone else who wants to conduct the inventory and compare notes. The insights that you gain could become the foundation for developing a new approach to time management. When you complete this exercise, why not reward yourself by scheduling a night out?

Finally, consider reading the Mayer book or Covey's chapter entitled "Principles of Personal Management," both listed in the References and Recommended Readings section.

References and Recommended Readings

Covey, S. R., Merrill, A. R., & Merrill, R. R. (1994). *First things first*. New York: Simon & Schuster.

Mayer, J. J. (1995). *Time management for dummies*. Chicago: IDG Books.

G.O.: Get Organized

Friendly Reminders

❏ Estimate the time it will take to read Chapter 6 and enter it on your Weekly Worklist. Compare the actual with the estimated times and try to account for major differences.

❏ As you read Chapter 6, identify skills of the covert curriculum that could transfer to your intended career.

❏ As you read Chapter 6, ask yourself whether your ability to get organized has an internal or external locus of control.

"It is best to do things systematically, since we are only human, and disorder is our worst enemy."

Hesiod (eighth century B.C.),
Greek poet

Can you envision a self-employed business person working successfully in a disorganized, poorly lit, noisy environment, indifferent to efficiency, productivity, or time?

Not likely. However, as a college student you are your own employer. You are investing several years of time, energy, and money in a venture designed to help you reach your long-range goals. You have responsibilities to discharge, people to whom you are accountable, work to complete, and pressures to contend with. You must learn how to structure your working environment for success, *and* you do not have a secretary to assist you. So, go! Get organized! In the previous chapter you learned *when* to do your work but not *how* to do it in an organized manner. This chapter will show you how to

- design your external and internal environment to improve concentration

- develop efficiency in your everyday activities

- obtain and use feedback to evaluate your progress

Construct an Environment for Concentration

As a student, you may find that you are not only without a secretary, but also without a well-designed work setting. However, you can become the architect and builder of your external and internal environment: the physical setting in which you learn and the mental skills needed for learning. *Concentration* is your ability to direct and maintain your attention to the act of learning. It is a skill and a power that fuels your motivation and actions. It is often the key factor to success for the athlete, the executive, the skilled worker, the burdened parent, and the pressured student. You improve your ability to concentrate when you

- *remain aware* of those external and internal conditions that promote and hinder concentration

- *forcefully* create and *construct* the proper external and internal environment

The term *construct* is used because *you* are the architect and builder of your daily life. If you act on the belief that you have the power to organize and direct most of your day's activities (you can't control your teacher's lecture or your boss's directives), you can improve your power to concentrate.

Construct Your External Environment

Your external work environment includes all the places where you learn including classrooms, laboratories, libraries, and study areas. Some settings you can influence, others you can't. You can't change the light fixtures, seating, or acoustics in a classroom, but you can arrive early the first day of class and sit toward the front of the room. Similarly, you can try to avoid distracting doorways, windows, students, and glaring lights.

What can you do to influence your study areas? A residence hall student cannot make major changes to a room, but some distractions can be avoided. Commuter students living at home or in apartments may be required to share space with family or roommates. But there are ways to make studying in these settings easier. As you read these sections, take notes on ways that you can reconstruct your work environment into an office for the self-employed business person you are.

❏ Get the Study Habit

The first step for getting organized is to develop the habit of regular study. Studying at regular times in the same places is a conditioning process, in which the cues from your physical study environment (room, desk, chair, lighting, sounds) become associated with the *process* of studying (thinking, reading, writing). The repeated association of your study behaviors with the physical cues of the environment causes you to connect and visualize the act of studying with that particular environment. In short, the physical environment evokes (go ahead, look up the word in the dictionary if you don't know its meaning) study behavior. Likewise, thinking about the specific time that you always study will evoke thoughts of study. For example, when you wake up Tuesday morning you think, "It's Tuesday. Therefore, I will study at the library from 1:00 to 3:00 P.M. and from 7:30 to 10:00 P.M. and in my room from 11:00 to midnight."

Take time now and identify periods in your term schedule that enable you to study in *regular* places at *regular* times.

❏ Construct a Distraction-Resistant Study Area

The ideal study environment is free of distractions. A *distraction* is any visual, auditory, olfactory, or tactile stimulus that diverts your attention away from your work. To assess the quality of your work area, check each item in the Directory of Distressing Distractions that accurately describes your study environment.

Directory of Distressing Distractions

_____ 1. There are usually people moving about the room where I study.

_____ 2. On my study desk/table there are pictures, mementos, photos, magazines, correspondence, or similar items.

_____ 3. My desk is located near a window or a door.

_____ 4. My typewriter or computer requires so much space that I do not have enough room to spread books and notes.

_____ 5. I like to study in an easy chair, on the couch, or in bed.

_____ 6. I know that I can study effectively while listening to music.

_____ 7. The room where I study is usually very warm (or very cold).

_____ 8. I like to study in the kitchen or family room.

_____ 9. I normally study near a phone.

_____ 10. I do not pay much attention to lighting because it is not that important.

Let's dissect these distressing distractions and apply them to your study environment.

Your Room (items 1, 7, 8, 9)
Studying in a high-traffic area is incompatible with concentration (item 1). If there is no better place to work, try to negotiate the right to silence. Many residence halls and homes enforce, with varying degrees of success, quiet times when socializing and entertainment are forbidden.

A room that is too warm (item 7) causes you to relax, a condition your body cannot fight even if your mind wants to. A cold room is also distracting. If you cannot change the temperature, dress accordingly.

The kitchen or family room (item 8) is an appealing place to study with its large table and bright lights, but it is the source of other distressing distractions. The blending of cookies, calories, and concentration is a poor recipe for learning. If you must "graze" in the refrigerator, snack before, not after, you begin your work. A kitchen is usually a high-traffic area and home to a phone (item 9). Not only is the sound of a phone distracting, but a busy phone makes you anticipate subsequent calls.

Your Desk: For Study or Storage? (items 2, 3, 4)

Studying is most often associated with a person leaning over a desk reading a book. But can you concentrate with a photograph of a loved one, the stuffed animal you won, or a stack of unanswered correspondence only inches from your book (item 2)? Remove such distractions from the desk when you study. The top of your study desk should contain only the items you need at that time. To avoid glare from the desk or table surface, buy a desk pad from your local stationery store.

Try to locate your desk away from a window or a door (item 3). Having a study desk face a glare-free, unadorned wall is one occasion when it is desirable to "draw a blank." If your typewriter or computer crowds your desk (item 4), consider buying a portable desk or table to augment your study space.

The Sounds of Silence? (item 6)

Ask some "A" students if they study listening to music. Probably a few will say yes, but so will several "D" students. The merits of studying with music are often debated, but most experts believe that students learn more effectively without it.

Perhaps the real issue is the definition of a distraction, not the presence of music. If the music is pleasant, familiar, and at low volume, you *might* be able to study effectively, if you work at it. Beethoven or Brahms at low volume may not distract the classical music fan, but it could irritate the roommate who prefers the latest rock group. Perhaps each of you likes New Age–type "mood" music, with low-definition sound patterns that are less distracting than other forms of music.

As a rule of thumb, if you are aware of the music while studying, it *is* a distraction. Turn it off. You are kidding yourself to think that

Locate a Backup Study Area

If your home or room sometimes contains too many distractions, what is the alternative? After experimenting with different areas, select one or two that are most conducive for study and make them your headquarters. Depending on your circumstances, you may need two or more regular study areas.

Pat was a commuter student whose family lived near campus. He could not study at home in the evening because his family lived in a small apartment and enjoyed television. After supper Pat went to the college library. During the first few months he chose a space along the aisle near the main entrance, a perfect place to be distracted by friends and members of the opposite sex.

When he realized his error, Pat moved to a remote area of the library where distractions were fewer. He arrived early enough to "stake out" a study carrel and returned to it regularly. Furthermore, Pat made it his goal not to look up whenever someone walked by. In only a few weeks his concentration improved markedly. When Pat returned home later in the evening, his family was retiring for the night. After a short break he resumed studying in the quiet of his room until bedtime.

Ask your librarian about reserving a quiet room or a study carrel. If there are no quiet areas in your college or public libraries, search for other areas on campus, such as an empty classroom or a quiet lounge. However, if an area seems too quiet or remote, observe how often it is patrolled by security and bring along a friend who is equally committed to serious study.

your brain can simultaneously process two different kinds of incoming information, one from your eyes, the other from your ears. In fact, the messages of ads and disc jockeys are intentionally designed to gain your attention.

Sometimes you can use one kind of sound to block out another. A student named Joan lives in a residence hall that has thin walls. When she becomes annoyed by voices in adjacent rooms, Joan turns on her portable fan, which creates a sound loud enough to mask the voices. But its quiet, constant hum is not distracting. "Elevator" music can have similar effects at low volume. Consider keeping a pair of earplugs or headphones handy for those times when you need to hear the sounds of silence.

Lighting for Learning (item 10)

Avoid extremes of light. Very bright or dim lighting can cause eye fatigue, which reduces study time. A light can be bright and not induce fatigue if it is diffused (indirect lighting). Avoid high-intensity lighting when it is the only source in the room. It creates a disturbing, sharp contrast with darkness.

One student, Neil, thought that he could study for two hours after his roommate went to bed. But the only light Neil could use was a high-intensity desk lamp. Although he was motivated and mentally alert, he experienced eye strain after an hour of reading. Because circumstances did not permit him to study elsewhere, he was forced to readjust his study schedule.

Seating: The Bottom Line (item 5)

Relaxing and studying are incompatible. You've been conditioned to associate couches, comfortable chairs, and beds with relaxing, resting, and sleeping, not with concentrating. Don't deceive yourself into thinking that you can remain alert while reading a textbook in bed, sprawled across a couch, or jackknifed in your favorite chair. If you *are* learning while in a relaxed position, you may learn considerably more in an attentive position. Do not let your body seduce your mind into relaxation. Avoid chairs that are too soft or too rigid. An ergonomic chair (one designed to promote good posture) may be a costly but worthwhile investment.

Construct Your Psychological Environment

Organizing the tangible objects in your external environment is sometimes easier than organizing the ideas, feelings, and attitudes that comprise your internal, psychological environment at any given moment, especially if you are experiencing stress. Your ability to concentrate is influenced by your motivation, goals, and physical condition.

❏ Motivate Yourself Throughout the Day

Concentration requires not only a well-designed physical environment, but also self-discipline and strong mental habits. For example, what should you do when you don't want to study, but must? How do you prepare yourself to study? The best time to motivate yourself is at the beginning of your day. While you shower, dress, exercise, or eat breakfast, mentally review the day's activities. Checking your appointment book, the weekly work list, and your daily DO-list is a minute well spent. Visualize the places you must go, your classes, the homework to be submitted, your appointments, and the personal business to be accomplished. Review when and where you plan to study. If you wrote your goals on the 3 × 5 cards as suggested in Chapter 2, review them briefly. Remind yourself how fortunate you are to be in college. Congratulate yourself for having the wisdom and the support systems to reach that goal. In short, begin each day goal-oriented: You know what you have to do and why. Be ready to remotivate yourself later in the day as your energy diminishes.

Monitor Your Motivation for Each Assignment

Motivate yourself before you begin an assignment by asking Deep Strategy (chapter 1) questions that make the assignment meaningful.

- How does this particular assignment fit into the course as a whole?

- What thinking skills will I strengthen by performing this assignment?

- How will the skills I use and the information I obtain help me in my academic major?

- How can I connect this assignment to my personal interests or career plans?

Do not expect answers to all these questions each time you prepare to study. However, such self-directed inquiry ("taking charge") places that work or study period in the context of your short-term, intermediate, and long-range goals. Your answers will guide your mental energy, reduce boredom, and improve the quality of your learning.

Sometimes you cannot motivate yourself or concentrate because personal problems or recent frustrations dominate your thinking and emotions. When that occurs take time out to create a short-term plan for contending with the problems, at least temporarily. The plan may involve calling someone, talking to a friend, visiting a counselor, or taking a long walk.

Some authorities (Pauk, 1993) recommend that you keep a sheet next to your textbook (or lecture notes) and make a check mark each time you are distracted. Count the number of times that you are distracted during that period and note the sources of the distractions (e.g., noises, daydreaming, anxiety, physical discomfort). Many students report a decline in the number of check marks after using the score sheet for one or two weeks. If some thought or feeling is distracting you, write it down and deal with it at a later time. By collecting data about your distractions, you become aware of the nature and frequency of the distractions, and you then have clues for reducing their influence.

Set GOals for Each Assignment

The first half of the word *goal* is *GO*. GOal setting focuses your time and energy, which in turn strengthens concentration. Apply the three principles described in Chapter 3, "Setting and Monitoring Goals": Set specific goals, set realistic goals, and obtain feedback.

Before you begin a study or work period, ensure that you have the books, papers, and other materials needed. Review your weekly work list and course syllabi to confirm the assignments and their context within the course.

Set specific goals for each work assignment. For instance, think about an assignment this way: "I need about 5 hours to complete my political science paper. I will work 3 hours today and 2 hours tomorrow." If your study goal is long or complex like the essay paper, divide it into smaller goals. Several small goals are easier (and will seem easier) to attain than one large goal. As you reach each small goal, you feel satisfied and confident that you can reach the larger goal. For example, divide the political science essay into parts: reading, outline, rough draft, revision, and hard copy. Estimate the amount of time required to complete each of the smaller goals. Be ready to revise your estimate of the total time needed and record it on your weekly work list.

Completing a major project is like painting a house. The task seems overwhelming until you divide it into smaller jobs (scrape old paint, paint trim, paint siding) and further divide those jobs into each of the four sides of the house.

❏ Monitor Your Performance while You Work

During your study or work period, periodically stop and monitor your performance by asking yourself questions such as

- Am I doing specifically what I'm supposed to be doing, or am I deviating from the assignment?

A Note to Parent/Students

Students who are parents are quick to point out problems with creating the ideal climate for concentration. Often it's impossible, no matter how hard you try. At home there are frequent interruptions and distractions; you may be forced to study in the kitchen or near the phone. You may not have the luxury of studying in a library. If you are a single parent, it may be particularly difficult to find significant amounts of quality study time. With toddlers around, you are continually challenged to keep them content with toys, books, and television. Once the children are in bed, you may be too tired to study for your most demanding courses.

If you are a parent/student, there are some things you can do to alleviate (look up the word if you don't know it) the conflicts between your needs and your children's. The solutions are few and may be limited, but they may prompt you to think of alternatives.

1. When possible, enlist the support of your spouse, children, and other family members. Let them take over some of the household responsibilities. Ask them to respect your need for quiet study time. Consider offering your children external rewards for certain tasks. Diplomatically remind family members that everyone will ultimately benefit from your education. And when you receive an A on an important test or paper, make it a family celebration.

2. If you have school-aged children, try to schedule study times and rest breaks together, so that home becomes like a school. Let them know you can help them, but that you too are a student who needs time to do your homework. When necessary, schedule play time together.

• Am I using my time properly, or am I spending too much time on some things and not enough on others?

• Am I really focused on my work, or am I being distracted?

Keeping track of what you are doing while you are doing it can lead to greater efficiency and higher productivity.

❏ Promote Concentration through Mind-Body Connections

Concentration was defined as the ability to direct and maintain your attention to learning. Maintaining attention in the face of many distractions requires self-discipline and toughness. In his book *Toughness*

3. Look for and use the "time pockets" of your day, those 10- to 45-minute free periods when you can study, join family members, do chores, or relax. Make every minute count.

4. Review your expectations of yourself and others; be open to moderating them. Like Dorothy, the nurse described in Chapter 3, you may have been an "A" student in high school. Is it reasonable to expect As in your current situation? Is it realistic to keep your house as clean as the television commercials demand? Or to entertain guests as often as or in the style you once did? Or to continue major commitments to volunteer work? Contrary to the illusion often depicted in the media, people do have their limitations. Superman and Superwoman *are* fantasy figures.

5. Inquire at the student affairs office about a parent-support group. Most colleges with significant enrollments of adult students have parent-support groups that meet regularly to share experiences.

6. Be patient and persistent. You will make it. Of those adult students who drop out of college, most withdraw during the first term. The majority complete their program. Years from now your success as a parent will not be measured by a grade point average, but by having done what you could for your family and yourself using the resources that were available.

Training for Life, sports psychologist James E. Loehr identifies concepts and techniques used by successful athletes and applies them to cultivating mental toughness in various life situations (Hanson, 1994). Although it is beyond the scope of this chapter to summarize Loehr's principles of toughness, they seem equally applicable to college life, especially to developing and maintaining concentration. Study the recommendations below thoughtfully, for you will encounter most of them in subsequent chapters.

1. Give yourself breaks. Study breaks influence your motivation to continue and remain alert. Build a 10-minute break into each hour of study. Decide in advance how you will use the time and try to

build in physical activity. At various periods of the day, plan a 15- to 30-minute break when you can relax, meditate, remotivate yourself, substitute positive emotions for negative emotions, and recharge your physical and psychological energy.

2. Use visual imagery. Many athletes create a visual image of the steps they follow to complete an activity. Use visual imagery to prepare for a speech (imagine yourself speaking to your audience), lead a group project (anticipate questions and your responses to them), contribute to class discussion (visualize interchanges with the instructor and your peers), plan the steps of a library assignment (using the computer, locating books or periodicals, taking notes), or learn new software (executing commands, making hard copy).

3. Make nutrition a high priority. To be mentally fit, don't skip meals. Eat a nutritious breakfast, a light lunch, and healthy snacks. Avoid heavy meals; be willing to eat smaller meals four or five times daily.

4. Exercise regularly, three to five times weekly for at least 30 minutes each time.

5. Establish a regular sleep cycle. Construct your bedtime environment to promote restful sleep. Before bedtime avoid bright lights, heavy reading, and worrying. Try to go to bed and get up about the same time each day; try to get enough sleep so that you wake up refreshed.

Some students think "Yeah, yeah, I've heard that before" when experts advise about nutrition, exercise, and sleep. You can creep through college with mediocre grades and poor health habits. You can beat up on your body and your mind still functions, even if marginally. If you don't believe that proper nutrition, exercise, and sleep is necessary, look yourself in the eye (a mirror helps!) and ask how you *really* feel when you are sitting in class on an empty stomach, only partially awake, connected (perhaps) to a body that feels like the living dead. Check your ability to concentrate. Could it be better?

In summary, the first major step to getting organized is to strengthen your concentration skills. You build concentration skills by constructing an external and psychological environment that is associated with learning and by attending to your physical health. Rome was not built in a day, and neither are concentration skills. Furthermore, they are facilitated by habits of efficiency, the second major topic of this chapter.

Tune Up Your Efficiency

Webster's New World Dictionary (Neufeldt, 1988) defines *efficiency* as the "ability to produce a desired effect, product, etc. with a minimum of effort, expense, or waste" (p. 433). There are several little things that you can do to reach your goals (desired results) with minimum expenditure of time and effort. The following suggestions may not transform you into an "A" student. But they enable you to buy time for other activities and generate confidence that you are in control of your work. Remember, you are still your own secretary.

Using Time Efficiently

Although time-management techniques were presented in Chapter 5, here are some specific, readily implemented suggestions that increase your efficiency. Chances are that you can add new ones to the list below.

1. Use your wake-up time to plan your day and bedtime to evaluate your accomplishments.

2. While listening to your favorite radio or television show, write checks, answer correspondence, straighten your room, care for clothing, or exercise.

3. When you feel tired or restless after a tough class, relax, take a brisk walk, or perform some other exercise.

4. Write definitions of key concepts you must learn on 3 x 5 cards and review them on your way to class, while waiting in lines, or during other time pockets.

5. If your employer permits you to study during the quiet times on your job, take books or notes to work.

6. When you have only 10 to 15 minutes before your next class, arrive early and review the assignment.

7. Work on one assignment at a time to keep your desk free of clutter.

8. Keep a notepad beside your bed to jot down ideas you get before bedtime or as soon as you awaken in the morning.

9. Allow some time for the unexpected.

10. Save 10 to 15 minutes each evening to clean up the clutter and organize your materials for the next day.

Add your suggestions here.

1. _____

2. _____

3. _____

4. _____

The late British prime minister Benjamin Disraeli once remarked, "He who gains time gains everything."

Your Academic Office Supply Kit

As a self-employed business person, consider purchasing the following items for your office.

1. A backpack, bag, or attaché case. Some mail-order companies offer book packs designed for students.

2. A compact portable office kit containing items such as a ruler, stapler, staple puller, three-hole punch, pen, and space for a calculator and tape.

3. A two-drawer file cabinet for storing course papers, notes, receipts, correspondence, and registration and financial assistance materials.

4. Reference books, including a standard dictionary, spelling dictionary, thesaurus, biographical dictionary, atlas, and guide to good writing.

5. A standard-size electric or suction cup pencil sharpener.

6. A small bulletin board for messages, notes, and DO-list items. Some colleges permit residence hall students to place a small bulletin board on the outside of their rooms for notes to and from friends.

7. Book shelves or plastic storage crates.

8. A calculator adequate for your most complicated math class, but not so sophisticated that you are unable to operate it when pressed for time or during an exam.

9. A typewriter with word-processing capabilities or a computer. Whatever you choose, learn how to operate it *before* your first major paper is due.

10. A reliable mechanical alarm clock with a loud bell or a battery-powered clock radio. They don't stop when the electricity goes off.

11. A two- or three-tier in/out basket to centralize your assignments.

12. Various sizes and colors of self-adhesive notepads. These handy pads with their sticky reverse sides can be used as single item DO-lists or for notes that stick anywhere they can be seen, including phones, notebooks, refrigerators, books, and mirrors. Carry a pack with you; they have unlimited uses.

As you browse through your favorite office supply store, look for other items that could tune up your efficiency. Can you imagine how impressed your family and friends would be if you suggested office supplies as potential gifts?

Remember, these suggestions are not the expressway to efficiency; they are thought starters and switches to energize your search for better ways to do your work. Efficiency is not just a series of short-cuts; it's an attitude, a continuous search for a better way. Once you have this attitude, getting organized is no longer a chore—it's fun.

Obtaining and Using Feedback

So far, getting organized has been described as a set of skills or techniques in concentration and efficiency. But how do you know when you are learning, concentrating, operating efficiently, managing time properly, or being honest with yourself? How do you become aware of the results of your behavior?

From Chapter 3, "Setting and Monitoring Goals," you learned that the third step in setting goals is feedback. Getting and using feedback from yourself and others is one of the most powerful learning-how-to-learn habits you can develop. It is essential for growth and development in any aspect of life. Proficiency in anything demands feedback. Feedback is information in the form of knowledge, opinions, feelings, and actions from yourself or others.

This chapter concludes with two popular and contrasting forms of feedback: journal writing and self-contracting. Study each carefully.

Choose the one method that best fits your personal style, then follow it for several weeks. Work hard to make it work for you. Be patient (it's a new skill) and be willing to make adjustments. If the feedback, or data, produces positive changes, even small changes, stay with it. If it does not work after giving it a good chance, switch to the other approach. As psychologist Rollo May stated, "The more self-awareness a person has, the more alive he is."

Journal Writing

Journal writing is an autobiographical approach to self-awareness. It produces feedback by letting you reflect on and connect the specific ideas and suggestions described in this book to your everyday experiences. The journal is an autobiographical approach to making *Learning Skills for College and Career* personally meaningful with each chapter you read (Hettich, 1990).

❑ Procedures

1. Purchase or recycle a spiral notebook and write *Journal* on its cover.

2. Set a goal to write two or three times each week at a time when you have a chance for reflection. But don't overdo it—you may have other writing assignments to complete.

3. Keeping a journal is a flexible technique that permits you to write a variety of entries. You can

   • record your experiences with the learning skills contained in this book

   • write about your successes and failures, your strengths and weaknesses

   • express feelings such as joy, frustration, anger, discouragement, and accomplishment

   • prescribe action: start doing . . . , stop doing . . . , continue doing . . .

   • integrate studying, learning, and living

   • review your motives and goals for college

   • write anything, but keep the highly personal entries to yourself

With journal writing you are the student *and* the teacher.

4. Review your journal entries weekly and determine what you learned about yourself. Then select one or two new learning skills that you want to try during the next week. Write about these skills on the days that you practice them.

5. Most important, be honest with yourself.

❏ Benefits of Journal Writing

1. Journal writing puts you in regular contact with your thoughts, feelings, and attitudes in a systematic way. Your entries are tangible evidence of your thinking and learning, your struggles, and your victories.

2. The journal is another way to become actively involved in your learning process.

3. Journal writing is a healthy means of blowing off steam, discharging tension, or saying things in writing that you may not want to communicate orally.

4. Journal writing is *writing*. Many instructors use journals in their courses as a supplemental measure of student learning.

❏ Sample Journal Entries

Below are sample journal entries written by students while enrolled in a study-skills course that required journal writing.

This week especially I've forced myself to review my notes for 10–15 minutes after I come back from class. I used the word *force* because it's a great effort and so easy to push off. Because I've done this, when I read the material covered in lecture (which I've already briefly gone over before class) ideas are familiar—kind of, "Oh yeah, I remember that!" It's a pleasant feeling. K.N.

While sitting in my car waiting for it to warm up, I decided to review the notes from the class that I had just attended. The next time I went to that class, it seemed that I had remembered more pertinent facts than previously. I find it a useful technique to review notes before a class and immediately after leaving one. R.L.

I find that when I start to study, my greatest problem is daydreaming. I'll sit down with a book and fall into past memories. Being it's difficult to concentrate on two things at once, I don't get the work done. I think the value of breaks really expresses itself here. By giving yourself a five- to ten-minute break, you are making room for both work and dreams. S.U.

We had our first exam in English. By following some basic rules for test preparation, there was no need to cram, nor did I experience panic. Continuous review, repetition, study scheduling (including exam review), and obtaining of general test information from the instructor made the exam an entire learning process. Early preparation and well-organized study helped me to avert panic, which could have impeded effective study. After the exam I felt confident and relaxed because I was receiving feedback on the work I had done in English. Any kind of feedback is positive and a form of motivation. The exam itself is a tool for future review. D.E.

Some thoughts on writing a journal: This was my first experience of keeping a journal, and I have to admit that I did not care for the idea at first. As the course progressed, I found journal writing to be less of a chore, and decided that there are some definite advantages. (1) Journal writing provided an opportunity to apply . . . concepts to my past and present life experiences. This is a definite learning aid, for concepts that are applied are not readily forgotten. (2) Because I was always on the alert for 'suitable journal materials,' I found myself thinking about different ideas, even when I wasn't studying or participating in class. (3) Journal writing provided an opportunity to express myself through the written word. It's a good rehearsal for a written exam, and one I sorely needed after a long absence from the academic world. (4) If a favorite topic of mine is not covered in an exam, I can write about it in my journal. (5) All right, I'll admit it—keeping a journal can be enjoyable! L.D.

What rich insights are gained by keeping a journal, and lost without one! One of the many rewards of journal writing is that it provides incentive for continuing to practice effective learning skills. However, if you do not experience insights, satisfaction, or incentive (intrinsic motivation) after you write entries for several weeks, then consider giving yourself an extrinsic reward until you feel intrinsically rewarded. For example, treat yourself to dinner or a movie each week that you wrote at least two thoughtful journal entries. Sooner or later self-awareness becomes its own reward.

Self-contracting

A self-contract is a written agreement between you and yourself to perform specific actions and in return receive specified rewards. A method of behavior modification, self-contracting has been used in a variety of educational settings to establish new habits of learning. It is beyond the scope of this book to describe all aspects of self-contracting as a behavior-change technique. Yet knowing the key components should help you use self-contracting to obtain feedback about your learning skills.

Self-contracting employs the three principles of goal setting described in Chapter 3. As such, it forges another link to your future. It links your daily experiences to your short-term, intermediate, and long-range goals.

❏ Procedures for Writing a Self-contract

1. Make a list of the learning skills that you want to develop or strengthen. Be as specific as possible. Do not write, "I will improve my time-management skills." Instead, write, "I will prepare a weekly work list each Sunday evening for the next week of classes" or "I will review my time-management techniques each morning before I go to class."

2. Choose two or three new skills (behaviors) and enter them on the learning skill line as shown in the sample self-contract in Figure 6.1. The number of skills that you select each week is less important than your ability to successfully complete those you do select. For example, if you choose a difficult skill, then choose another that is easier. If you choose only the hard skills, chances are that you will fail, feel guilty, and become discouraged.

As you improve, *add* one or two new skills to the list. When you add new skills gradually, you increase your chances of succeeding with them. Students who attempt to practice too many skills at once, in spite of good intentions, are asking for frustration, failure, and guilt.

3. At the end of each day

   • record the number of attempts (tries) you make to practice that skill

   • record the number of successes (hits) you achieved

   • enter a dash on the days when there is no opportunity to practice the skill (see Figure 6.1)

SELF-CONTRACT FOR LEARNING SKILLS

I, *Chris Elder*, contract with myself to practice the following learning skills during the week of *Oct 24th* to *Oct 31st*. I will record the number of times that I practice the behavior (# tries) and the number of times that I succeed (# hits). At the end of the week I will sum the total number of tries and hits for each skill and then calculate the percentage of hits by dividing # hits by # tries for each skill.

	Learning Skill		Sun.	Mon.	Tue.	Wed.	Thr.	Fri.	Sat.	Total	%
1st week	Review day's notes	# tries	–	0	1	1	1	1	–	4	50%
		# hits	–	0	0	1	1	0	–	2	
	Review week's notes	# tries	1	–	–	–	–	–	1	2	100%
		# hits	1	–	–	–	–	–	1	2	
	Do weekly work list	# tries	1	–	–	–	–	–	–	1	100%
		# hits	1	–	–	–	–	–	–	1	
		# tries									
		# hits									
2nd week	Regular Study Place	# tries	1	1	1	1	1	1	–	6	67%
		# hits	0	1	0	1	1	1	–	4	
	Plan the day	# tries	–	0	0	1	1	1	1	4	50%
		# hits	–	0	0	1	0	1	0	2	
		# tries									
		# hits									
3rd week	Skim N.Y. Times	# tries	–	0	1	0	1	0	–	2	100%
		# hits	–	0	1	0	1	0	–	2	
	Survey & Proofread tests	# tries	–	–	–	1	–	1	–	2	100%
		# hits	–	–	–	1	–	1	–	2	
		# tries									
		# hits									

REWARD MENU

Learning Skill	Specific Reward	Amount of Reward
Review day's notes	money	$1.00 per day
Review week's notes	money	$5.00 per week
Weekly work list	Sunday night T.V.	2 hours
Regular Study Place	Leisure reading	45 minutes ea. night
Plan the day	~~Breakfast treat~~ Relaxation	~~1 jelly donut~~ 1 half hour
Skim N.Y. Times	Snack	1 candy bar
Survey & Proofread tests	Self-recognition	"pat on the back"

Figure 6.1 Self-contract for Learning Skills

Learning skills differ widely and are applied in diverse ways. Therefore, clearly defining the precise meaning of tries and hits for each skill is impossible. *You* decide when you have attempted a new skill and when you have succeeded or failed in your attempt. The number of tries and hits forms the data that become feedback from you to you.

4. At the end of each week

- add the tries and hits for each skill

- calculate your success rate (percentage) by dividing the number of hits for each skill by the number of tries for each skill, as shown on the far right side of Figure 6.1

- compare your success rates from week to week as a measure of progress

When you begin to practice a skill, expect a low ratio of hits to tries, especially with skills that are tough to learn. It is hard to break old learning habits and replace them with new habits. With practice your ratio of hits to tries will improve and you'll be pleased with your progress.

If the ratio does not increase as fast as you want, carefully examine

- your expectations (are they too high?)

- the particular skill that you are practicing (is it more complex than you imagined?)

- the reward that you selected

5. Reward yourself (the fun part!). Perhaps you have a mother or grandmother who says, "After you eat your vegetables, then you'll get your dessert." If getting dessert were not dependent on eating vegetables, your experience with vegetables might be non-existent.

The situation is similar to rewarding the performance of study skills. Like eating vegetables, developing new learning skills may be an unappealing activity for some students. If you are not intrinsically rewarded by practicing new skills, then identify specific extrinsic incentives that, like a dessert, will reward you until your intrinsic motivation takes over. The following steps show how to select and record rewards on the reward menu in Figure 6.1.

a. Identify a specific concrete, self-administered reward for each learning skill you plan to develop: a coin, a small piece of candy, a ten-minute phone call, a half-hour TV program, or an hour with your favorite magazine. The reward must be something that will bring you satisfaction.

b. Let the reward fit the behavior. Choose rewards that are sufficiently strong to motivate you, but realistic to obtain. For instance, buying a sports car for taking good notes is unreasonable; visiting a showroom to look at a sports car is not unreasonable! Skills that are very difficult to learn deserve stronger rewards than those that are easy to learn.

c. Match the reward to the behavior so that the reward's influence does not deteriorate or have potentially unhealthy effects. For example, a candy bar may be an appropriate reward for something you do once or twice a week, but not for a skill performed several times daily. Similarly, use different rewards for different behaviors. Money, for example, can lose its effectiveness if used too often.

d. If possible, administer the reward or a symbol of the reward (for example, an "I.O.Me") soon after you perform the desired skill. Spend a few minutes at the end of the day to administer or record your rewards.

The process of rewarding specific behaviors with external rewards can be more complicated than these general instructions suggest. However, following the steps outlined above should be sufficient for using a self-contract effectively.

Your success in gathering and benefiting from feedback with a journal or the self-contract depends on your personal commitment to work with either technique for several weeks. As suggested earlier, choose carefully, be patient, and persist. Switch to the alternate technique *only* if after several weeks you can honestly admit that you are not learning anything about yourself.

A Memo to the Messy and the Meticulous

This chapter will benefit primarily those students who have difficulty organizing their environment. There are many of you who *must* get organized if you want to survive in college. On the opposite end of the organizing spectrum are those meticulous students who have a

passion for organizing *everything* they can get their hands on. For them this chapter has been like chocolate to a "chocoholic." Techniques of organizing can become rituals, compulsions, and ends in themselves rather than means to an end. If you happen to be on one end of this spectrum (messy or meticulous), try to meet someone on the other end. You may not want to be roommates, like Felix Unger and Oscar Madison in *The Odd Couple,* but you *can* learn from each other.

This chapter has suggested three approaches for getting organized: concentration, efficiency, and feedback. The next chapter, "Getting Around," builds on your organizing skills and shows you how to identify and use your institution's resources.

Connecting Getting Organized to Your Career

A student operates like a self-employed business or professional person. To succeed in any occupation, you must learn how to simultaneously adapt to and modify your work setting to serve you efficiently. Several suggestions presented in the past two chapters are often mentioned in training sessions of business and professional conventions. Organizing and concentration skills readily transfer to the workplace, whatever it may be for you. By then, perhaps you will have a secretary to whom you can teach these skills!

Action-Oriented Thought Starters

1. Survey the areas where you currently study. Using information contained in this chapter, note the advantages and disadvantages of each place.

   a. What can you do to change these settings?

   b. What are the things you cannot change and must adapt to?

2. Everybody knows an efficiency expert, whether a parent, sibling, friend, neighbor, or teacher. Ask your favorite efficiency expert whether you can follow him or her around for an hour to observe how work is accomplished. If you are unable to perform a walk-around, learn what the person does to improve efficiency. Apply what you learned from this interview to your work habits.

3. Some individuals learn concentration skills through various approaches, including the study of the ideas and techniques derived from Eastern philosophy, religion, and martial arts. Consult library sources or individuals you know and learn the differences among these terms. Although concentration is only one aspect of these practices, learn what mental/psychological dimensions they share in common, as well as how they differ, and how those dimensions can be applied to student life.

- Transcendental meditation
- Tae Kwon-Do
- Yoga
- Zen
- Qigong
- Tai Chi Chuan

References and Recommended Readings

Covey, S. R. (1989). *The seven habits of highly effective people.* New York: Simon & Schuster.

Hanson, C. (1994, February 27). "Working smart: Winning the gold in business requires Olympic discipline." *Chicago Tribune,* p. 9.

Hettich, P. (1990). Journal writing: Old fare or nouvelle cuisine? *Teaching of Psychology, 17,* 36–39.

LeBoeuf, M. (1979). *Working smart: How to accomplish more in half the time.* New York: Warner Books.

Loehr, J. E. (1993). *Toughness training for life.* New York: Dutton/Penguin Group.

Neufeldt, V. (Ed.) (1988). *Webster's new world dictionary of American English* (3rd ed.). New York: Webster's New World Dictionaries.

Pauk, W. (1993). *How to study.* Geneva, IL: Houghton Mifflin.

Watson, D. L., & Tharp, R. G. (1993). *Self-directed behavior: Self-modification for personal adjustment.* Pacific Grove, CA: Brooks/Cole.

Winston, S. (1978). *Getting organized.* New York: Warner.

CHAPTER 7

Getting Around

Sonia Powell
Olive-Harvey College

Paul Hettich
Barat College

Friendly Reminders

❏ How much time on your weekly worklist did you schedule for reading this chapter?

❏ Before you read this chapter, check your physical study environment and set goals for this study period.

❏ Preview Chapter 7 using the Preview Checklist on page 11.

"He who starts behind in the great race of life must forever remain behind or run faster than the man in front."

Benjamin E. Mays (1895–1984),
American educator and civil rights proponent

One of the most significant benefits *and* challenges of your college experience is your exposure to people who are different from you. Students differ in culture, socioeconomic status, educational preparation, life experiences, family settings, value systems, sophistication, and familiarity with the U.S. educational system, to name a few of the most significant differences. To the extent that the student community reflects major differences contained in U.S. society, a college is a microcosm of the larger culture. Just as there are groups in our society who start behind and remain behind unless they run faster, many students start college "behind" in one way or another.

If you are one of the fortunate students who did not start college behind the majority of your peers, don't skip to the next chapter. You will gain considerable insights from reading this chapter.

College is an excellent place in which to learn with and from individuals whom you might not ordinarily encounter. Such experiences help empower you to become a more fully functioning participant in society, perhaps a leader who will make a significant contribution someday. Besides, people who work well with diverse groups possess social skills that are highly marketable.

Starting from Behind

For those of you who feel like outsiders to the college culture, getting the most from your education requires learning new customs, ideas, skills, and attitudes, in addition to seemingly endless hard work. However, by learning the system you will likely get through college with fewer problems, better grades, more friends and fun, and better career preparation than if you ignore or fight the system.

Learning to get around is all the more critical for students with limited financial means. They do not have the safety net of expendable money and time to correct a poor start in college. They risk never being able to cross the finish line if they initially fail to make the most of any available opportunities.

Many students who start behind grew up in lower socioeconomic backgrounds, are the first in their generation or family to attend college, belong to racial or ethnic minorities, or are older returning adults, foreign students, or students with disabilities. Not every student who identifies with these groups is or feels behind, but many do. This chapter is for everyone, but especially those who have not sat around the dinner table with college-educated family members or friends and discussed how to get around and, ultimately, thrive in college. Specifically, you will learn how to assess your needs and identify campus resources that can help you.

The First Step: Determine Your Needs

Students who start from behind come from several different backgrounds. Many inner-city or rural students who are products of poorly functioning school systems have suffered accumulated academic deficiencies and require extensive help to manage the rigors of college. Returning adults, many with families and jobs, may lack confidence in their ability to survive in college after a long absence from the classroom. Foreign students, sometimes stereotyped for their high academic achievement (real or perceived), may face a strange, complex, and sometimes hostile new culture. Finally, some students do not think they are starting from behind but, in fact, grossly underestimate the academic demands, peer competition, and stresses they face. These students may have achieved at the good or excellent level in an unchallenging high school, but overestimate their level of preparedness for college-level work.

To determine whether you must run faster to catch up, check the alternatives in each item of the Needs-Meter that best describes you.

The Needs-Meter: Checking Your Distance from Other Runners

1. What was your overall academic average in high school?
   ___ D or below   ___ C   ___ B or above

2. If you completed the ACT or SAT, in what range did you score?
   ___ Lower third   ___ Middle third   ___ Upper third

3. To what extent do you read daily or weekly news magazines, read information-oriented books, and follow current national and international events?

    ___ Very little   ___ Somewhat   ___ Very often

4. How many members of your immediate family and close relatives obtained a college degree?

    ___ None   ___ 1 to 3   ___ 4 or more

5. How would you characterize your socioeconomic background?

    ___ Lower   ___ Lower to middle   ___ Middle or above

6. Are you a member of a racial or ethnic minority or a first-generation American?

    ___ Yes   ___ No

7. How familiar are you with the U.S. culture?

    ___ Not very   ___ Somewhat   ___ Very

8. How many semesters or quarters of college have you completed?

    ___ None   ___ 1 to 2   ___ 3 or more

9. How many years ago did you graduate from high school?

    ___ 8 or more   ___ 4 to 7   ___ 0 to 3

10. To what extent do you depend on yourself for financial support?

    ___ Completely   ___ Considerably   ___ Very little

11. How many people depend on you for financial or emotional support?

    ___ 3 or more   ___ 1 to 2   ___ None

12. Do you have children 18 or under who live with you?

    ___ Yes   ___ No

13. Do you have physical or psychological disabilities that make it difficult to learn or to attend classes?

    ___ Yes   ___ No

14. How old are you?

    ___ Over 35   ___ 24 to 34   ___ Under 23

15. How difficult is it for you to establish good relationships with your peers?

___ Very difficult   ___ About average   ___ Fairly easy

16. Do you enjoy meeting new people and starting new relationships?

___ No   ___ Yes

17. How often do you attend social gatherings?

___ Almost never   ___ Sometimes   ___ Frequently

18. To what extent are you a "self-starting" independent person who takes the initiative to do what must be done?

___ Not at all   ___ Somewhat   ___ Very much

19. How would you describe your level of self-esteem?

___ Below average   ___ Average   ___ Above average

20. How confident are you in your ability to succeed in college?

___ Not very   ___ Somewhat   ___ Very

21. How motivated are you to obtain a college education?

___ Not very   ___ Somewhat   ___ Very

The Needs-Meter is a checklist intended to help you reflect on and take steps to improve your situation. It is not a diagnostic instrument. There is no scoring key because your answers to such diverse questions could not be "weighted" properly. However, it is probably safe to conclude that if your answers tend to be those on the left side of the page, you may be behind many of your peers. In some areas you may need considerable assistance. Learning to get around your campus should be a high priority for you. However, confidence, proper motivation, hard work, and a good self-image can help you get on the right track.

If most of your answers were the middle choices, you may need some assistance. If your responses were mainly on the right side, you are not home free, but you are probably prepared for what lies ahead. Appreciate your position; try to understand and empathize with those who are behind you.

The items in the Needs-Meter are grouped into the following different areas to help you interpret them.

Academic Preparedness: Items 1–3

A solid academic preparation in high school is generally regarded as a key predictor of success. However, average or higher grades should not make you feel secure if you attended schools whose academic standards are below national norms. The ACT or SAT scores give you a much better picture of your preparation. Although such tests are often criticized for being racially or culturally biased, they *are* somewhat objective measures with norms (standards) that have been derived by nationwide testing of people like you and your college peers. Chances are they are more accurate gauges of your academic preparedness than your high school grade point average alone. Together, your test scores and high school GPA are strong predictors of success during your first terms of college. Do not hesitate to ask a counselor, admissions officer, or your advisor for an interpretation of this issue.

If you regularly read news magazines and information-oriented books and are familiar with current events from watching thought-provoking television programs, you can compensate for some aspects of average or below-average achievement reflected in your high school transcript. Success in college and later in your career is a measure of how well you can analyze and integrate individual events within the social context. Reading beyond your discipline is an excellent practice.

Exposure to College: Items 4–9

Collectively, items 4 to 9 measure how attuned you are to the culture of U.S. colleges. Generally, the closer you identify with mainstream values and the more exposure you have to college, the easier your adjustment will be. College-educated relatives and friends can share their insights. To minimize pressures and to test the waters, many prospective students enroll in a college course prior to matriculating as a degree student.

Independence and Responsibilities: Items 10–14

The greater your responsibilities for children, spouse, parents, or others, the more likely that you will experience demands on your physical and mental resources. You may be caught between the rock and hard place we've all heard about: Personal or job advancement requires further schooling, but obtaining that education increases your stress.

Box 7.1

Between a Rock and a Hard Place

Sharon faced the typical dilemma of many returning adult students. She was a single parent with two small children under the age of 10. Sharon decided that a college degree was her ticket out of borderline poverty to a better life, but she did not want to spread her program over several years as a part-time student. However, after enrolling full-time she began to notice a loss of quality in her family life. The demands on her time and energy were so great that she was no longer able to help her children with their homework or put nutritious meals on the table. The house began to resemble a touchdown zone that had been ravaged by several tornados. When her children's grades slipped and complaints about disruptive behavior increased, she began to feel exhausted and depressed.

Finally, Sharon dropped all of her courses and enrolled in job-related courses at the local community college. She decided that until the children were older, she couldn't pursue a full-time college program. She discovered that the responsibilities that push people toward more education may, at the same time, prevent them from achieving it in a timely manner.

Social Skills: Items 15–17

If socializing is difficult for you, you may fail to achieve one of college's most important, most rewarding, and most marketable outcomes: the development of interpersonal skills. Make it a personal goal to increase your social activities. Study the suggestions offered in this chapter and in Part Three of this book.

Determination and Locus of Control: Items 18–21

Julian Rotter's notion of locus of control was summarized in the Chapter 2 discussion of motivation. Self-starting, motivated students with positive self-esteem and strong self-confidence possess an internal locus of control that empowers them to take charge of life and strive to work successfully. Such students see themselves as the initiators of action; they accept responsibility for their behavior.

Unfortunately, many students may not have had the life experiences that strengthen these characteristics. Yet with the help of the college's resources (advisors, teachers, counselors, staff), students can begin to construct their personal environment for success. College is often the best opportunity an individual receives for developing these characteristics. Determination, self-discipline, sacrifice, and hard work are the key ingredients for achieving your daily, short-term, and long-range goals.

The Next Step: Getting Around to Your Resources

By admitting you, your college has expressed its confidence that you *can* succeed, *if* you use your own and the institution's assets. What are the typical resources available on campus that enable you to get around? They include the

- teaching faculty
- counselors
- library services
- learning resource centers
- administrative offices
- health services
- campus bookstore
- campus activities
- fellow students

Teaching Faculty

On the road to their baccalaureate degree, students are likely to encounter 30 to 40 different teachers. Long after you have forgotten a course's subject matter, you will remember its instructor, especially the idiosyncrasies, insights, and the overall emotional and intellectual impression that person left on you. Teachers project several images to their students, including authority, role model, adversary, friend, surrogate parent or sibling, advisor, counselor, and leader.

❑ Working with Faculty

Because professors differ widely, don't expect them to treat you in identical ways. Similarly, do not treat them the same. Your good teachers are not just subject-matter specialists. They are role models and resources willing to help you inside and outside the classroom, if you work with them. As role models, your instructors reflect attitudes, value systems, and habits that you may want to emulate (go ahead, look it up in the dictionary) or avoid. As resources, teachers are willing to meet and discuss course topics, test grades, and career-related issues. Listen attentively, take notes, and ask questions because many of your most significant insights occur during such meetings with teachers.

Obviously, teachers can be wrong on issues, but they probably spent considerable time and thought to develop their views. You are not obliged to agree with them (although agreeing may help on some tests), but examining their ideas is one reason you are in college.

When you meet with faculty, be businesslike and courteous. Make an appointment in advance for a specified time during the professor's regular office hours. Be prompt; call ahead if you must cancel the

---

Box 7.2

A Tale of Two Students

Do not expect teachers to think kindly toward students who wait until the end of the semester to start dealing with problems that became evident after the first exam. Teachers are not miracle workers. They are willing to help you, but they expect you to accept responsibility for your behavior as the problem develops.

When you see a problem developing, get help immediately. Don't be like Bruce, who chalked up three Ds on his tests, missed several classes, and waited until the end of the term to meet with his instructor. By that time only a miracle would have brought Bruce's final grade up to a C. Bruce expected that his teacher would offer extra assignments to raise his grade. However, the instructor, like many teachers, felt that extra assignments would distract Bruce from learning the material assigned. Bruce's failure to take responsibility for his behavior earlier and learn the material resulted in a final grade of D–.

Desiree, on the other hand, was so bothered by the D she received on her first test that she made an appointment with her instructor immediately. Because she was genuinely committed to learning the material (not simply raising her grade), her instructor explained the questions she missed, discussed the test criteria, and showed her a technique for analyzing her errors. Desiree used this information on her subsequent tests. Not only did her grade improve, but she also applied the skills she learned to exams in other courses.

appointment or arrive late. Come prepared with your questions or concerns so that valuable time (yours and theirs) is well spent.

If you want to learn from your professors, expect constructive criticism. The truth may hurt, but be open to viewing criticism as a prerequisite for growth and change. Regard criticism as feedback directed to your specific behaviors, such as a poorly written paper, wrong information on an exam, or a thoughtless remark. But don't take criticism personally. If you do not believe that the criticism is valid, diplomatically ask for the evidence on which the criticism is based. The ability to accept criticism maturely is an essential life/learning skill.

Teaching and learning is a two-way process and students have responsibilities to professors. Attend all classes and arrive on time. If you must be late or absent, inform the instructor as soon as possible. Many instructors assume that absences and tardiness are due to apathy. In class ask questions, participate in the learning process, and show genuine enthusiasm.

Most instructors appreciate students who contribute to the teaching/learning process. If the teacher seems open to it, bring in relevant books or articles. The best professors learn from their students too. Many are open to feedback about their teaching, when suggestions are presented in a constructive manner.

❏ Teachers as Advisors

Although most teaching occurs in the classroom, academic-advising sessions are another occasion for learning. Your advisor is there to help you learn how to make decisions about your academic program. Good advisors will answer your questions about courses, ensure that you understand college procedures, offer suggestions, and try to assist you in integrating your personal and professional goals with your current experiences. Before you begin your courses, learn about your institution's advising system from the catalog, the student handbook, or the admissions counselor. Expect advising procedures to differ at least a little from school to school.

Some advisors are directive in their remarks to new students but become less directive as students mature and accept responsibility for their own plans. One of the best things you can do to earn your advisor's attention is to have read the catalog, especially those parts that pertain to your general education requirements and your academic major. Know the catalog well; it is an unofficial contract between you and the institution. Similarly, read and understand the student handbooks and related publications. If you cannot find an answer to your question, ask your advisor. Remember that advisors occasionally make mistakes, so don't hesitate to check with other sources to clarify important issues and procedures.

Finally, recognize that the teacher-student relationship can evolve into a mentor-mentee bond that endures throughout college and the years beyond. Such relationships are often among the most valuable outcomes of your college education.

Counselors

Because the term *counselor* has different meanings, responsibilities may differ from school to school. In community colleges a counselor may serve as an academic advisor, a career counselor, and a personal counselor. In 4-year institutions these functions may be handled by three different *and* differently trained individuals.

❏ Career Counseling

Students typically begin college convinced that career counseling is something that they will investigate during their last term, if time permits. WRONG! Even if you have chosen an occupation, but especially if you have not, visit the career planning and placement office during your first semester.

Why? Chapter 3, "Setting and Monitoring Goals," showed how long-range goals, when connected to intermediate and short-term goals, help make the daily routine of college meaningful and obstacles surmountable. By investigating career possibilities during your first term, you can make your course work meaningful. Browse through the materials of your career planning center. Counselors will respect your wishes if you do not want to talk about careers that particular day.

❏ Personal Counseling

When your car breaks down, do you expect it to fix itself? When you incur a serious injury or contract a disease, do you go untreated? If you are experiencing personal problems with relationships, substance abuse, an unwanted pregnancy, sexually transmitted diseases, or any other source of serious distress, can you expect your problem to correct itself? College counseling centers are staffed by professionals trained to treat a wide array of personal problems, including those you may experience. Students who do not seek help reduce their chances of finishing their education. When the student is

What Distresses Students?

If someone told you that college is supposed to be a happy time in your life, guess again. Although most students experience some pleasant times, most students also experience considerable stress. In a nationwide survey of 5200 students from 39 colleges and universities, counselor-researchers David Alexander and Gus Baron (1995) asked students how much they were "currently distressed." Sixty percent of the students surveyed were seeking counseling at the time of the survey (the Clinical group), whereas 40% were not (Nonclinical group). On 42 items, each representing a different type of stress, students were asked, "How much are you currently distressed by . . . ?" using a five-point rating scale. Below are the rankings of the top 15 sources of stress reported by each group, in the order of most stressful to least stressful.

Rank	Clinical group	Nonclinical group
1	Academic school work, grades	Academic, school work, grades
2	Anxiety, fear, worries, nervousness	Finances
3	Self-esteem, self-confidence	Decisions about career, major
4	Depression	Uncertain about future, life after college
5	Uncertain about future, life after college	Procrastination, getting motivated
6	Finances	Anxiety, fear, worries, nervousness
7	Procrastination, getting motivated	Weight problems, body image
8	Stress management	Time management

forced to face the problem outside the college environment, treatment is likely to be expensive and inconvenient. Read Box 7.3 for additional information about personal counseling.

Library Services

Have you toured your college library? What hours is it open? Are there study carrels? Where are the reference books and the current

Rank	Clinical group	Nonclinical group
9	Decisions about career, major	Test, speech, and performance anxiety
10	Relationship with romantic partner, spouse	Self-esteem, self-confidence
11	Concentration	Stress management
12	Breakup, loss of relationship	Concentration
13	Weight problems, body image	Perfectionism
14	Relationship with parents, family, or siblings	Dating concerns
15	Irritability, anger, hostility	Reading, study-skills problems

A few points need to be made about the information above. First, the variety of distresses reported indicates that counselors are accustomed to dealing with these and several other sources of distress. Second, students who receive counseling and those who do not share many of the same distresses. Consequently, students should not assume that their problems are unique. By seeking counseling, students are showing good judgment in trying to manage the problem before it becomes too serious. Finally, note those topics that are addressed in this book: motivation (Chapter 2), time management (Chapter 5), concentration (Chapter 6), stress management (Chapter 8), reading (Chapter 11), study-skills problems (Chapters 9–15), and, to an extent, relationships (Chapter 16). In summary, if you are experiencing these problems to the extent that they prevent you from doing your best, seek the services of a professional personal counselor. You are not alone, nor is it likely that your source of distress is unique. *Take control of your problems before they control you.*

periodicals located? What is the reference librarian's name? Are there rooms where small groups can work? Walk through the stacks and browse through the books and periodicals that interest you. If your library's holdings are limited, ask about its interlibrary loan system and how long it takes to obtain books and journal articles from other libraries. You need to know the answers to these questions long before you begin a major paper, not the week before the paper is due.

Each week browse through the newspapers and magazines when you have a 10- to 45-minute time pocket. Skim the *Wall Street Journal,* the *New York Times,* and the local papers; read articles that attract your attention. Skim magazines that interest you, especially those you like but cannot afford. Make a mental file of the articles you read because they may become useful topics for a subsequent class assignment.

What kinds of computers do you have access to in your library and what software is available? If you are not familiar with the software, does the library staff provide instruction?

Many courses require students to conduct library research and write papers. If bibliographic instruction (learning how to use the library's resources) is not explained by your instructors, ask librarians if training sessions are available. Some colleges and universities offer credit-based courses in bibliographic instruction. The time you invest in learning how to use your library will pay high dividends with each paper you write. As a life/learning skill, competency in library research pays even higher dividends if you enter any of the numerous occupations that demand research skills.

Learning Resource Centers

Do your basic reading, writing, or math skills need strengthening? Don't wait for that first D for proof that you need help. Most colleges have centers staffed by trained professionals with graduate degrees who can help you further develop your learning skills. On some campuses, you go to separate departments for help in math, English, or other courses. Most universities and colleges centralize their learning-support services in a learning-assistance office or learning resource center.

If the Needs-Meter showed that you are running behind other students, chances are that you need help in reading, writing, math, critical-thinking, problem-solving, and study skills. Smart students face the reality of their deficiencies and seek help. If you feel too ashamed of your deficiencies or too proud to ask for assistance, you can hide your feelings for the one to two terms it takes before low grades force you to drop out of the important race you want so much to compete in. In fact, the learning resource center should be appreciated as the place that can help you step out in front of the competition and take the lead of the race. It can not only help the D student earn Cs, but also help the C student earn Bs and As. Recall the skills identified in Chapter 4, "The Covert Curriculum: Connecting College to Career," as workplace basics. You will not get a *good* job without them.

Administrative Offices

The administrative offices are responsible for providing services to students and employees of the college. Each term your records are updated in the offices of the registrar, cashier, financial assistance, student affairs, health services, security, and others. You should maintain a file for all materials you receive from each office in case of changes or errors. Avoid problems by learning institutional policies and procedures that are described in the catalog and the handbooks. Periodically check with administrative personnel to see whether there are new policies or information that you should be aware of.

Get to know the secretaries because in most organizations they are major conduits of information. If you have a question about someone, something, or some event, a secretary can usually answer it. They have access to schedules ("Dr. ____ will be in only until 3:30 today even though his schedule shows 4:30."). They know policy and procedures ("The last day to submit that form was yesterday, however . . ."). They are unsung power brokers ("Just a minute and I'll check to see if she is available.") who can help you or frustrate you. Remember your favorite secretary on her birthday or on Secretary's Day. Similarly, get to know other staff who are there to serve you when you need them: security, maintenance, housekeeping, and food service. Learn who they are; understand the roles they perform.

Health Services

Become familiar with the institution's health services, policies, hours of operation, and special programs. Most students underestimate the importance of maintaining their health. Yet apathy toward your health can produce a tragic domino effect. Irregular or insufficient sleep, lack of exercise, poor diet, and substance abuse make you vulnerable to illness, class absences, poor performance, and dangerously low grades. It is not unusual for students placed on academic probation to trace the origin of their problems, not to low motivation or poor study habits, but to poor attitudes about health. Attend wellness workshops or similar events sponsored by the health services. Finally, view the sports center as a resource for staying well. Developing healthy habits about health is another minicourse in the covert curriculum that pays dividends for the rest of your life. Remember that a great deal of energy will be needed to reach your goals. Good health is imperative!

Box 7.4

"But I Didn't Know the Test Was Today!": KNOW Your Written Resources!

"How would I know I needed a prereq to get into the course?"

"So why do I have to be immunized to use the library?"

"Where does it say that my out-of-town guest can't stay in my room?"

"Just because I missed the drop/add deadline, why can't I get a tuition refund?"

"If I can drink at home, why can't I drink in the dorm?"

"I didn't realize that I could do an internship in this program."

Such agonizing exclamations of frustration and anger are heard too often by administrators, staff, and faculty. However, problems like these could be reduced if students took the time to study and abide by the many rules and regulations that govern their behavior. Reading your written resources is essential not only to prevent problems, but also to help you maximize your opportunities. The information that helps you navigate the challenges confronting you during college exists in many forms. Sometimes people will simply tell you what they expect of you, but don't depend on verbal communications alone. An organization's published resources disseminate essential information and policies publicly, efficiently, and reliably. Let's review the most common written resources.

Course Syllabi

When you receive your course syllabus on the first day of class (be sure to attend that important first class!), enter the dates that tests and major assignments are due into your appointment book and on your room calendar. Read your syllabus at least once a week during the first month of the term to understand everything you can about the course. The syllabus is the course blueprint that reflects the teacher's expectations and the students' obligations.

Course/Term Schedule

The college's schedule of classes for each term contains essential information and often lists course prerequisites and drop/add and withdrawal deadlines. Keep a copy of the course schedule throughout the term as it usually lists drop/add and withdrawal deadlines and other useful information.

Catalog of Courses/Academic Bulletin

The catalog describes your institution's programs, opportunities, policies, and services. It lists the academic majors, courses, and course requisites. Read your academic bulletin carefully; it is type of contract that prescribes the mutual responsibilities that you share with your college. Save your academic bulletin at least until graduation because it contains those policies and regulations that were in effect when you matriculated (go ahead, look up the word if you don't know its meaning!).

Handbooks

Most colleges and universities publish specific academic and nonacademic policies in handbooks that supplement the academic bulletin. The problems identified above regarding course prerequisites, immunization, tuition refunds, out-of-town guests, and drinking could have been avoided if the students *understood and obeyed* the regulations that govern those activities.

You incur significant costs when you fail to abide by your institution's regulations. The personal costs to you may include frustration, lowered self-esteem, waste of time, stress, penalties, or loss of opportunities. For example, the student who pleaded ignorance to the test was in a course in which makeup tests are a major irritant to the teacher. The student who missed the drop/add deadline lost several hundred dollars in tuition. Colleges are rarely willing to make exceptions, no matter how valid the excuse seems to you. Students who attempt to complete a course without the appropriate prerequisites typically experience frustration and failure. The student who attempted to have a friend stay the weekend was embarrassed when the Head Resident denied the request. Students caught with illegal substances are vulnerable to dismissal and legal action. The student who did not read about internships lost out on a significant learning experience. Your college education contains enough stressful events. Why increase your stress by ignoring your published resources!

Your written resources may not be exciting reading, but when you ignore them, the people who have your best interests in mind may have to pay the costs.

(continued on next page)

Box 7.4
continued

For example, the mother of the student denied library privileges because he failed to get immunized made over 100 phone calls before the problem was solved. The student who failed to complete the drop/add form on time created a financial loss for the family. Why bite the hand that feeds you?

Ignoring rules also generates inefficiency and administrative costs to your institution. For instance, the business office must process your late drop/add form. You waste your advisor's time when she or he has to explain information from the catalog that you are responsible for knowing. The instructor who gives you a makeup test must divert time from other activities, even if your excuse is valid. The student affairs office becomes involved in residence hall infractions.

When you fail to use your written resources, you create the impression in others that you are immature and not yet able to "take charge" of yourself. Most of all, you take one step backward in the journey toward the discovery of your true potential.

Finally, knowledge is power. When you acquire the habit of knowing your written resources, you increase your chances of succeeding in any organization you enter, college or the workplace. After all, how can you lead the pack and win the game if you don't understand and follow the rules?

Campus Bookstore

One way to catch up with the person in front of you is to read. Buy a weekly news magazine such as *Time, Newsweek,* or *US News and World Report*. Read articles that interest you; skim the rest of the magazine. Student discounts make it easy for you to subscribe. You'll be amazed at how much reading about current events helps you in classroom discussions or conversations with friends and increases knowledge, builds self-confidence, and nurtures motivation.

Are you looking for leisure reading? Browse through the paperback best-seller list. Or look for the biography or autobiography of one of your heroes or heroines. Biographies are valuable sources for learning how others have survived, thrived, and caught up with the people in front of them. Consider using books on audio tape when driving or exercising.

Use the campus bookstore to learn about books teachers use in courses that you might take. Finally, many bookstores carry the kind of office supplies recommended in Chapter 6, "G.O.: Get Organized," and the time-management devices described in Chapter 5.

Campus Activities

Try to attend as many college events as your schedule and responsibilities permit. Campus-wide activities, student organizations, lectures, concerts, and field trips are opportunities to learn and meet people. Once you take charge of your time and commitments, consider joining an organization. The activities in most clubs teach you organizational and interpersonal skills and teamwork.

If you identify with a racial, ethnic, age, or other special group, consider joining its campus organization. Often it takes substantial emotional energy to function effectively in an environment that is different from your own or, worse yet, hostile to you. It is important to remain in contact with those values you identify with strongly. It is equally important not to remain exclusively within your particular group.

The emotional support you can derive from your special group may be vital for your survival. For example, single parents account for an increasing number of students on many campuses. The student affairs or counseling offices in many universities and colleges sponsor support groups where single parents meet regularly to share their experiences. Black, Hispanic, Asian, and other racial and ethnic organizations are common on campuses, especially in larger universities.

Look for events sponsored in your academic major. Departmental events and student clubs, such as the Computer Club or French Club, are ideal opportunities to learn about your professors, peers, and the subject matter of your career interests. Try to meet the full- and part-time faculty. Engage them in conversations about their professional interests or your career interests. At one college, the Psychology Club has sponsored a wide variety of campus-wide events including speakers from social-service agencies, psychology alumni who connect their college and career experiences, faculty speakers from related departments, discussions of social issues, movie nights, hypnotists, and bake sale fund-raising activities. Club meetings are occasions to meet other students, establish friendships, develop leadership skills, and identify work opportunities. Some of the most memorable experiences of college life can come from your club activities.

Box 7.5

Choosing Your Friends

Not everyone you befriend is someone you want to learn from, as Jim discovered. Jim came from a top-notch, nationally acclaimed high school. Though his GPA was in the lower third of his class, he was accepted into the engineering program at an excellent state university.

Jim was invited to join a study group with some high-achieving students. He attended a few meetings and his quiz grades improved. However, Jim grew bored and irritated with his study group's incessant talk about class projects. He began "studying" with another group of students who were more fun to be with. When his new circle of friends was not socializing, they spent considerable time complaining about their courses and professors. Although this routine was more exciting to Jim, his grades dropped rapidly. As it turned out, Jim and his friends stopped sharing good times and started sharing the depressing experience of being placed on academic probation after only one semester of their "friendship."

Some "friends" will distract you from your academic goals, *expect* you to party when you shouldn't, or try to infect you with values and attitudes incompatible with your own. When that occurs you must clarify the meaning of friendship and assess the costs and benefits of your relationship as it influences your goals. If you are highly motivated, feel self-confident, and have high esteem for yourself, you can handle the situation maturely.

Fellow Students

Last but not least, view your peers as resources. Get to know the students sitting next to you in class. Exchange phone numbers for those days when one of you must be absent. Share a coffee break when time permits. That attractive student sitting next to you may be a fascinating person, a real help in understanding a complicated lecture, the offspring of an IBM executive, or the spouse of the local TV anchor. Make a special effort to know the individual if he or she comes from a background that is different from yours.

Finally, do not be afraid to discuss your fears and aspirations with *good* friends. You'll discover that they share most of your concerns and are able to assist you in developing self-awareness. Perhaps one of the most enduring legacies of your college experience will be found 20 years from now in the college friendships that you continue to nurture.

Getting Around the Downside

Unfortunately, college life is not always as rosy as some of our remarks suggest. America is a country of "isms," including some that are found on the typical campus. Racism, sexism, and elitism are among the most abominable and common attitudes you may encounter. Prejudices regarding age, disabilities, and social origin are also commonplace. Such prejudices are one of the reasons that people can be difficult to work or coexist with. Try to learn how to minimize conflict and maximize rapport. People who are prejudiced are showing limitations that they will have to contend with long after your paths have crossed. Recognize that people have the capacity to change, but do not change as rapidly as we might like or need. In the meantime, remember your rights, continue to pursue your goals, and strive for excellence in whatever you attempt. If your rights are violated, deal with the situation. Make sure you have all the facts because it is easy to distort or misinterpret communications and behaviors. State the facts and complain directly to the person involved. Try to reach an agreement privately, avoiding embarrassment, because most issues are better handled that way.

If your rights continue to be violated, the system provides the means to redress grievances. Contact the student affairs, counseling, administrative, or student government offices and obtain the documentation that shows you how to proceed. Take control of your emotions, avoid exaggeration, follow the grievance procedure most carefully and, again, make sure that your facts are correct. A grievance stated in writing is a compelling, permanent document. Fortunately, most problems can be settled without declaring a world war, so be optimistic.

If you are challenging a school policy that you consider discriminatory, work within the system first. Chances are the institution's legal resources can explain their policy to your satisfaction. If not, you may need to seek legal counsel outside of the institution.

Crossing the Finish Line

To repeat Benjamin Mays: "He who starts behind in the great race of life must forever remain behind or run faster than the man in front."

This chapter has offered helpful advice and practical suggestions for getting around college a little faster and crossing the finish line a little sooner.

Ultimately, perseverance is your most important attribute in this race. Furthermore, *you* are responsible for exploiting the opportunities that lie ahead. When failure occurs, as it will, get up and get back into the race again as soon as possible. The fact that you did not start in the mainstream is not likely to motivate other people to treat you with fairness and compassion. Don't feel sorry for yourself. Avoid blaming others. Besides, a master at getting around always thinks of alternatives and always anticipates the future.

Connecting Getting Around to Your Career

Whether or not you feel part of the mainstream of college students, the information in this chapter has significance for your career. It reflects an attitude and a strategy for successfully adjusting to new situations in which you feel like an outsider. When you enter a new organization, conduct an assessment of your strengths and weaknesses relative to those who are insiders. Discover the ways in which you are behind others, if you are truly behind. Next, become familiar with the organization's resources, both human and financial. What opportunities are available for training and advancement? What is the total scope of the organization's activities? What are its strengths and weaknesses? How is it viewed by the community? Finally, meet the people who work there and expect more diversity than meets the eye. While you are learning to get around an organization, you will probably also discover how to stay ahead in the race and move up.

Action-Oriented Thought Starters

1. Getting Around Your Campus
    To learn how much you really know about your campus and your college policies, try answering the following questions, by yourself or with a friend.

    a. Where is the health center and what are its hours?

b. What is the name of the library? Are there other libraries on campus?

c. Who is the chairperson of the department in which you plan to major? Where is his or her office?

d. How often do job recruiters visit campus each term?

e. What is the phone extension of security and where is the security office located?

f. What is the name of the college newspaper?

g. How much is the library fine for books that are returned late? Are all books charged the same fine?

h. Where can you go to use a word processor? What software is available?

i. What is the last day to drop and add a course? To withdraw from a course?

j. Does the registrar/records office have evening hours?

k. What are the hours of the counseling service?

l. What is the procedure for obtaining a parking sticker (and paying parking fines)?

m. Who is the director of financial assistance?

n. Where are three student lounges located?

o. Where can you cash a check?

p. What is the tuition refund policy?

2. Throughout life you will be required to solve problems quickly in unstructured situations. For example, the senior author experienced a death of a family member from out of state during the writing of this chapter and was placed in charge of all arrangements and the settlement of legal matters. A considerable degree of getting around was necessary.

a. Identify similar events either on campus or involving family or friends where your getting-around skills are important for an immediate and effective response to an emergency situation.

b. What concepts presented in this chapter would help you with such situations?

References and Recommended Readings

Alexander, D. K., & Baron, A. (1995, October). *Nature and severity of college students' counseling concerns.* Paper presented at the meeting of the Research Consortium of Counseling and Psychological Services in Higher Education, Newport, RI.

Combs, P. (1994). *Major in success.* Berkeley, CA: Ten Speed Press.

Kanter, R. M., & Stein, B. M. (Eds.) (1979). *Life in organizations: Workplaces as people experience them.* New York: Basic Books.

Kaye, E., & Gardner, J. (1988). *The student's handbook for getting ready, moving in, and succeeding on campus.* New York: College Entrance Examination Board.

Tchudi, S. (1987). *The young learner's handbook.* New York: Scribner's.

CHAPTER 8

Passing the Stress Test

Camille Helkowski
Loyola University of Chicago

Friendly Reminders

❏ Preview Chapter 8 using the Preview Checklist on page 11.

❏ Name two or three resources presented in Chapter 7 that could provide you with information about stress management.

❏ Adjust your external environment to limit distractions that may reduce concentration, then motivate yourself to concentrate.

"Adaptability is probably the most distinctive characteristic of life. . . . It is the basis for homeostasis (establishing a new steady state) and of resistance to stress."

Hans Selye (1907–1982),
Canadian endocrinologist

According to Carl Rogers, adaptability is the sign of a truly educated individual. According to endocrinologist Hans Selye, it is the hallmark of a healthy person, one who knows how to manage stress. Effective stress management is an ongoing test of your ability to keep your life balanced in a roller-coaster world. "Passing the Stress Test" helps you identify the external and internal circumstances that are most likely to throw you off this roller coaster. Also, you'll learn some healthy approaches to regaining your physiological composure and your emotional perspective. Losing your balance is not necessarily awful or dangerous. In fact, some stress-management strategies enable you to enjoy the ride!

You probably noticed there are a few assumptions in the previous remarks. *Assumption 1:* Stress is inescapable, no matter who you are or what you do. *Assumption 2:* Psychological and physiological health depend, to a great extent, on your ability to effectively handle the stress in your life. *Assumption 3:* Now is the right time to learn to manage your stress.

At the beginning of your college career, you might think you have plenty of time to become a skillful stress manager. However, the common stressors listed in Box 8.1 (pages 134–135) indicate that the college environment provides ample opportunities to experience stress. Spend a few minutes now to review those stressors.

Did you notice that many sources of stress for students are likely to recur at other points in life? Consequently, try to participate in a stress-management class (another non-credit minicourse in the covert curriculum) while you are in college. *The stress-management strategies you master now will help you keep your balance through the many stages of your career and relationships.*

Stress: In Theory and in Practice

Dr. Hans Selye, known for his research on the physiological effects of stress, describes stress as a side effect produced by any situation to which you respond in any way (Selye, 1974). It is the nonspecific response of the body to any demand made upon it. The demand may be pleasant—an A on a test—and still produce stress. When the demand is unpleasant—an F on a test—the accompanying stress is also unpleasant or damaging. Selye called the damaging type of stress *distress.*

Selye's research concluded that, although human beings are very adaptable, we cannot adapt indefinitely to unremitting (go ahead, look it up) levels of stress. We experience stress in three stages, which Selye calls the General Adaptation Syndrome.

Stage 1: Alarm Reaction—Your first exposure to the stressor produces characteristic physiological changes and lowered resistance.

Stage 2: Resistance—As your exposure to the stressor continues, the body adapts, producing above-normal energy. All signs of alarm disappear and then resistance to the stressor rises.

Stage 3: Exhaustion—Long, continued exposure to the stressor eventually depletes the body's adaptation energy. Alarm signs reappear and resistance begins to decline again. Over time, when an individual's adaptation energy is exhausted, death occurs.

You may think that you are a whole lot smarter than those lab rats Selye used in much of his research. You take better care of yourself. You make sure that you do not have to operate at above-normal levels of stress for very long. Most students believe this; many are correct. They manage their internal and external worlds by recognizing and dealing with stressors in their lives. Some students, however, do not deal effectively with their stressors. They do not recognize the problem, or they will not admit to it. In either case, their emotional and physical health is in jeopardy.

To observe the General Adaptation Syndrome outside of a laboratory setting, visit any college campus during the last two weeks of an academic term and note the "finals frenzy" (*alarm reaction*). You are likely to find formerly reasonable human beings who suddenly believe that they can function at optimal levels with only a few hours of sleep each night. They think that the four basic food groups are pop, pizza, nachos, and nicotine. Caffeine, nicotine, alcohol, and other substances are used to alternately keep them awake or calm them down.

You, the observer, are at first amazed by their stamina (*resistance*). Then you begin to notice the signs of deterioration: memory lapses, inability to concentrate, increased anxiety, diarrhea. The lack of sleep

Box
8.1

Common Stressors of Adulthood

Adulthood—especially early adulthood or the college years—can be a stressful time, bringing major life changes that require adjustment and accommodation. Listed below, in order of probable severity of effect, are 35 life events that you may experience. Clusters of these events may increase the likelihood that you'll become sick; they will certainly increase your stress level. If you find that the list includes events that you have experienced recently or expect to experience soon, take the time to develop and cultivate your coping skills—they'll serve you well, both now and in the years to come.

1. Death of a close family member

2. Divorce or separation from mate

3. Detention in jail or other institution

4. Major personal injury or illness

5. Death of a close friend

6. Divorce between parents

7. Marriage

8. Being fired from job or expelled from school

9. Retirement

10. Change in health of a family member

11. Pregnancy

12. Being a victim of a crime

13. Sexual difficulties

14. Gaining new family members (through birth, adoption, older person moving in, and so on)

15. New boyfriend or girlfriend

16. Major business or academic readjustment (merger, change of job or major, failing important course)

17. Major change in financial state (a lot worse or a lot better off than before)

18. Taking out a loan or mortgage for school or a major purchase

19. Trouble with parents, spouse, or girlfriend or boyfriend

20. Outstanding personal achievement

21. Graduation

22. First quarter/semester in college

23. Denied admission to program or school

24. Change in living conditions

25. Serious argument with instructor, friend, or roommate

26. Lower grades than expected

27. Major change in working hours or conditions or increased workload at school

28. Major change in recreational, social, or church activities

29. Major change in sleeping or eating habits

30. Denied admission to required course

31. Taking out a loan for a lesser purchase (for a car, TV, or freezer, for example)

32. Chronic car trouble

33. Change in number of family get-togethers

34. Vacation

35. Minor violation of the law (traffic tickets and so on)

and of proper nutrition and exercise, as well as the use of other substances, are taking their toll. Do they notice these reactions? Do they change their behaviors before they write that last paper or fall asleep during their last final (*exhaustion*)? Do their responses to stress pave the road to the Dean's List or to dismissal?

The General Adaptation Syndrome carries with it good news and bad news. The good news is that human beings are the most adaptable of earth's creatures, having the capacity to withstand tremendous shocks and overcome enormous obstacles. However, a person's ability to adapt has limits. The bad news comes when people refuse to recognize those limits, putting their minds and bodies in grave and imminent danger.

Your Stress Buttons: Identifying Major Sources of Stress

 The first step to handling stress effectively is recognizing what presses your stress buttons. What are the situations and people that are stressors *for you*? As the stressors listed in Box 8.1 indicate, there are certain transitions and traumas that are likely to cause anyone stress. Beginning college is a life transition that most people find stressful, though enjoyable. Beginnings of any kind are typically sources of pleasurable stress. The loss of a loved one is always accompanied by distress. Most people recognize that major life changes result in stress and most people are willing to take the steps necessary to cope with these changes.

The next part of this chapter identifies five *typical sources of stress* that can press your stress buttons. They include

- life's mosquito bites—the little things
- our thoughts and beliefs
- the lack of goals
- relationships
- decisions about finances, careers, and similar choices

As you read, keep a list of the types of situations that push your stress buttons. This list can help you determine which stress-management strategies will be most useful to you.

1. Life's Mosquito Bites—It's the Little Things

The greatest sources of stress in anyone's life are often the little things—life's mosquito bites. Individually they are irritating; in combination, their effect can be serious and sometimes deadly. College provides ample opportunity to get bitten.

- You wait in a long registration line only to find that the class of your dreams is closed.

- You discover the cafeteria's dinner choices are, once again, macaroni or fish on a bun.

- You have overslept, again, and missed your 8:00 A.M. philosophy class.

- Your final on Western civilization will consist of 500 fill-in-the-blank questions. (It actually happened to this chapter's author!)

- Your roommate loves the very same music you hate. (This happened to the book's author!)

- Your significant other wants to spend more time together and does not understand how the study of finite math will make a difference in your relationship.

- You fail to press the "Save" key on the computer and lose the five-page paper you just entered.

- Everyone in your family wants to know what you "intend to do with your degree."

Life's mosquito bites often do more damage than life's major traumas precisely because these bites occur continuously. Like the many small dips on a roller coaster, you seldom notice the little stressors, or your responses to them that indicate that you are experiencing distress. Unattended, the effects of these stressors combine. You end up with a headache, colitis, an anxiety attack, or any of a variety of stress-related physical or emotional ailments. An important rule of stress management is to *pay attention to the impact of the little stressors.*

2. Believing Is Seeing—The Impact of Our Beliefs and Thoughts

Dark Garden*

I once had a garden
filled with flowers
that grew only on dark thoughts

but they need constant
attention

& one day I decided
I had better things
to do.

Brian Andreas,
American poet and artist

Our own thoughts and beliefs can be major contributors to the stress in our lives. Everyone behaves and interprets the behavior of others through their own particular set of beliefs. Psychologists Aaron Beck and Albert Ellis are convinced that we cause ourselves great emotional pain when we operate out of a set of irrational or distorted beliefs. As the major creators of cognitive therapy, Beck and Ellis maintain that we should examine the beliefs that truly motivate our behavior, compare them to reality, and revise those beliefs that make goals unattainable and life difficult or impossible.

Each of us has some irrational beliefs. Consider the following common examples of irrational thinking of a student who

- believes that the only acceptable grade is an A

- has missed class and blames his roommate for not ensuring that he got out of bed

- is positive that her parents will hate her and withdraw their emotional and financial support unless she makes the Dean's List

- believes no one will want to go out with him, so he never asks

- believes she can make her boyfriend quit his excessive drinking

*Source: From *Mostly True—Collected Stories and Drawings*, by Brian Andreas. Copyright © 1993 Story People. Reprinted with permission.

Respectively, these are examples of perfectionism, blaming, "catastrophizing," emotional reasoning, and the belief that one individual has the power to change another. These examples are a representative sample of the irrational beliefs and distorted thinking that motivate behavior. Let's examine more closely in the following exercise those distorted thinking patterns that are the basis of some of our behaviors.

Styles of Distorted Thinking

Table 8.1 is a list of distorted thinking styles.

1. Place a checkmark next to the styles that reflect your own beliefs.

2. Rewrite the styles that you checked as rational, achievable belief statements. The rewritten statements of style should show that (a) you accept responsibility for and ownership of your own actions; and (b) you understand the need to set attainable, "real-world" goals.

3. Rewrite the examples, or write and rewrite your own example.

Did you gain insight into your behavior from this exercise? These distorted thinking and belief patterns exemplify "living on the edge." Yet, as Selye's research implies, the key to effective stress management is learning how to adapt to keep your balance on the roller coaster of life. Living on the edge and keeping balanced are mutually exclusive (contradictory) experiences. Consequently, a crucial step to stress management is to identify your irrational patterns of thinking, then revise and bring them into balance.

3. You're Not in Kansas Anymore: Setting Goals

As the scarecrow pointed out to Dorothy when she reached the crossroads in *The Wizard of Oz*, any way is just as good as any other if you don't know where you want to end up. Luckily for Dorothy, she did know. She had a goal. Do you? Although goal setting was discussed extensively in Chapter 3, the absence of goals can be a major stressor.

When you are in the midst of a transition, such as beginning college or a new career, your stress level is significantly increased if you lack goals or direction. Initially, your goals need not be crystal clear to provide direction and motivation. It is necessary to begin with *some*

Table 8.1 Styles of Distorted Thinking (suggested rewrites appear in Table 8.3, pages 160–162)

Distorted Thinking Styles		Rational Thinking Styles	
Style	*Example*	*Rewrite Style*	*Rewrite Example*
SAMPLE: Blaming Other people are responsible for your pain. Or you are completely responsible for every problem.	I studied hard for the test but got a C. The teacher must hate me.	I am responsible for my behavior and I accept the consequences. I am not responsible for every problem that occurs within a 50-mile radius of me.	I ran out of time and was unable to complete the test, which accounts for my grade. Next time I will bring a watch and pace myself better.
1. Emotional Reasoning If you feel something, then it must be true.	I feel so scared about making my biology presentation. I know I won't remember a thing when I get in front of the class. Then everyone will see how stupid I am.		
2. Catastrophizing You expect disaster. You wait for the worst and know that good events are only temporary interruptions from life's crises.	I have worked with the drama department all year and have finally gotten a lead. I know I'll blow it on opening night and never be cast in another role.		
3. Mind Reading You know what others are thinking and feeling and why they behave the way they do, without ever talking to them about it.	She didn't say hello to me when I walked into class. She must be angry with me.		

Table 8.1 Styles of Distorted Thinking *(continued)*

Distorted Thinking Styles		Rational Thinking Styles	
Style	*Example*	*Rewrite Style*	*Rewrite Example*
4. Myth of Change By the power of your will and/or the intensity of your love, you can make others into the people you want them to be. Your own self-worth is dependent on your ability to do this.	I know that he will stop drinking when we are married. I will make him so happy that he won't need to drink anymore.		
5. Myth of Fairness You alone determine the standard for fairness and are angered when others don't agree.	My English professor is making me do a research paper plus a take-home final exam. She just isn't being fair. After all, I have other classes too.		
6. Perfectionism You must never make a mistake, never achieve at anything less than an optimum level. Being wrong is unthinkable because it makes you unacceptable.	I can't believe I got a B in Spanish. Now I'll never get into grad school, and my parents will really be upset that I got such a terrible grade.		
7. Polarized Thinking You view events and people in terms of this or that, good and bad, right and wrong. There is no middle ground.	I'm going to pledge a fraternity and my best friend isn't. I guess we can't really be friends if that's how he feels.		
8. Overgeneralization You come to a global conclusion based on a single piece of evidence.	I can't believe she would go back to work so soon. Her baby is just a few months old. She is obviously not much of a mother.		

(continued on next page)

Table 8.1 Styles of Distorted Thinking *(continued)*

Distorted Thinking Styles		**Rational Thinking Styles**	
Style	*Example*	*Rewrite Style*	*Rewrite Example*
9. Shoulds You have a list of absolutes to govern your own actions and the actions of others. Any deviation from your rules is unacceptable.	If I don't understand something in a class, I don't ask questions. I should be able to get this stuff, and I don't want anyone to think that I'm not cutting it here.		
10. Victim of Circumstances You have no control over anything that happens in your life and are helpless to do anything about your life. You are not responsible for any outcomes.	It's not my fault that I couldn't study. My friends hounded me until I said that I'd go out with them last night. I know I failed that test this morning, but there was nothing that I could do.		

Source: Based on Thoughts and Feelings: The Art of Cognitive Stress Intervention, by M. McKay, M. Davis, and P. Fanning, New Harbinger Publications, 1981.

goals, such as completing the requirements for a degree within a specified period of time. Once you make it your goal to obtain a degree, then you can create plans to choose a major and develop your career direction. Without goals, your college experience is like an uncharted ocean, and unknowns can cause stress. As indicated in Chapter 3, goals are the compass that you follow to navigate your way through this transition in life. Because goals make the unknown knowable, goal setting is an important stress-reduction strategy. If your goals are vague, return to Chapter 3 and reread the three principles of goal setting.

4. *The Times They Are A-Changin':* The Impact of Transitions on Relationships

Bob Dylan's famous folk song of the 1960s alerted a nation to the changes it was going through. Of the many changes you now face, perhaps the most stressful are the changes in relationships.

❏ Traditional-age Students

If you are a traditional-age college student, entry into college life usually occurs with a burst of independence. Whether a resident or a commuter student, you are now free to structure your own work and leisure time. In fact, during college you may have more freedom to structure your schedule than at any other time in your adult life. Managing this freedom can be stressful. Whether you go to class or hang out in the student lounge, whether you study in the library or party with friends, whether you live at home or stay at school—these choices are often yours alone to make.

The rules on the home front probably have not changed much. Your parents have certain expectations of your behavior that may not fit with your new sense of independence. Parents are (or should be) learning how to let go. You are (or should be) learning how to be let go of. It is normal to feel the strain of conflicting expectations, and it is important to remember that all of you are probably doing your best to adapt to the situation.

❏ Returning Students

If you are continuing your education later in your adult life, competing demands for your time are often the most significant sources of relationship stress. By adding education to an already full life, you simply have less time to spend with your significant others. Consequently, you may feel guilty; those who are most important to you may feel left out. School is an enormous commitment of your time, finances, and intellectual and emotional energy. Your pursuit of a college degree cannot help but affect the amount of time that is available to family and friends. No matter your age, to keep your relationships healthy, you must reduce the amount and duration of stress that you experience in your relationships. The two most important steps that you can take are to communicate and evaluate priorities.

Keeping the lines of *communication* open is an essential ingredient to reducing stress in your relationships. Try to include those important to you in your new life. Visits to campus are wonderful opportunities for your significant others to actively participate in your college experiences. If campus visits are not practical, let these important persons know what you are doing and how you are doing. Ask them for the support that you need, and clarify in what form that support would be most useful. Ask them what they need from you. If there are conflicts (and there will be), negotiation is usually preferable to digging in your heels.

The second step to maintaining healthy relationships is to *evaluate or reevaluate your priorities and commitments.* No one in your life can always come first, nor can they always come last. Consider these examples.

- When faced with a choice of washing the kitchen floor or spending time with your children, it may be more important to be with the children. Wanting floors you could eat off is one of those irrational beliefs relegated to your former life. Besides, when was the last time your family actually ate off the floor?

- When faced with going home to celebrate your best friend's birthday or staying at school because there is a big party, you may need to go home. Birthdays are one day a year; parties happen all the time on a college campus.

- When faced with getting some much needed sleep or attending a committee meeting, sleep may be just what you need. You are no good to yourself or any organization if you are exhausted.

- When faced with missing a class or attending to a friend or family member in need, you may have to miss class. Let your instructor know why you were absent; most of them will understand.

In short, college life influences not only your relationships with your significant others, but also your attitudes toward yourself.

5. Other Stressors of College Life

Students often feel that they are under a great deal of pressure. That's because they are. Doing well academically, financing a college education, selecting an academic major, making solid career decisions, dealing effectively with intrapersonal issues, and developing positive interpersonal relationships are significant issues that most college students face at some point. If a major problem occurs in any one of these areas, a student can easily feel overwhelmed.

As indicated in the previous chapter, it is important that you discover and become familiar with the resources available on your campus. Working with a tutor, career counselor, financial-aid advisor, therapist, or an academic advisor will decrease your sense of crisis. Remember: There is no glory in suffering silently. To resolve most serious problems you need expert information and support. You only need to ask for help on most campuses to get it. Consult your college catalog and student handbook to locate the resources your campus offers.

Developing a Stress-resistant You

In the previous section, we emphasized the importance of understanding the stressors that press your stress buttons, whether they are life's mosquito bites, distorted beliefs, lack of goals, changing relationships, or decisions about life and career. You learned that for each stressor there are resources available for managing them. Let us now examine steps you can take to resist the effects of stress. They fall into two categories: the mind-body connection and discovering what's really bothering you.

Managing the Mind-Body Stress Connection

In Chapter 6 proper nutrition, adequate sleep, and regular exercise were highly recommended for getting organized. These conditions are equally crucial for effective stress management. Unfortunately, students often sacrifice nutrition, sleep, and exercise to the demands of their active academic and social lives. Inferior performance in your daily activities is the short-term result, whereas poor course grades are the long-term product of ignoring your physical needs. The good news is that these aspects of your life are relatively easy for you to control if you listen to the messages your body sends to you. The benefits of controlling them are striking.

❑ **Food**

Develop a food plan that matches your schedule to that of the college cafeteria or your home. Consult your student health service or a nutritionist if you need assistance. Limit your junk food intake, especially during intense academic periods (midterms, papers, finals). Research conducted on the effects of food on academic performance suggests that simple carbohydrates (candy, pop) slow you down, whereas proteins increase your alertness, memory, and ability to handle complex ideas.

According to *The College Student's Health Guide* (Smith and Smith, 1988), there are a number of tips that students can readily follow if they are concerned about their weight. You can

- reduce the amount of soft drinks and juice you consume to reduce sugar intake (drink water instead)

- increase intake of complex carbohydrates by eating rice, noodles, beans, and whole grains

- substitute fruit or sherbet for rich desserts

- choose low-fat protein foods

- reduce or eliminate alcohol

Smith and Smith also identify situations when students should consider seeking professional help for weight-related problems. These circumstances include

- experiencing a sudden weight change of 10 or more pounds

- feeling hopeless or depressed about your weight and being unable to eat in a consistently healthy way

- wanting to lose (or gain) weight but being unable to get started

- wanting to better understand the causes and solutions to weight-related personal issues

The types of help available for weight-related problems include medical diagnosis and treatment and nutritional and psychological counseling (Smith and Smith, 1988).

Although the primary purpose of food is to fuel your body, many people eat to reduce the tensions and feelings produced by stressful situations. At best, food camouflages these feelings only temporarily because they keep returning until you deal with them. Food is a delay tactic, not an answer. When food is used to reduce tension, the extra weight that usually results can create new tensions and a self-perpetuating cycle of eating to reduce increasing tension.

❏ Rest

Rest, like food, revives your body. Inadequate rest and sleep push students to the point where their concentration and capacity to deal with complex ideas are impaired. Obviously, poor sleep habits are not the road to academic or social success. Why not record your sleep habits in a journal for one to two weeks to determine how many hours you really need to feel good? Avoid disturbing your circadian rhythms. Do not sleep any more or less than the amount you need, and go to bed at regular times. Finally, many students with very active schedules can profit from a short rest, when there is time, to recharge their batteries.

❏ Exercise

Most colleges provide such a variety of exercise options that you ought to be able to find something that you enjoy. If you think that aerobics classes are the invention of the devil, don't sign up! Do something you like to do. Swim, lift weights, bowl, walk, bike, or play tennis. Choose something! A half hour of exercise at least three times weekly is an effective way to alleviate stress, maintain your health, and increase your metabolism, circulation, and muscle tone.

According to Smith and Smith, exercise can also improve your self-esteem and attitudes. This occurs because of an improved physical appearance; a reduction of tension, anxiety, fatigue, and aggressiveness; and an improved mental outlook and self-confidence.

❏ Listen to Your Body Talk

Your body is a wealth of information, if you know how to listen to its messages. Practice getting in touch with your own physical clues. These body signals alert you to increased levels of stress immediately (see Stage 1: Alarm Reaction on page 133). *The Wellness Book* by Herbert Benson and Eileen Stuart (1992) suggests that "Attending to these cues or signals, you can then recognize when the [negative stress] cycle is about to begin and can choose an effective preventive strategy" (p. 181). It is important to acknowledge which stress warning signals are most typical for you. The following list notes the most common cues.

- sweaty palms
- headaches
- racing heart
- grinding teeth at night
- changes in normal breathing patterns
- dramatic changes in normal breathing patterns
- dramatic changes in typical eating patterns
- major changes in grooming and self-care patterns
- use of alcohol, cigarettes, drugs "to cope"
- poor impulse control
- easily upset or angered
- emotionally numb, disconnected
- inability to concentrate
- forgetfulness
- poor decision making or inability to make decisions
- muscles tightening
- nausea, stomachaches
- shaking

Pay attention! Your body is trying to make you aware that you are in "dangerous" territory. Effective stress management requires that you respond quickly with a strategy or technique to reduce the stress that you are experiencing. Do not hesitate to consult your student health service or counseling center for additional information.

Three Techniques for Discovering What's Really Bothering You

Identifying the real sources of your stress is seldom easy, but the following techniques are useful tools for further developing a stress-resistant you.

- distinguish feelings from thinking
- keep a journal
- know your options

Notice that each technique is based on the learning-how-to-learn skill we called obtaining feedback. Feedback was discussed in Chapter 3 in relation to goal setting and in Chapter 6 as a means of getting organized.

❑ 1. Distinguish Feelings from Thinking

Recognize the difference between thinking and feeling and allow yourself to deal with both. People often disregard their feelings and choose to give credence only to rational thought. Yet your feelings are often the best clues to the source of your stress. Explore them without judging them as inappropriate. Once you recognize how you really feel, you can identify acceptable ways to deal with those feelings and alleviate your stress. Refer to the vocabulary of feelings in Table 8.2 for words that can help clarify the way you feel.

Table 8.2   Vocabulary of Feelings

Intense	Strong	Moderate	Mild
loved	enchanted	liked	friendly
alive	vibrant	excited	wide awake
	great	good	content
lustful	passionate	yearning	attractive
worthy	admired	popular	approved
respected	important	appealing	graceful
elated	delighted	pleased	turned on
courageous	valiant	venturous	daring
	brave	peaceful	
comfortable			
	brilliant	intelligent	smart
hate	disgusted	suspicious	unpopular
unloved	resentful	envious	
loathed	deserted	aversion	
angry	frustrated	dejected	listless
hurt	sad	unhappy	moody
miserable	depressed	bored	lethargic
pain	sick	bad	gloomy
exhausted	fatigued	weary	tired
worthless	worn out	torn up	indifferent

Now examine the case of Nancy and Bob in Box 8.2 as an illustration of the steps you can take to resolve thinking/feeling conflicts.

❏ 2. Keep a Journal

In Chapter 6, you were encouraged to maintain a journal as a means of obtaining feedback from you to you. Keeping a journal can also help you recognize stress patterns. If you discover that you developed a headache during every psychology class over the last two weeks, then you can safely assume that there is something about that class that is stressful. Without a journal, this pattern might be missed. A journal also helps you identify and clarify various physical and emotional reactions that you are likely to experience. In short, journal writing is a good way to become a better organized and stress-resistant you.

If you want support for keeping a journal, write a contract with yourself such as the one presented in Figure 6.1 or the one in Figure 8.1. Ask a friend or roommate for moral support in your effort. At the end of each month, evaluate the effectiveness of journal writing *as a stress-management tool* (apart from using it to monitor behaviors described in Chapter 6). Based on your evaluation, determine how journal writing will continue to fit into your lifestyle. Figure 8.1 also shows an example of journal writing as a stress-management technique.

❏ 3. Know Your Options

Once you determine the source of your stress, your possible responses are rather limited:

- You can leave it.

- You can change it.

- You can live with it.

Your task is to decide which of the three options is both desirable and "doable." For example, consider the course that gives you a headache. Looking more closely, you discover that you are feeling overwhelmed by the amount of the new material covered during each class. By the middle of the lecture, your head hurts so badly that you cannot concentrate. Your notes are sketchy at best and you are falling further behind with each class.

In reviewing your three choices, you reject the leave-it option. If you drop the class at this point in the term (the leave-it option), you will lose your tuition money, the credits, and eliminate the full-time student status you need to receive financial aid.

Box 8.2

Thinking and Feeling: A Case Study

Nancy and Bob have expensive tickets to a sold-out, once-in-a-lifetime concert. They have both looked forward to this concert for months. As they are leaving for the concert, Bob slips on a patch of ice and hurts his ankle badly. Instead of going to the concert, Nancy and Bob spend their evening in the emergency room. While Nancy is waiting for the doctor to examine Bob, she is flooded by conflicting thoughts and feelings.

To clarify her thoughts and feelings, Nancy writes the following:

Feeling: Disappointment
Thought: I really wanted to see that concert.

Feeling: Anger
Thought: Bob should have been more careful. I can't believe I'm stuck in this dumb waiting room.

Feeling: Guilt
Thought: How can I be so insensitive? He's really hurt and I'm worried about a concert. I have no right to feel disappointed when Bob's in so much pain.

Feeling: Care and concern
Thought: I hope this is nothing really serious. I want him to be all right.

What are the possible resolutions to this situation for Nancy?

1. Nancy feels only anger and disappointment. She leaves a message for Bob with the nurse, walks out of the waiting room, and goes to the concert.

2. Nancy cannot believe she would even dare to think of herself when Bob is hurt. She tells herself that she is shallow and does not deserve anyone as wonderful as Bob. She decides that the noise and crunch of people at the concert would have been a hassle anyway. She feels glad that she did not go to the concert.

3. Nancy allows herself to feel disappointed because she really was looking forward to the concert. She also knows that her concern for Bob's welfare makes her glad she can be there to support him. When Nancy is allowed to see Bob, she says, "I'm really sorry that we missed the concert, but I'm also really glad that I can be here for you."

Resolution 3 is the best solution. It allows Nancy to validate her feelings and select the behavior that is most appropriate, given the limitations of the situation. What do you think Bob thinks and feels?

Spend a minute now to identify possible resolutions for him that acknowledge *his thoughts and feelings*. Use the vocabulary of feelings in Table 8.2 to clarify Bob's feelings. To what extent would your reactions to this case be different if Nancy, not Bob, had slipped on the ice?

PERSONAL CONTRACT

october 24, 1997
_____
(date)

I promise to: keep a journal
_____
(name of stress-management strategy)

I will: _____ make an entry daily _____ for: _____ the entire month _____
(specific behavior) (how often)   (how long)

my roommate/friend
_____
(name of resource person)

has agreed to support this endeavor and will assist me if I am tempted to
ignore the terms of this contract. At the end of the month, I will evaluate the
effectiveness of ___ journal writing ___ as a stress-management tool.
Based on my evaluation, I will determine if and how ___ journal writing ___
will continue to fit into my lifestyle.

_____
(your signature)

_____
(signature of resource person)

SAMPLE JOURNAL ENTRY

october 27, 1997

I had a difficult time making it to my psych class today. Once
again, I developed a headache mid-morning and wasn't feeling
good enough to sit from 11:30 to 12:30 in that overcrowded classroom.
It's always so claustrophobic in there. I forced myself to go but
I didn't take any notes, because my head hurt so badly. I'll have
to ask someone for their notes tomorrow. Actually, I should get
the notes for the entire week because the same thing happened
on monday and wednesday. There is a test in a week. Come to
think of it, I had a dream about taking a test last night. The
dream took place in the same classroom that my psych class
is in. I sat there staring at a blank sheet of paper while
everyone around me was writing furiously. I need to get a grip on
this class. There are better things to dream about.

Figure 8.1 Personal Contract and Sample Journal Entry

The change-it option is not within your power. You have no control over the amount of material the professor chooses to cover. You are left with the live-with-it option. Living with it does not mean suffering through the course. It means developing responses to reduce the stress caused by the class. Your responses could include contacting a course tutor, attempting to change your attitude toward the material or the instructor, relating the course to your career plans, taping the lecture, and developing relaxation techniques such as daily meditation, deep breathing, and creative visualization before you enter class.

Once you understand the process of examining your options, you can apply it to almost any situation. Not every case is as clearly defined as this example. However, knowing your options is a most effective stress-management skill. Use Chris's case in Box 8.3 to become more familiar with the process of determining whether you should change it, leave it, or live with it.

Some factors that create stress can be changed; others cannot. If you want to know what you can or cannot change with regard to anxiety, panic behavior, and eating disorders, read the Seligman article cited at the end of this chapter.

A famous invocation by Saint Francis of Assisi characterizes the essence of the "change it, leave it, or live with it" approach to reduce stress: "God, give me the serenity to accept things which cannot be changed; give me courage to change things which must be changed; and the wisdom to distinguish one from the other."

Passing the Stress Test: Some Final Thoughts

The paradox of effective stress management is that it requires you to *actively embrace* the very thing that is causing you stress—change. To reduce your stress, you must first identify the source. Then, implement strategies to bring your roller-coaster life back into balance. This process is often fun, sometimes difficult, and always necessary.

Robert Sapolsky, the author of *Why Zebras Don't Get Ulcers: A Guide to Stress, Stress-Related Diseases, and Coping* (1994), has spent more than a decade researching the causes and effects of stress. He offers some general strategies to use in the face of stressors.

- Find an outlet for life's frustrations that is personally compatible and can be used consistently. Use the *Action-Oriented Thought Starters* at the end of the chapter to generate some possibilities.

Box 8.3

Change It, Leave It, or Live with It: Case Study

Chris graduated in June with a GPA of 3.4 and a major in business administration. His area of concentration was human resources management. He focused his job search on positions that had recruitment as the primary responsibility. Jobs in human resources, especially recruitment positions, are hard to come by for a new college graduate with no personnel background. It took Chris six months to land a job.

Chris was hired as a recruiter for an executive search firm. Although the search firm environment was not his first choice, he knew it would give him extensive interviewing experience that he could use to make his next job search less painful. Chris took the job with the intention of staying at least one year. He had heard that less than a year's experience looks bad on a resumé. His six months of unemployment was not easy to explain to a potential employer. Chris accepted the job offer and, that week, moved into an apartment with two college friends. He had finally met his graduation goals: his first professional position and his own living space.

Two weeks into the job, Chris discovered a few facts that were not clearly explained during his interviews. Chris was under the impression that he would receive a salary plus commission. His salary, however, was *completely dependent* on commissions he would earn as a result of placing people in jobs. He would take home a small draw (funds based on future commissions) twice a month for the first six months. This was supposed to help him get started in the business. However, commission checks would be kept by his firm until they surpassed the draw he had already been paid.

Chris also found himself working at least ten hours each day, six days a week, which was the company norm. Saturday work was never mentioned in his inter-

- Strike a balance between holding on to an optimistic view of even the most stressful situations and allowing a small part of you to prepare for the worst. In other words: "Hope for the best. Cope with the rest."

- Look for small footholds of control in any stressful situation. If you try to scale a wall in a few steps, you'll have little control and find the wall insurmountable. But when you create several small footholds from which you can control your movements, the wall can be surmounted. Control those aspects of a stressful situation

view. His boss made it clear that he did not have to work Saturdays, but that Chris's success depended on his ability to push himself and work long hours. Three months into the position, Chris was indeed getting the experience in interviewing that he had lacked. He enjoyed his coworkers and had made a few friends. Unfortunately, he was barely making enough money to pay his bills, and his long work hours left him little time for any kind of social life. Some days he was sure he wanted to quit immediately. Some days he thought he would be better off if he stayed there a year. Most of the time he felt confused.

In the last month, he had gotten some really bad headaches. His appetite had all but vanished, especially since he rarely had the time or energy to make himself a decent meal. He found himself less inclined to call friends or to exercise.

Using the "change it, leave it, or live with it" strategy, identify Chris's options. The following questions might be of assistance.

1. What things does Chris have the power to change in his work environment?

2. What does he have the power to change in his personal life?

3. What are the positive aspects of remaining in his position?

4. What are the negative aspects of remaining in his position?

5. What changes would you recommend that Chris make if he leaves his present position?

6. What changes would you recommend that Chris make if he stays in his job?

7. What would you do if you were Chris?

that you can. They give you a sense of empowerment and provide support for your continued stress-management efforts.

- Predictable, accurate information can reduce stress if it is available in a timely fashion, and if it is not far more data than you need or far worse than you want to know.

- Social networks that provide you with affiliation and support are crucial. Feeling truly connected to others is an important component of stress management.

Each of us has probably had the positive experience of dealing successfully with a stressful situation. We recognized the signals and responded with the best techniques in our stress management arsenal. On the other hand, each of us has faced a stressor and been completely unable to respond. When your typical strategies are not working, it is important to ask for help. Most colleges and universities have counseling, student health, and campus ministry centers. Professionals in these areas can help you work through the situation at hand, provide ongoing support, or direct you to the appropriate resources.

Connecting Stress Management to Your Career

The techniques that you master and the lifestyle changes you make now will not only help you stay healthy in college, but also work for you in your personal and professional activities. In addition, if you learn to understand and manage stress in the real world of college, you can *begin* to evaluate your capacity to handle the stresses you are likely to encounter in your career.

New college graduates often find that adjustment to their first professional position is very stressful. All the major stress categories seem to be represented in this life transition. Changes in self-image (student to worker), in social support networks (geographic separation from friends or family), in personal achievement measures (grades to raises and promotions), not to mention crowded commutes, limited free time, and student loan payments typically occur during the year after college graduation.

Career change is another prospective source of stress. You can expect to change careers four to six times in your career life span. Each of these times brings a lack of predictability, a change in professional roles and goals, as well as financial and interpersonal shifts. The necessity of career change often propels adults to return to school, adding yet another role to an already crowded life. The need to balance your many life roles also can produce stress.

Unmeasurable human suffering and hundreds of millions of dollars are among the annual costs of work-related absences and illnesses caused by mismanaged stress. The kinds of stress-management techniques presented in a corporation's training workshops may not differ significantly from those available through college counseling centers. Educate yourself now about stress management so that you can continue to connect college to career.

Action-Oriented Thought Starters

1. You should have a variety of stress-management techniques and strategies at your disposal. The following checklist can help you identify the techniques you have already mastered and the ones you would like to learn more about. Mark both columns as appropriate. After you finish, reflect on the insights you gained about yourself.

	I am able to do this			*I am willing to do this*		
	very often	*sometimes*	*never*	*very often*	*sometimes*	*never*
Maintain a sense of humor	___	___	___	___	___	___
Reevaluate and rewrite my irrational beliefs	___	___	___	___	___	___
Communicate openly and honestly with myself and with others	___	___	___	___	___	___
Eat well, regularly	___	___	___	___	___	___
Get adequate rest each day	___	___	___	___	___	___
Exercise regularly	___	___	___	___	___	___
Keep a journal	___	___	___	___	___	___
Accept that what I feel is real and needs a response from me	___	___	___	___	___	___
Recognize bodily signs of stress	___	___	___	___	___	___
Become familiar with relaxation techniques: deep breathing, visualization, meditation, and tensing and relaxing muscles	___	___	___	___	___	___
Spend some quiet time with myself each day	___	___	___	___	___	___
Use music, art, and nature as calming forces in my life	___	___	___	___	___	___

	I am able to do this			I am willing to do this		
	very often	sometimes	never	very often	sometimes	never
Focus my attention on one problem at a time	_____	_____	_____	_____	_____	_____
Learn to play; play each day	_____ '	_____	_____	_____	_____	_____
When negative thoughts enter my mind, I yell "Stop!"	_____	_____	_____	_____	_____	_____
Avoid those who are carriers of anxiety and depression	_____	_____	_____	_____	_____	_____
Choose friends who make healthy, positive lifestyle choices and who support my efforts to do the same	_____	_____	_____	_____	_____	_____
Discover the resources of my campus and community; give myself permission to ask for help when I need it	_____	_____	_____	_____	_____	_____
Create a personal contract as shown in Figure 8.1	_____	_____	_____	_____	_____	_____

2. Would you like to learn more about stress? Perhaps you could turn this exercise into a term paper for another course. The purpose of this Action-Oriented Thought Starter is to combine one of your major resources for "getting around" college (see Chapter 7) with the material contained in this chapter. The following steps are among those a librarian would recommend for learning more about stress and stress management.

   a. Conduct an on-line search in your library using terms such as *stress* or *stress management* to access references. Some on-line systems have a directory containing specific words or terms you can enter to locate the print or nonprint material.

   b. Check the reference library shelves for encyclopedias, dictionaries, or handbooks that might contain relevant information.

   c. Review periodical indexes in print or on line.

d. Browse through the shelves containing appropriate books or periodicals. Page through books, magazines, and professional journals that interest you.

e. Ask the reference librarian to show you other sources of information about stress and stress management.

f. Quickly review other campus resources mentioned in Chapter 7. Can you identify at least two other sources that may have information about stress and stress management?

Before you complete these steps, you will likely be overwhelmed by the variety of resources that address the issue of stress and stress management. Don't panic. Your challenge will be to narrow your topic, organize the information you have, and keep in mind the specific purpose of your search (e.g, the objectives of the paper you must write). The ability to locate, organize, select, and evaluate from an array of resources in today's information-driven society is a highly valuable skill of the covert curriculum (Chapter 4) that will serve you well in college and in most occupational areas.

Table 8.3 Suggested Solutions to Styles of Distorted Thinking Exercise in Table 8.1. (Compare your responses to this solution sheet and try to analyze why the solutions are stated the way they are.)

Style	Distorted Thinking Styles		Rational Thinking Styles	
	Example	Rewrite Style	Rewrite Example	

Style	Example	Rewrite Style	Rewrite Example
SAMPLE: Blaming Other people are responsible for your pain. Or you are completely responsible for every problem.	I studied hard for the test but got a C. The teacher must hate me.	I am responsible for my behavior and I accept the consequences. I am not responsible for every problem that occurs within a 50-mile radius of me.	I ran out of time and was unable to complete the test, which accounts for my grade. Next time I will bring a watch and pace myself better.
1. Emotional Reasoning If you feel something, then it must be true.	I feel so scared about making my biology presentation. I know I won't remember a thing when I get in front of the class. Then everyone will see how stupid I am.	There is nothing sacred or automatic about how I feel. Feelings and events are two different things.	Everyone feels nervous before they make a presentation. I have made successful presentations before and I know that my nerves will calm once I begin speaking.
2. Catastrophizing You expect disaster. You wait for the worst and know that good events are only temporary interruptions from life's crises.	I have worked with the drama department all year and have finally gotten a lead. I know I'll blow it on opening night and never be cast in another role.	Life has its ups and downs, but real crises are actually pretty rare. What are the chances that my worst fears will occur? Usually, the odds are very slim.	I have been involved in theater since grade school. I have always done a good job, and this role won't be any different. If I make a mistake, I know I can recover without the audience ever suspecting. The show not only will go on—but I will do a fine job.
3. Mind Reading You know what others are thinking and feeling and why they behave the way they do, without ever talking to them about it.	She didn't say hello to me when I walked into class. She must be angry with me.	I don't have a crystal ball and cannot know what others think and feel. I can make assumptions, but that's all they are until I get direct information from those involved.	If she didn't say hello to me, maybe it's because she didn't see me. I can approach her after class and check this out.

Table 8.3 Suggested Solutions to Styles of Distorted Thinking Exercise in Table 8.1 *(continued)*

Style	Distorted Thinking Styles Example	Rewrite Style	Rational Thinking Styles Rewrite Example
4. Myth of Change By the power of your will and/or the intensity of your love, you can make others into the people you want them to be. Your own self-worth is dependent on your ability to do this.	I know that he will stop drinking when we are married. I will make him so happy that he won't need to drink anymore.	The only person I have the power to change is myself. My happiness depends on me, not others.	His choices to drink or to stop are his own—not mine. My choice is whether or not I want to marry him, given that I cannot change his drinking habits.
5. Myth of Fairness You alone determine the standard for fairness and are angered when others don't agree.	My English professor is making me do a research paper plus a take-home final exam. She just isn't being fair. After all, I have other classes too.	"Fair" is often in the eye of the beholder. I need to own my preferences and recognize that others may not agree.	My English teacher has a right to set the standard for her classes; however, I would certainly prefer that she assign less work. If the workload is too intense, given my other classes, I can choose to take the course at a later time or with another instructor.
6. Perfectionism You must never make a mistake, never achieve at anything less than an optimum level. Being wrong is unthinkable because it makes you unacceptable.	I can't believe I got a B in Spanish. Now I'll never get into grad school, and my parents will really be upset that I got such a terrible grade.	Perfection is both unachievable and undesirable. Mistakes can be embraced as a part of the learning process. There is a difference between what I do and who I am.	My entry into a graduate program will not be determined by one grade—especially a B. Bs are not terrible grades; they are perfectly acceptable to the vast majority of the world!

(continued on next page)

Table 8.3 Suggested Solutions to Styles of Distorted Thinking Exercise in Table 8.1 *(continued)*

Distorted Thinking Styles		Rational Thinking Styles	
Style	Example	Rewrite Style	Rewrite Example
7. Polarized Thinking You view events and people in terms of black and white, good and bad, right and wrong. There is no middle ground.	I'm going to pledge a fraternity and my best friend isn't. I guess we can't really be friends if that's how he feels.	Events and people are not usually characterized by extremes. Most often the truth is somewhere in the middle. I will work to evaluate things on a continuum as opposed to an "either/or" approach.	Two people can make different choices without having either choice be wrong. It is only important that my choice to join a fraternity is the best choice for me; and that my friend's choice not to pledge is the best choice for him. We can come to different conclusions about the same thing and still be friends.
8. Overgeneralization You come to a global conclusion based on a single piece of evidence.	I can't believe she would go back to work so soon. Her baby is just a few months old. She is obviously not much of a mother.	The best decisions are made with adequate information. One or two points is usually not enough to draw a correct conclusion.	She must have a number of reasons for returning to work so quickly after the birth of her baby. Her choice to work is not—of and by itself—an indication of her commitment to motherhood.
9. Shoulds You have a list of absolutes to govern your own actions and the actions of others. Any deviation from your rules is unacceptable.	If I don't understand something in a class, I don't ask questions. I should be able to get this stuff, and I don't want anyone to think that I'm not cutting it here.	Absolutes in life are very rare. Almost all rules have exceptions. Because people have different values, they will draw different conclusions.	Because I value the opportunities I have to learn, I have a right to ask for clarification or to question things I don't understand.
10. Victim of Circumstances You have no control over anything that happens in your life and are helpless to do anything about your life. You are not responsible for any outcomes.	It's not my fault that I couldn't study. My friends hounded me until I said that I'd go out with them last night. I know I failed that test this morning, but there was nothing that I could do.	I have control over my actions and reactions and I accept the consequences of my behavior.	I chose to go out with my friends rather than study for my test. I knew that my decision had the potential to jeopardize my grade, but I made it anyway.

Source: Based on *Thoughts and Feelings: The Art of Cognitive Stress Intervention*, by M. McKay, M. Davis, and P. Fanning, New Harbinger Publications, 1981.

References and Recommended Readings

Andreas, B. (1993). *Mostly true—Collected stories & drawings.* Decorah, IA: Story People.

Benson, H., & Stuart, E. M. (1992). *The wellness book.* New York: Birch Lane Press.

Black, C. (1989). *"It's never too late to have a happy childhood."* New York: Ballantine.

David, M. (1991). *Nourishing wisdom: A mind/body approach to nutrition and well-being.* New York: Tower.

Guterman, M. S. (1994). *Common sense for uncommon times: The power of balance in work, family, and personal life.* Palo Alto, CA: Consulting Psychologists Press.

Hay, L. L. (1988). *Heal your body.* Santa Monica, CA: Hay House.

Insel, P., & Roth, W. (1994). *Core concepts in health* (7th ed.). Mountain View, CA: Mayfield Publishing.

Kurtz, E., & Ketcham, K. (1992). *The spirituality of imperfection.* New York: Bantam Books.

McKay, M., Davis, M., & Fanning, P. (1981). *Thoughts and feelings: The art of cognitive stress intervention.* Richmond, CA: New Harbinger Publications.

McLean, A. D. (1979). *Work stress.* Reading, MA: Addison-Wesley.

Peck, M. S. (1985). *The road less traveled.* New York: Simon & Schuster.

Sapolsky, R. M. (1994). *Why zebras don't get ulcers: A guide to stress, stress-related diseases, and coping.* New York: W. H. Freeman.

Seligman, M. E. P. (1994, May/June). What you can and what you cannot change. *Psychology Today.* 33–41, 70, 72–74, 84.

Selye, H. (1974). *Stress without distress.* New York: Signet.

Smith, S., & Smith C. (1988). *The college student's health guide.* Los Altos, CA: Westchester.

Watson, D. (1993). *101 simple ways to be good to yourself.* Austin, TX: Bard Productions.

PART TWO

Essential Study Skills

CHAPTER 9

Listening to Learn

Friendly Reminders

❑ Remember to use the techniques of stress management to reduce tension.

❑ If you want to learn more about listening after reading Chapter 9, what campus resources would you consult?

❑ Construct your external and psychological environments to promote concentration while you read Chapter 9.

"Listening well and answering well is one of the greatest perfections that can be attained in conversation."

François de La Rochefoucauld (1613–1680),
French epigrammatist and man of letters

Take a few minutes now and recall the many hours that you spent in high school learning the basic communication skills.

Do you remember the hours you spent

- *writing* those innumerable papers for English, history, and other courses?

- *reading* thick, formidable textbooks and obscure novels and plays?

- preparing anxiously to *speak* in front of your class?

- learning how to *listen?*

If you are having trouble remembering when you were taught how to listen, your memory is not failing. You, like most people, probably received little or no formal instruction in how to listen. From toddler to teens you were told *to* listen, but not *how* to listen. Yet Norma Costner (1988) maintains that up to 9 out of every 10 hours of high school classes are devoted to lecture and discussion, situations that demand listening skills.

Larry Barker and his associates surveyed college students about their use of time. The results showed that communicating accounts for about three-fourths of our waking hours (Steil, Barker, and Watson, 1983). Of greater significance, and perhaps more surprising, is the percentage of time spent in the four communication modes:

Listening	53%
Reading	17%
Speaking	16%
Writing	14%

Listening is the communication skill we learn first, use by far the most, but are seldom taught. The brevity of this chapter testifies to the dearth (go ahead, look it up in your dictionary) of information on listening compared with other topics covered in this book.

Consequently, any instruction in listening is at the remedial level for most college students. But don't feel discouraged; you're not alone! By the time you complete this chapter, you will have obtained a fundamental understanding of the listening process and several suggestions for building your skills. "Listening to Learn" is another learning-how-to-learn minicourse in college's covert curriculum.

The Listening Process

Hearing is a passive, generally involuntary process in which the brain receives and interprets sounds from the external environment. In contrast, *listening* is an active, voluntary process in which the listener deliberately pays attention to, interprets the meaning of, and responds to a message.

Steil, Barker, and Watson (1983) believe that listening consists of four connected activities: sensing, interpreting, evaluating, and responding. *Sensing*, the first and most basic activity, is the listener's ability to detect a message. For example, a student buried in a daydream probably will not hear a teacher say, "This class's performance on the last quiz was well below average." A student who is mildly daydreaming may detect that a message was sent but fails to *interpret* its meaning. An alert student will sense and may interpret the same message this way: "The *class's* performance on the *last quiz* was *well below average.*"

After sensing and interpreting a message, a listener will often *evaluate* it—that is, agree or disagree with its content. The message about the quiz could be evaluated in various ways such as, "So what!" "I agree," or "It wasn't that bad, was it?" Poor listeners begin evaluating a message too soon and tune out the speaker when they hear something disagreeable. Good listeners continue to concentrate on the speaker's message but suspend or carefully consider a judgment.

The final activity in the act of listening is *responding*. Sensing, interpreting, and evaluating are internal activities that can occur in the span of seconds. Responding is an external behavior that may occur immediately (frowning, sighing, speaking) or at a later time (studying harder for the next quiz). Listening begins as the passive, involuntary, sensing, and interpreting of sounds, but becomes (when you take charge of it) an active process of attending, evaluating, and responding to the message.

The Four-Factor Framework for Learning How to Listen

As a communication skill, listening can be described in terms of a general model of communication that includes three components: *sender, message,* and *receiver.* This model will be used in subsequent chapters to explain notetaking and public speaking. The three components of this model, plus a fourth (the *environment*), combine to form the framework for learning to listen. The four factors include

- the physical environment for listening
- the message (message component)
- the speaker (sender component)
- you (receiver component)

You are involved in all four aspects of listening, but you have limited control over the first three.

1. Your External Listening Environment

Effective listening requires concentration. In Chapter 5 you learned that to concentrate you must actively construct or organize your external environment to reduce distractions. Although you do not have much control over your classrooms, you can take the following steps to reduce distractions and promote concentration.

1. Do not sit next to classmates who talk excessively or whose personality and looks are a constant source of distraction (Yes, that may be difficult at times!).

2. Sit toward the front and center of class, but not in the front row if you feel self-conscious. A close seat is especially important in courses where the professor uses a blackboard or audiovisual materials regularly. Similarly, sit where light does not reflect directly on you or the blackboard. Think twice before sitting behind basketball players or classmates who wear hats in class.

3. Avoid distractions such as doorways, windows, and desks with interesting graffiti.

4. Avoid checking the time more than once or twice during class.

If you are forced to listen in a room that contains irritations, be aware that *you* must compensate for them with an additional dose of attention and effort. If you believe that the instructor can improve the listening environment, ask for assistance.

2. The Message

The message is the particular information you wish to listen to. Listening is easy when you like and understand the message. However, if an emotionally arousing or complex message interferes with your ability to sense, interpret, evaluate, and respond, you must be prepared to remove the listening barriers. Let's examine the emotional and intellectual barriers to listening.

❏ Emotional Barriers to Listening

Since grade school a student named Jan deeply admired Abraham Lincoln, especially his 1863 Emancipation Proclamation. However, in her political science course Jan was told that Lincoln would have supported slavery to preserve the Union. Shocked, Jan stopped listening to the instructor and refused to read the text for the next class. With regard to the listening process, Jan sensed and interpreted the message, but she short-circuited the evaluation phase by her instant defensive judgment and premature response.

Jan's immediate reaction is not unusual. When cherished political, cultural, religious, or philosophical beliefs are challenged, your natural response is often emotional and defensive. For example, your religious affiliation could be criticized in a history course, your attitude toward U.S. business pummeled in economics, your party affiliation attacked in political science, your beliefs about creation questioned in biology, or your attitude toward a supreme being ridiculed in a philosophy text. Your first impulse is to close the book, tune out the teacher, and shut down your mind. Then you worry about having to recall the threatening information on the next exam.

Tuning out threatening ideas may be a normal response, but it is not an *educated* response. Unless you quickly take charge of your emotions, you may generalize them from a particular comment on a specific topic to all subsequent comments on similar topics. Before you know it, you have cursed your textbook and attached the proverbial pitchfork and horns to an instructor who simply challenged one of your values. Occasionally, the opposite effect occurs when a teacher's affirmation of your cherished beliefs persuades you to place a halo around all subsequent remarks. Whether you hang halos or horns on your professor, you have ceased to listen. Your emotions take control of the evaluation and responding phases of the listening process.

How do you remove the emotional barriers to the message? Start with hard work, an open mind, and the decision to act on these recommendations.

1. *Be prepared.* As you plan your day each morning, think of classes that are likely to address your personal beliefs. Imagine what might be said; anticipate how you might respond. Remind yourself that college is supposed to challenge your ideas and sharpen your critical-thinking skills. Read the assignments before class; review your notes after class.

2. When your emotions begin to bubble in class, *be cool!* Take a deep breath, continue to listen carefully, and take notes. Suspend judgment until you have time after class to evaluate the issues. Besides, while you are wallowing righteously in your emotions you could be missing important points. Ultimately, you do not have to agree with views that conflict with your own. At least hear them out. If experts are wrong, chances are they spent considerable time and thought reaching their conclusions. You may benefit from understanding their reasons; you could learn something that strengthens your beliefs. One way to deal with these situations is to find a quiet spot, think about the issues (express your feelings in writing if it helps), and reexamine your options and goals.

Outside of class you could be involved in discussions about U.S. foreign policy, war, gun control, abortion, premarital sex, substance abuse, and other controversial issues that are debated on lively college campuses. Participate and listen. However, people who insist that you make a quick judgment about a complex issue seldom understand the issue, nor are they good listeners. Similarly, when you feel pressured into quick decisions that can have serious consequences (for example, pressures to use drugs, have sex, or cheat), rely on the core values that helped you discern right from wrong in the past.

3. *Ask questions.* When confronted in class with ideas that conflict with your own, organize your thoughts, control your emotions, and ask for clarification or elaboration. You will defuse your defensiveness when you phrase your remarks carefully so that you won't be embarrassed by them in class on a later date. For example, do not preface a question by saying, "I was taught by my family to believe . . . ." Such

words put you *and* the instructor on the defensive. Instead, state confidently, "Some people believe . . . What do you think are the strengths and weaknesses of that position?" By detaching your thoughts from your emotions, you state the question objectively and enable the teacher to respond fairly. However, expect an instructor to solicit your opinion. Asking questions can be risky business, but it is the business of your college education. Besides, instructors respect students who ask thoughtful questions; they learn too.

4. *Pursue the issue on your own.* Responding, the fourth stage of listening, can be immediate *or* delayed. Do not expect clear answers soon. Value-related issues reflect diverse perspectives, evolve over time, are affected by new information, and merit further analysis. Discuss them with friends and family. Read respected magazines, newspapers, and books for contrasting views. Watch in-depth television news programs where the issues are debated by experts. The controversy could become the subject of a term paper. College should be one of life's best opportunities for exploring the shades of gray that intervene between life's seemingly black-and-white issues.

❏ Intellectual Barriers to Listening

When your listening shifts from a hallway conversation about last night's television shows to a classroom analysis of phenomenology and existentialism, what happens? Why do you feel at ease listening to discussions of foods, fashions, and family but not philosophy or physics? Not only are the former topics *familiar,* the words and concepts used to discuss them are *concrete and tangible.* In contrast, your course topics are unfamiliar and your instructor's language is abstract and technical. To their own delight (and your dismay), teachers reason methodically and quickly through forests of facts, mountains of data, and theoretical labyrinths using polysyllabic words and abstract terms that blow your mind. You *struggle* to listen. Similarly, if English is a second language for you or your instructor, listening is a constant challenge.

How do you remove the intellectual barriers? The first two suggestions are extensions of previous recommendations.

1. Be prepared for the barriers by reading the assignment in advance of class. If you do not know whether you should read the material at a general level or in depth, ask the instructor.

2. Ask questions. Inquiry is a right and an obligation. Yet students often hesitate to ask teachers to clarify or repeat difficult material be-

cause they feel self-conscious. Or students believe that their question may be viewed as dumb. In fact, attentive students seldom ask dumb questions and classmates benefit from the exchange. Besides, questions often help the teacher communicate material more clearly.

In her book *Listening—The Forgotten Skill* Madelyn Burley-Allen (1995) discusses the art of asking questions and provides examples for several listening situations. Some of the situations she presents have been adapted below to classroom listening.

Situation	Sample Student Questions
Unfamiliar phrases: The teacher has used an unfamiliar phrase.	"Could you elaborate on what you mean by _____?"
Digressing: The teacher seems to have digressed from the previous topic.	"Perhaps I missed something. Could you please relate _____ to _____?"
Clarification: The teacher says something that does not appear to agree with an earlier statement.	"I thought you said earlier that _____. Now I hear you saying _____. These statements seem to conflict. Could you clarify?"
Obtaining ideas: You want to obtain the ideas of the teacher about something said by the teacher, you, or a peer.	"I think that ___. What are your thoughts?"
Obtaining feedback: You or a peer stated the strengths or benefits of an idea and you want the teacher's feedback.	"What is your opinion about the strengths of ___?"

Don't hesitate to ask such questions in the classroom, but be sure to ask them in a positive, friendly manner. Your active involvement with the listening process is in keeping with the "Taking Charge" theme of Part One of this book. Moreover, your questioning promotes clear understanding of the material in a nondefensive manner, and it enlivens the teaching-learning process.

3. Use the dictionary. When you hear an unfamiliar term, check its meaning in your text's glossary, a technical dictionary, a standard dictionary, or on your computer. Write the definition, carry it with you, and try to use it in conversations or papers. To avoid being overwhelmed by too many new terms, select those that are most important and likely to appear on the next test. Terms that you do not master now may reappear in the same or subsequent courses.

4. Study the teacher's teaching methods. Your best professors know that students must work hard to grasp difficult concepts, so they

use teaching techniques that facilitate listening. Because listening and notetaking use similar learning strategies, some suggestions below will be elaborated on in Chapter 10. Your instructor is helping you develop listening skills when she or he

a. begins class with a review, states the objectives of the current class, ends by summarizing main points, and previews the next class

b. uses a chalkboard or projector to show important names or to outline main points

c. distributes handouts or study guides

d. takes time from a lecture to pause, ask questions, encourage comments, or create discussion groups to gain your involvement

e. helps you organize your thoughts with verbal cues such as "The main points are . . ."; "It is important that you know . . ."; "There are three steps . . ."; "Let me illustrate by . . ."; "For example, . . ."; or "The evidence that supports this idea is . . . ."

f. speaks slowly enough to let you take notes, but fast enough to maintain your attention

In summary, a major step to effective listening is to identify and surmount the emotional and intellectual barriers created by the message component of the communications.

3. The Speaker

When Dr. Remoht, Raphael's physics teacher, lectures, he leans on the podium, stares out the window, periodically looks at students, mutters in a low voice, appears disorganized, and wears clothes that clash. Sometimes he gives long reading assignments at the end of class to augment the subsequent assignment. He is very critical in his remarks on student papers. Dr. Remoht would, no doubt, score low on a course-evaluation questionnaire. His behaviors irritate Raphael and other students to the point where they sometimes lose interest in the subject matter. They know that he is unlikely to change, even if they approach him.

However, Raphael is a senior and has considerable experience with the idiosyncrasies (go ahead, look it up in the dictionary if you don't know its meaning) of teachers. Raphael knows that he must *concentrate on the message and not the messenger* to master the material and obtain a good grade. Consequently, he sits where he can listen, forces himself to ignore the instructor's idiosyncrasies, concentrates on

Box 9.1

When the Message and the Speaker Interact

You might infer from our separate analyses of the message and speaker aspects of communication that they operate independently. WRONG! Often the major barrier to listening is due to a particular combination of the speaker, the particular message being delivered, *and* our stereotypes and prejudices. Analyze the contrasting situations in each example below to determine how you might react if you were the student.

1. You are a northerner attending
   a. a southern university and your history teacher, in his heavy southern accent, sharply criticizes Civil War–era northern politicians
   b. a northern university and your history teacher, in his northern accent, sharply criticizes the Civil War–era northern politics

2. You are a white male, in your personnel management class, and
   a. a "laid-back" middle-aged, white male teacher presents evidence of discriminatory hiring practices in small corporations
   b. an assertive, young, black female teacher presents evidence of discriminatory hiring practices in small corporations

3. Your family has voted Republican for generations. In political science, the teacher,
   a. an avid Democrat, evaluates the 1996 Democratic presidential campaign
   b. an avid Republican, evaluates the 1996 Democratic presidential campaign

4. In an ethics course discussion of abortion,
   a. a pro-choice professor interprets the rights of the mother and the fetus
   b. a pro-life professor interprets the rights of the mother and the fetus

In these and other situations, your effectiveness as a listener is strongly influenced not only by the content of the message, but also by the particular characteristics of the instructor and your prior beliefs and stereotypes. *Stereotypes* refer to preconceived beliefs about a particular group (southerners, black women, Republicans, pro-life partisans) that fail to account for individual differences among members within the group. Because each of us harbors stereotypes, we must struggle to listen objectively; we *must* listen.

the material, and holds himself responsible for what must be learned. Actually, Dr. Remoht is a fine teacher who challenges his students and has inspired several to pursue graduate studies.

Most teachers exhibit at least a few annoying characteristics; others seem to define themselves by their eccentricities. Some students are easily distracted by such behaviors. Instead of listening they criticize the teacher's mannerisms, speech, and clothes, or attribute low test grades to the teacher.

The prescription for dealing with instructor idiosyncrasies is contained in Raphael's behavior.

1. Monitor the message, not the messenger. He knows that long after Dr. Remoht retires, the material he presented will be important to remember.

2. If the irritating behavior directly impedes the teaching-learning process, speak with the instructor. Clashing clothes is not a cause for concern. However, if a teacher continually speaks too fast or too slow, too loud or too soft, or exhibits mannerisms that impede listening, students have a legitimate reason to ask for change. Most new and many experienced teachers are receptive to constructive criticism when it is made in private, in a diplomatic manner, and by a student who has demonstrated a serious interest in class.

3. If the irritating behavior is not amenable to change, force yourself to adapt. Adaptation to unpleasant situations is a necessity of life and, according to Carl Rogers, the sign of an educated person. In spite of the instructor's idiosyncrasies, you are still responsible for learning the material.

4. You (the Receiver)

Although you have limited control over the speaker, message, and environmental factors, the suggestions presented can help you manage them. The fourth and final factor that enables you to listen effectively is *you*. The remaining suggestions are completely under your control.

1. Motivate yourself to listen. It is easy to listen when a stimulating instructor is discussing topics that interest you. When the teacher, the topic, or both seem dull, remotivate yourself to learn and earn a satisfactory grade. Remind yourself that

- you are in college to achieve your long-range goals

- learning to listen to dull topics or dull teachers is an excellent preparation for many of life's dull moments

- you can still learn *how to think* regardless of the message or the speaker

- quite possibly, it is *you* who is dull, not the teacher or the topic

- although the material is difficult or the teacher dull, you are still responsible for learning

- when you prepare for the class in advance, you will listen to the material at a higher level

 2.   Listen *and* look. Teachers, consciously or unconsciously, emit a variety of nonverbal signals that convey meaning to their words. Look for changes in loudness, pitch, and clarity of voice; posture, facial expression, hand movement, and movement from place to place in the room; eye movement; and pauses between remarks.

However, resist the urge to give quick and simplistic interpretations to nonverbal behaviors. It is easy to err when you make generalizations that go beyond simple nonverbal expressions of approval and disapproval or enthusiasm and disinterest. For example, the teacher who stands with arms crossed might not be conveying arrogance; he may be chilly. Still, if you study a speaker's nonverbal behavior over an extended period of time (and expect to be wrong sometimes), you can discern distinct attitudes and feelings toward the material being presented. Those nonverbal cues can promote listening.

3.   Physically respond to the speaker. Communicate nonverbally by maintaining eye contact, nodding to show you understand, and being attentive. Don't pretend to be attentive when you're not. Teachers know that true attention will manifest itself in your participation in class and on the next exam.

Ask questions but don't interrupt. Wait until the instructor reaches the end of a particular point, lowers her or his voice, and pauses. For teachers who talk fast, be ready to launch your hand into outer space as soon as the pause begins. If a class ends without time for questions, ask them after class or at the beginning of the next class. Some professors give distinctive pauses during which questions are welcome. Cynthia Hamilton and Brian Kleiner (1987) maintain that responding to the speaker reflects courtesy and common sense as well as good listening skills.

4. Be a thinking listener, not a tape recorder.

- Stay alert and assume that an important point could be made anytime.

- Don't try to take notes verbatim on every statement you hear, but don't walk out of an hour's lecture with only a few paragraphs of notes.

- Use long pauses to review the main points, to keep the big picture in view. For example, glance at the main headings in your notes or in the text. Recall the instructor's introductory remarks. Skim your notes from the previous class.

- During long pauses it sometimes helps to think ahead. Anticipation can help ideas become meaningful; it takes advantage of your mind's ability to think faster than your teacher speaks.

- When your personal beliefs are challenged, stay cool. Keep thinking.

5. Practice listening. Ask permission to tape-record an instructor's lecture. Then analyze it in terms of the recommendations given in this chapter. Compare what you heard to your notes and try to explain the discrepancies.

Take notes on a videotape of a political speech, *Nightline, NewsHour with Jim Lehrer,* or similar thought-provoking news programs. Replay the videotape and compare your notes with the points presented. Pay special attention to the role of nonverbal cues.

6. To remain an alert listener, get enough sleep, eat nutritiously, and exercise regularly. You have heard this message before. You will hear it again. And it's true!

To summarize, the process of listening consists of four connected activities that include sensing, interpreting, evaluating, and responding. They operate in conjunction with the environment and the message, speaker, and receiver factors to influence your listening effectiveness. Some suggestions offered here will be repeated in the next chapter, in which notetaking (an outcome of listening) is discussed.

Although you have completed your first lesson in listening, it should not be your last. Why not?

Connecting Listening to Your Career

Do you recall the percentage of time that college students spend communicating through listening? According to Zane Quible (1989), most business employees spend about 40% to 60% of their workday listening. If you establish effective listening habits in college, you are likely to be as good a listener in your job. However, the consequences of poor listening in college may not be as serious as those in many career positions. To illustrate, consider the implications of poor listening for

- the nervous job applicant who daydreams about salary instead of listening to the employer's statement of expectations
- the health-service provider who must listen to details of a patient's condition and treatment procedures
- the executive who negotiates the fine points of a multimillion dollar contract
- the police officer who must listen to conflicting versions from two motorists whose cars collided
- the marketing manager who ignores product-testing warnings

Necessary to these and similar situations is the ongoing interpersonal communication, the give-and-take among individuals who work together. Research shows that managers devote a significant portion of their time to resolving personnel conflicts that are often caused by failure to listen. Corporations such as AT&T, General Motors, Xerox, IBM, Coca-Cola, and General Electric place such high value on listening skills that they include an instructional component in the inservice training offered to executives and supervisory personnel (Costner, 1988).

Finally, consider the career called marriage (or other long-term intimate relationships) and the extent to which listening or failing to listen affects the quality of the relationship. La Rouchefoucauld was right.

Action-Oriented Thought Starters

1. Make several photocopies of the Listening Checklist below and take it to two or three of your toughest courses for a week or two. Make notes after each class for each category. Review your comments to determine which listening skills are satisfactory and which could be strengthened.

The Listening Checklist: Problems and Prompts

The Physical Environment

_____ Distractions: noises, students, doorways (change seats?)

_____ Seat location: view of teacher, chalkboard, screen (change seats?)

Message Factors

_____ Emotional barriers to listening: teacher/text activates your emotions (read assignment in advance; remain cool; ask questions; pursue issues)

_____ Intellectual barriers to listening: teacher/text is abstract or terms are unfamiliar (read assignment in advance; ask questions; use dictionary; observe teaching)

Speaker Factors

_____ Teacher's idiosyncrasies: speed of speaking, gestures, accent, etc. (monitor the message, not the messenger; speak with teacher; adapt)

Receiver (Listener) Factors

_____ Your motivation: Are you *really trying* to listen? How do you feel, physically and emotionally? What can you do to remotivate yourself?

_____ What nonverbal cues does the teacher use to communicate?

_____ Are you responding with sufficient attention, eye contact, nodding, questioning?

_____ Are you a "thinking listener" who stays alert, takes notes thoughtfully, reviews, and anticipates subsequent remarks?

Observe how teachers promote good listening when they:

____ begin with a review, state objectives, summarize, or preview the next class

____ use the chalkboard, distribute materials, present materials audiovisually

____ pause to ask questions, encourage comments, speak at moderate speed

____ [others: you add] _____

What other factors affected your ability to listen attentively? _____
_____

2. Listen and laugh. Do you have access to old radio broadcasts of the 1940s and 1950s? Listen to a few of the comedy and dramatic programs from that era. Compare the voices and sounds you hear with the ideas and feelings they express and with the images you create while you are listening. There may not be scientific evidence to support it, but this exercise could be a useful means of improving your listening skills and your ability to visualize—and it's fun!

3. Each day for one week keep a log of the approximate amount of waking time that you spend listening.

   a. Divide (or color-code) listening into classroom listening, social listening, and, if appropriate, the amount of listening you do on your job.

   b. Add the total listening times for all categories and calculate the percentage for each.

   c. In which settings is your listening best? Poorest? What can you do to improve your listening in each setting?

References and Recommended Readings

Burley-Allen, M. (1995). *Listening—The forgotten skill: A self-teaching guide* (2nd ed.). New York: Wiley.

Costner, N. (1988). Developing basic listening skills. In *National Business Education Yearbook* (pp. 11–19). Reston, VA: National Business Educational Association.

Hamilton, C., & Kleiner, B. H. (1987). Steps to better listening. *Personnel Journal, 66,* 20–21.

Quible, Z. K. (1989). Listening: An often overlooked communication skill. *Business Education Forum, 43,* 19–20.

Steil, L. K., Barker, L. L., & Watson, K. W. (1983). *Effective listening: Key to your success.* Reading, MA: Addison-Wesley.

CHAPTER 10

Taking Notes in Class

Friendly Reminders

❏ Reading this chapter *before* class will break down many barriers to listening and increase what you learn.

❏ With a good set of notes you will save time when you study for your next exam.

❏ Preview Chapter 10 using the Preview Checklist on page 11.

"He listens well who takes notes."

Dante Alighieri (1265–1321),
Italian poet

After reading the previous chapter on listening, you might be tempted to ask, "If I become an effective listener, why do I have to take notes?"

First, taking notes compensates for deficiencies in our memory. On the average, we forget about 50% of what we learn within a day and about 80% within two weeks. Notes serve as an *external storage* device for memory, like a computer disk. Having easy access to a "hard copy" (our notes) of what we heard in class, we need not depend on our imperfect memory to hold the information in focus.

Second, notetaking enables us to *focus attention* on the speaker's message. Focusing is enhanced by our intention to be attentive and by involving our motor sense (the muscles used in writing) in the learning process. Together, attention and motor movement enhance the permanency of learning.

Third, when we take notes, we *encode,* or organize and translate the speaker's message into our thoughts and words. Researchers believe that encoding strengthens memory and increases achievement.

Fourth, most students are *deficient* in note-taking skills. According to Kenneth Kiewra and Stephen Benton (1987), students generally record less than 50% of a lecture's main ideas. *When you combine the inefficiency of notetaking with the inefficiency of memory, the amount of information we lose from a typical class lecture is astounding!* Think of the potential that you have for improvement! First, let's examine why some students don't take notes, and then we can examine the nature of taking notes and suggest techniques for strengthening this learning-how-to-learn skill.

Why Some Students Avoid Notetaking

When you learned that fewer than 50% of a lecture's main ideas are recorded, did you wonder why many students are such poor notetakers, or why you may be a poor notetaker? Let's examine three likely answers to this complex issue. First, there is a popular misconception among students that only *the most important* words should be recorded. Major terms are a crucial but insufficient part of your notes. Most teachers expect you to know several specific facts and details that support general concepts. Although recording the instructor's words verbatim is nearly impossible and unwise, students should plan to take several notes *throughout* a class, unless the teacher suggests otherwise.

How many pages of notes should you take each class? There is no simple answer to this question because several factors are involved. Follow these two guidelines. First, it is better to err on the side of taking too many notes than not enough. In other words, it is better to possess information you may not need than to omit information you will need. Second, let your test results guide the amount and type of notes that you take. If your performance is below your goals, insufficient or poor quality notetaking may be the cause. In fact, researcher Kenneth Kiewra (1987) believes that extensive notetaking is positively related to achievement in a course: generally the more notes, the better the grade. In addition, the amount and content of your notes depends on the types of test questions you answer. If the only information you recorded consists of facts, you can answer only fact-based test questions. However, if the test questions contain such verbs as *compare and contrast, analyze, demonstrate,* or *evaluate,* knowing facts will be insufficient. **Notes must reflect factual information *and* thinking.** The relation of notetaking to test questions will be discussed further in "Pretest Reviews" and in Chapter 13.

A second major reason why students are not effective notetakers is due to the discrepancy in speeds of speaking and notetaking. According to Kiewra, teachers tend to speak between 45 and 240 words per minute, whereas students tend to write about 20 words per minute. Many students simply give up trying to take notes or are content with sketchy notes when faced with the continuous dual challenges of what to select and how to record it quickly.

Finally, for several possible reasons, the earlier educational experiences of many students did not promote the value of notetaking as an essential component of the learning process. Thus, most students enter college seriously deficient in a skill that most professors believe should be well developed in college freshmen.

Notetaking as Selective Recording

Taking notes is the process of *selecting* and *recording* information contained in a spoken or written message. Selecting portions of a message is a process that operates at all phases of communication in the typical college course. Study the Pyramid of Selective Learning in Figure 10.1; read up from the bottom.

Textbook authors select their information from original sources such as research studies, scholarly books, and personal experience, or from secondary sources such as textbooks and reviews. These resources are cited in the reference or bibliography sections of textbooks. The second level of the pyramid represents information that your teacher selects and integrates from primary and secondary sources.

Although you have little control over the first two levels of the pyramid, *you* determine what to select, record, and remember from the teacher's message, the pyramid's third level. The volume at this level may be large or small depending on your ability to listen, take notes effectively, and remember.

The time allocated during a course for exams seldom permits a professor to test students on all of the material. Consequently, the pyramid's fourth level represents your instructor's selection of the most important material from the total presented. Typically, you prepare for exams by selecting and mastering what you believe are the most essential facts and concepts.

The top of the pyramid represents what you remember weeks, months, or years later. Although it is only a very small fraction of the information presented, the amount depends on your listening, note-taking, and remembering skills. Perhaps you prefer to compare the pyramid of selective learning to an iceberg. All that is known about a particular topic is the bottom, what the teacher selects is below the surface, and what you remember is exposed.

Do you feel discouraged to discover that the knowledge you retain from a particular course is, at best, a modicum of what is known? (Go ahead, look up *modicum* in your dictionary.) If you are preparing for a technical field, your reaction may be compounded by the continuous explosion of new ideas and the obsolescence of old ones. Given that your 40 to 50 hours of class time exposes you to a small portion of the subject (level 2), and given that you select (level 3) and remember (level 5) a fraction of that portion, learning to take class notes effectively is *crucial*. The goal for the rest of this chapter is to offer suggestions that will increase the middle level in your pyramid of selective learning. Chapter 11 contains recommendations for improving your reading skills. Chapters 12 (remembering) and 13 (taking exams) enable you to expand the top level of your pyramid. Because notetaking consists of selecting and recording, each phase is discussed separately.

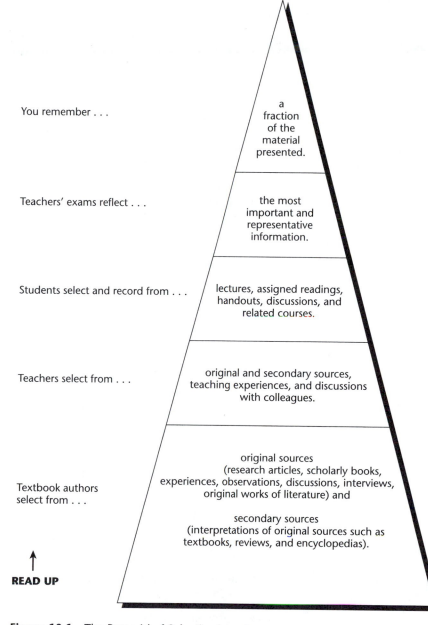

You remember . . .

a fraction of the material presented.

Teachers' exams reflect . . .

the most important and representative information.

Students select and record from . . .

lectures, assigned readings, handouts, discussions, and related courses.

Teachers select from . . .

original and secondary sources, teaching experiences, and discussions with colleagues.

Textbook authors select from . . .

original sources (research articles, scholarly books, experiences, observations, discussions, interviews, original works of literature) and

secondary sources (interpretations of original sources such as textbooks, reviews, and encyclopedias).

↑
READ UP

Figure 10.1   The Pyramid of Selective Learning

Selecting: Detecting Cues

Perhaps the most common frustration that students voice about notetaking is not knowing what to record and what to omit. A good notetaker is like a detective sifting thoughtfully through a barrage of evidence, searching for relevant cues and clues. There are several cues that enable you to sift through the words and thoughts of your instructor. Because notetaking is the transformation of information you hear to "hard copy," some suggestions presented in the previous chapter are briefly repeated below.

1. During the first class, ask your instructor for guidance. Would you take a cross-country road trip without a map? Your teacher's review of the course syllabus on the first day of class provides important directions for reaching your course goals. For example, should you perform a general or a specific reading of the material in advance? To what extent will lectures parallel the reading assignments? How much emphasis should be placed on main ideas? How much on details? What percentage of an exam is taken from class notes and what percentage from the text? Some teachers follow the text closely; others use it to augment their notes. *Knowing what to expect helps you decide what to select.*

2. *Read the assignment before class.*

3. Search for cues in the instructor's style of teaching. According to Mary Beirne-Smith (1989), teachers facilitate notetaking when they

- provide *advance organizers* (preparatory information) such as topic outlines, lists of terms, or notes

- repeat or restate their remarks that signal important concepts or to reinforce learning

- use visual aids such as projectors and chalkboards

- pause or slow down to give students time to record important points

- summarize, draw conclusions, or integrate ideas after presenting a topic

- use voice inflection, hands, posture, facial expression, or movement to communicate or dramatize an idea

Look and listen for these cues. Your instructor is trying to help you select the important facts and ideas.

4. Take notes when you hear cue words and phrases, such as

- "It's important (crucial, critical, vital, significant, essential) to remember that . . ."

- "Also (likewise, in addition, ditto, furthermore) . . ."

- "Here's an example (illustration, demonstration, representation) of . . ."

- "There is (are) 1 (2, 3, 4, 5, 500) causes (reasons, motives, purposes, explanations) for . . ."

- "The consequences (results, effects, outcomes, outgrowths) of . . ."

- "Still (yet, in spite of, but, nevertheless, though, on the other hand, in contrast) . . ."

- "Everyone (all, the public, the people) believes . . ."

- "Some (part, a portion, a few) believe . . ."

Cue words and phrases indicate how an instructor's thought processes are organized. Underline the cue words in your notes. Learn synonyms such as those shown in parentheses above. Try to anticipate how your instructor might include cue words in test questions.

Recording

Knowing what to select is the first and, usually, the most difficult aspect of notetaking. *Recording* is facilitated through preparation, mastery of note-taking formats, and practicing shortcuts.

❑ Be Prepared

Before you complete your first page of notes in your first class, do the following:

1. Sit smart. Arrive early and select a seat close to the front, one with a good view of the chalkboard and free of distracting noises, views, and people.

2. Use a ring binder. Obtain a three-ring loose-leaf binder for $8\frac{1}{2} \times 11$-inch paper. Purchase dividers or tabs to separate the notes for each course. A ring binder permits you to add handouts and reorganize the pages as needed. Transfer all notes no longer needed for class to another binder in your room. Why? How would you feel if you lost your notes or had them rain-soaked the week before final exams?

For an added touch of efficiency and security, consider using one small ring binder for each course.

As an alternative to this procedure, some students bring a pocket folder to class containing course syllabi and loose-leaf paper that is coded and dated for each course. After returning home, they transfer the notes to their loose-leaf binder and number the pages.

3. Create space. As you take notes, leave plenty of white space for editing after class. Use wide margins, skip lines between topics, and write only on one side of the paper. Leaving one side blank also prevents ink from bleeding through the sheet on your notes, and it makes your notes appealing. Like an eye-catching advertisement, visually attractive notes will capture your attention when it is needed the most—as you prepare for an exam.

4. Motivate yourself to *understand* the material using Deep Strategies of learning (Chapter 1). Avoid taking notes mechanically, to memorize at a later date. Think hard about the meaning of what you write while you write.

❑ Note-taking Formats

The most popular formats for taking notes are the outline and column methods.

The Outline Format

Figure 10.2 is an example of the outline format that was used to take notes on the topic of research methods in a consumer psychology course.

Note why the outline format is appealing. The topics are organized and categorized neatly into major headings and subheadings. Ample space was left for margins and between lines. The notes will be easy to review for an examination. The information is so easy to follow in outline notes that it is tempting to use this format in all classes. However, choosing the outline method depends on the instructor, the material, and the student. Outlining is effective when the lectures *and* you are well organized—that is, when you can readily identify the major topics and subtopics. However, if the lecture appears disorganized, or if the instructor digresses or rambles rather than lectures, you may become frustrated trying to determine the major and minor headings. The outline format is usually appropriate when you read textbook assignments before class because familiarity with the topics helps you know what to expect and when, relative to other topics, to expect it.

Three approaches / Methods for Gathering
  Consumer (C) Information (Info)

A. Observation (ob.) - collecting info / data by ob.
    some aspect of behavior (B)
    1. Types
        a) Direct ob. of B by researcher (R) with or
           w/o C's awareness he's being watched

        b) Mechanical ob.
            i. Cameras observe shoppers' B
            ii. automatic scanning devices (scanners) read
                UPC codes at check out

    2. Evaluation
        a) Advantage (+) can ob. C's B in natural
           setting w/ little interference of C's B

        b) Disadvantages (-)
            i. data from direct ob. can be biased by
               selective perceptions of R
            ii. data may or may not represent C's B
            iii. can't control variables causing C's B

B. Experimentation (Exp.) - R designs situation where
   specific variable (e.g., size of magazine ad) is
   intentionally manipulated to study its effects on
   B (e.g., attention span). Other variables (e.g., age,
   preferences of C) are extraneous & are controlled
   to prevent R from misinterpreting results.

Figure 10.2 The Outline Format of Notetaking

1. Types

   a) Lab. exp. permits high control over extraneous variables but setting is contrived & artificial

   b) Field exp. provides more natural setting but some control is lost

2. Evaluation
   a) Adv. (+) Generally, exp. offers R considerable control over variables that affect C's B. Thus R is able to understand cause & effect relationship among variables

   b) Disadv. (−) To achieve control R designed setting so contrived & artificial that it doesn't resemble real world of C

C. Survey (Sur.) used here includes interviews, questionnaire, & surveys. Sur. is process of gathering data in somewhat structured somewhat natural setting

   1. Types
      a) Interview. Direct face-to-face interaction w/ C in which much data can be gathered through pre-determined questions and follow-up probes of C's response
      b) Telephone surveys
      c) Mail surveys

   2. Evaluation

Figure 10.2   The Outline Format of Notetaking *(continued)*

The Column Format

Figure 10.3 shows how the column format is used to record notes on a question/answer discussion presentation of the material presented in Figure 10.2. To use the column format, divide your paper into the content column (about two-thirds of the right side) and the critical-concept column, the left third. Some stationery stores carry loose-leaf paper marked with a two-thirds margin.

The critical-concept column consists of one or more key words that best describe the information you record on the content side. The critical concept may be recorded before, during, or after you record the content. When an instructor introduces a new topic, listen carefully so that you may record it before you begin your notes. If you are unsure about the critical concept, ask for clarification or record it when it becomes clear. Record specific information that supports the critical concept in the content column. Typically, that information takes the form of facts, details, evidence, or examples, depending on the cue words chosen by the instructor to organize the material.

The column method is appropriate in classes where topic organization may be unclear or has been modified by the instructor in a way that discourages outlining. Also, some teachers prefer to present their information as a series of questions rather than as a lecture; the questions become the critical concept, the responses the content side. Certain courses revolve around the discussion of key issues in which facts and illustration are integrated.

Designer Notes

Work hard to become proficient with the outline and column formats because they are the most useful note-taking methods. During the first few weeks of a new course pay close attention to the professor's particular style of teaching and the cues she or he emits as well as the material. If you experience difficulty with both formats, make adjustments that help you learn. Occasionally, there are situations for which the best approach to taking notes is a combination of the two formats plus your own techniques. However, do not be quick to modify the basic formats unless the results of your first exam and a meeting with your teacher warrant change. Ask your teacher if you can tape-record one or two classes to evaluate your note-taking format.

❏ Note-able Shortcuts

To increase the amount of notes you take, practice hard to master these shortcuts.

Three Approaches/Methods for Gathering Consumer (C)
   Information (Info.)—What are They?

Observation (Ob.)	Info./data gathered by ob. of behavior (B)

Types?	- Direct ob. of B with or w/o being seen
	- Mechanical ob.
	    Cameras ob. shopping B
	    Auto. scanning devices (scanner)
	    at checkout counters of UPC codes

How evaluated?	- Adv. B is ob. in natural setting,
	  little interference w/ C
	- Disadv. - Data from direct ob. biased
	  by selective perceptions of observer
	    - Data may/may not represent
	      C's B

Experimentation (Exp.)	- Researcher (R) designs situations where
	  specific variable (e.g., size of magazine ad)
	  is intentionally manip. to study its
	  effects on B (e.g., C's attention span).
	  Other variables (e.g., age, preferences of C)
	  are extraneous & controlled to prevent
	  R from misinterpreting results

Types?	- Lab exp. permits high control over
	  extraneous variables but setting is
	  contrived and artificial
	
	- Field exp. provides more natural
	  setting but some control is lost

Figure 10.3 The Column Format of Notetaking

How evaluated ?	- Adv. Generally exp. offers R considerable control over variables that affect C's B. Thus R able to understand cause and effect relationship among variables
	- Disadv. To achieve control, R designed setting so contrived + artificial it doesn't resemble real world of C.
Survey (Sur)	- Used here includes interviews, quest. + sur. Sur. is process of gathering data in somewhat structured + somewhat natural setting
Types?	- Interviews - Direct face-to-face interaction w/ c. Much data can be gathered through pre-determined questions + follow-up probes of C's response.
	- Telephone Surveys
	- Mail Surveys
How evaluated ?	- Interviews
	- Adv. face-to-face gives flexibility to interact + use probes
	- can get much data
	- Disadv. - Time consuming + requires →

Figure 10.3   The Column Format of Notetaking *(continued)*

1. Decide to either print or write. To conserve time and muscle movement during notetaking, ascertain whether it is faster for you to print or write to produce legible notes. Also, simplify your handwriting or printing by omitting unnecessary curls or long lines. If these suggestions seem trivial, calculate the number of hours you are likely to spend writing or printing notes during the 40 to 50 courses that comprise your college program!

2. Reduce words to abbreviations and symbols.

   a. Substitute the prefixes contained in your course schedules (BIO, SOC, MAT, CHM, BUS, HUM, ECN, PSY) for discipline names.

   b. Learn the meaning of key Latin abbreviations used in textbooks and research studies: *e.g.* for *for example, i.e.* for *that is, viz.* for *namely,* and *vs.* for *versus.*

   c. Use only the first one or two syllables of a word (for example, *esp* for *especially, illus* for *illustration, rel* for *relevant, exper* for *experiment, crit* for *criticize*).

   d. Omit prepositions (for example, *in, by, to, of*) and articles (*a, an, the*), if their omission does not change the meaning of the statement.

   e. Omit vowels (*bk* for *book, pnt* for *point,* or *crcl* for *circle*).

   f. Substitute symbols for words: = for *equal,* ∴ for *therefore,* > or < for *greater* or *less than,* w/ for *with.* Use arrows to symbolize change and movement.

   Introduce your abbreviation system gradually so that it doesn't confuse you. Oh yes, be sure to keep a master list of your abbreviations in your ring binder so that you don't forget what they mean!

Reviewing: Getting the Most from Your Notes

Now that you are familiar with basic principles of notetaking, shouldn't this chapter end? For too many students, the end of class signals their last contact with their notes until the night before an exam. To ignore your notes is unfortunate. Kenneth Kiewra (1985)

Box 10.1

Creating Shortcuts for Your Toughest Class

Take time to create shortcuts for your least favorite course. Begin by spending 5 to 10 minutes reviewing notes from the last two classes. Then record some shortcuts that you could begin to use at the next class.

Name of Course: _____

Shortcut:

1. Discipline prefix: _____

2. One- or two-syllable words: _____

   _____

3. "Vowel-less" words: _____

   _____

4. Symbols for words: _____

   _____

5. Other abbreviations: _____

   _____

6. Other shortcuts? _____

   _____

maintains, "Simply recording notes . . . is ineffective unless those notes are reviewed" (p. 396). In fact, recent research indicates that recording lecture notes but not reviewing them is as ineffective as just listening to a lecture without taking notes (Kiewra et al., 1991). To get the most from your notes, plan to review them at least three times before you are tested on them. The importance of review will be reiterated (go ahead, look it up in the dictionary) in Chapter 13, "Evaluation and Test-taking Tips."

First Review

The first review should occur as soon as possible after class. If you do not have time immediately after class, find a 10- to 15-minute period before day's end. If you have evening classes, force yourself to review your notes before bedtime or early the next day. The first review is crucial because it is an opportunity to *edit, rehearse,* and *reflect* on the material while it is still fresh in your mind.

In *editing,* use the first review to

- finish incomplete thoughts or statements

- rewrite illegible words

- clarify the organization of an outline format

- complete the critical-concept section in column notes

- reorganize notes, if necessary, to gain clarity

- decipher note-taking shortcuts that you used

If you recorded your notes on one side of the paper, left ample margins, and skipped a line between topics, you should have sufficient room for these editorial changes.

Reviewing notes is a *rehearsal* (repetition) of the information in your own words. Thoughtful repetition strengthens learning and increases what you remember. Do not forget to review handouts, especially if they are outlines or summaries of the material covered.

Finally, as you rehearse during this first review, *reflect* on the material's relevance to past classes and its personal significance for you.

Second Review

A good time-management plan should contain 2 or 3 hours on a weekend for reviewing that week's notes. Having edited your notes during the first review, you are free to concentrate on content and organization. The second review refreshes your memory, strengthens comprehension, and facilitates the integration of major ideas and facts.

As you review, underline or highlight key concepts as you would in a textbook (Chapter 11 contains suggestions for marking textbooks). Using the Deep Strategies for learning summarized on page 9, take time to reflect on the relevance of the ideas to the course, your academic major, and your daily life when appropriate. To the extent that you try to make such connections, the material will "stick."

Students often ask about the benefits of typing notes. *If* you have very poor handwriting or printing, *if* you have considerable time to spare, and *if* you are such a good typist that it will not distract you from thinking about the material, then typing notes may be helpful. Otherwise, typing notes is likely to be a poor use of your time.

Similarly, students inquire about the value of audiotaping a class. Unless you have a physical or learning disability for which taping is a necessary aid, taping lectures regularly is time consuming. It is time consuming because you replay the whole class; it is unwise because you are depending on a machine to remember for you. However, as indicated in the previous chapter, occasional taping to strengthen listening skills can be beneficial.

Pretest Reviews

At the risk of stealing the thunder from the Chapter 13 discussion of test-taking skills, here are suggestions for your pretest review sessions.

The fourth level in Figure 10.1 represents the instructor's selection of information for an examination. Tests are a reality that students must face. Having reviewed your notes twice, problems in reading, editing, and organizing notes should be minimal. In fact, you have the right to feel a bit confident and pleased with yourself; classmates who have never reviewed notes must face those problems before mastering the meaning of the notes, and time is running out.

Although research on *how* to review notes is inconclusive, experience suggests that exams influence note-taking habits, and vice versa. You can best use your notes before an exam if you can answer these questions:

1. What type of test will it be?

If the test emphasizes factual information and detail, your notes should contain several pages of facts and details. Multiple-choice and short-answer essay tests usually require mastery of specific information to *recognize* the differences among details or *recall* factual information. Long-answer essay or take-home exams assume that you went beyond the mastery of specifics during review sessions. Such tests measure your ability to apply, connect, compare, or critically evaluate major concepts and support your reasoning with sufficient facts and details. Box 10.2 shows one method of using your notes to study for this type of exam.

2. Are your notes sufficient?

Many students assume that with a detailed set of notes they do not need to study anything else. For some but not all teachers, good notes are sufficient. If a teacher assigns and discusses additional readings or creates summary sheets, outlines, or charts, that information is probably important. Your notes should contain clues about the importance of such handouts.

3. Should you reread the text?

If the professor's presentation corresponds with the text, chances are that you should reread it to gain more detail. Because time seldom permits adequate coverage of textbook material, students may be held responsible for pages not discussed in class. Ask the professor. If the text is used mainly to augment the instructor's lecture, do not ignore the text, but devote most of your attention to the notes. Remember, if you are not sure, ask.

Is Notetaking Second-guessing?

Trying to determine how much emphasis the instructor gives to class notes, handouts, and text material can be viewed from many perspectives: psyching out the teacher, playing games, detecting clues, solving problems, or using common sense.

Knowing that the professor's particular use of notes and text is consistent from one test to another is valuable information. If the relationship among text, notes, and tests is unclear, frustration occurs. Whether the unpredictability reflects the professor's game playing, lack of experience, or conviction that such practices reflect the unpredictability of real life may be hard to judge. In any case, plan on adapting your note-taking and reading habits to the exams. Do not hesitate to create a set of notes that combines your class notes

Box 10.2

Self-questioning to Learn from Notes

Depending on what your teacher wants you to know, you may conduct a pretest review of your notes to demonstrate that you *understand* the material or can *analyze* and *apply* it to other topics.

Researcher Alison King (1992) found that small groups of students trained to generate questions from their notes scored higher on an exam than students who simply reviewed their notes. Although differences exist between the structured conditions of her study and those that characterize your note-taking review sessions, applying King's 13 "generic" questions to a well-written set of notes may help you prepare for exams that require high-level thinking skills.

1. What is the main idea of . . . ?

2. How would you use . . . to . . . ?

3. What is the difference between . . . and . . . ?

4. How are . . . and . . . similar?

5. What conclusions do you draw about . . . ?

6. Explain why . . . .

7. Explain how . . . .

8. What is a new example of . . . ?

9. What do you think would happen if . . . ?

10. How does . . . affect . . . ?

11. What are the strengths and weaknesses of . . . ?

12. What is the best . . . and why?

13. How is . . . related to . . . that we studied earlier?

with textbook information. Many experts recommend taking notes on the text, as Chapter 11 indicates.

In summary, taking notes is the process of selecting and recording information from a large body of knowledge. Authors select from their sources. Teachers select what to present and what to test for. Students select what to record and, later, what to review. Selecting is enhanced by seeking cues from the teacher's organization and communication patterns. Recording is facilitated through preparing, choosing the appropriate format, using shortcuts, and conducting timely reviews. What relevance does notetaking have for careers?

Connecting Notetaking to Your Career

On my first day of work at a midsize corporation, proud of my new doctorate and new job title, I was surprised to discover that my notetaking days were not over. After listening attentively while my supervisor briefed me about my responsibilities for various research projects, I returned to my office to jot down his remarks. Immediately, I began confusing my responsibilities on one project with those on other projects. Similarly, my boss's valuable suggestions for approaching these projects were blurred or forgotten. Embarrassed, I returned to his office for clarification. From that day on, I always entered his office and attended his meetings carrying a pad of paper and a pen. In essence, my supervisor was another teacher, his office the classroom, and my new job the beginning of a new educational experience in which listening and note-taking skills were essential tools in the learning process.

Many jobs involve meetings, briefings, reports, evaluations, conferences, negotiations, and similar activities where accurate notes must compensate for an imperfect memory. If you develop a respect for skills in notetaking as a college student, carrying a pen and pad will become natural in your job.

Action-Oriented Thought Starters

1. This exercise is similar to an activity suggested in Chapter 9, "Listening to Learn," except that the emphasis is on notetaking. Obtain a videotape of a major segment (about 10 to 15 minutes) of the PBS program *NewsHour with Jim Lehrer*, ABC's *Nightline*, or a similar in-depth news program. Take notes as if you were going to be tested on it.

   a. Which note-taking format is more appropriate? Why?

   b. While you take notes, practice your shortcuts.

    c. Replay the program and compare your notes with the speakers' remarks. What were the strengths and weaknesses in your notetaking?

2. Choose one of your less demanding classes to conduct an experiment about the relationship between notetaking and test taking. Ask a classmate whose note-taking skills are similar to yours to act as your coparticipant.

    a. Choose a particular class period and agree that one of you will take notes as if you will receive a multiple-choice test, whereas the other takes notes for a long-answer essay test.

    b. At the next class, reverse the testing roles. Then compare and discuss your sets of notes in terms of the number of pages recorded, the amount of details and facts recorded versus statements of concepts and principles, and the format used. What can you conclude about the connection between notetaking and test taking?

3. Photocopy the notes you recorded for the class in which Chapter 10 material was discussed. Using the checklist below, evaluate the strengths and weaknesses of your notes by comparing them with the concepts and techniques covered in this chapter. Write your comments on the photocopy or on a separate sheet.

___ The use of instructor cues such as advance organizers, repetition, visual aids, and summaries.

___ The recording of cue words and phrases such as "for example."

___ The amount of space between lines and in margins.

___ The proper use of the outline or double-column note-taking format.

___ The use of abbreviations.

___ Performing the first review after class or before day's end.

___ Other note-taking concepts: _____

References and Recommended Readings

Beirne-Smith, M. (1989). A systematic approach for teaching note-taking skills to students with mild learning handicaps. *Academic Therapy, 24,* 425–437.

Kiewra, K. A. (1985). Examination of the encoding and external-storage functions of notetaking for factual and higher-order performance. *College Student Journal, 19,* 394–397.

Kiewra, K. A. (1987). Notetaking and review: The research and its implications. *Instructional Science, 16,* 233–249.

Kiewra, K. A., & Benton, S. L. (1987). Effects of notetaking, the instructor's notes, and higher-order practice questions on factual and higher-order learning. *Journal of Instructional Psychology, 14,* 186–194.

Kiewra, K. A., DuBois, N. F., Christian, D., McShane, A., Meyerhoffer, M., & Roskelley, D. (1991). Note-taking functions and techniques. *Journal of Educational Psychology, 83,* 240–245.

King, A. (1992). Comparison of self-questioning, summarizing, and notetaking-review as strategies for learning from lectures. *American Educational Research Journal, 29* (2), 303–323.

CHAPTER 11

Getting Involved with Your Reading

Pamela B. Adelman
Barat College

Friendly Reminders

❑ Search for specific cues in your instructor's presentation to strengthen your listening and note-taking skills.

❑ Which "note-able" note-taking shortcuts can you use when your instructor presents this chapter?

❑ Preview Chapter 11 using the Preview Checklist on page 11, and learn its major ideas using the Deep strategies on page 9.

"Reading is to the mind what exercise is to the body."
Richard Steele (1672–1729),
British essayist, dramatist, and politician

Are you in better shape since you started exercising? Can you lift heavier weights or run longer distances? Everybody knows abilities, including reading, improve with practice. In college, improving your reading ability allows you to tackle longer and more challenging assignments. It is also time to become a more *flexible* reader. The knowledge you bring to a topic, your prior knowledge, also affects the speed with which you will comprehend the material. Material with new vocabulary, complex sentence structure, and new concepts may require several readings before you comprehend it. For books and articles used for research papers, you can skim several pages to get an overview of the material or scan for a specific piece of information. However, one paragraph of technical information could take an hour or longer to accurately comprehend. As an *efficient* reader, you can quickly identify the skills and strategies you need to read a particular selection.

Whether you are reading to master complicated information, to do research in the library, or to enjoy a good novel, the key is *to take an active role* in the reading process and *to interact with the text*. While you read, you should communicate with the author. How can you communicate with an author? Ask questions. Relate information to prior knowledge. Make predictions about what you are going to read. Use context to figure out the meaning of new information.

To become an active reader, you must understand the skills and abilities required for reading. The following skill assessment will help you determine what you need to do to improve your comprehension and your retention of the material.

Reading Strategies: A Self-assessment

Have you ever thought about the strategies and skills you use when you read? Take a few minutes now and check each statement that describes your reading strategies.

_____ 1. Before I start reading, I think about the author's purpose for writing the material and my purpose for reading it.

_____ 2. I preview my textbook to learn its features.

_____ 3. I preview each chapter before starting to read.

_____ 4. When I come to a word in my reading that I cannot pronounce, I look up the pronunciation in the dictionary.

_____ 5. I know how to use the pronunciation guide in a dictionary.

_____ 6. I take the time to look up the meanings of words I do not understand.

_____ 7. I try to use context to figure out new words.

_____ 8. As I read, I stop periodically and ask questions or make predictions.

_____ 9. When I read, I note the main ideas and identify details the authors are presenting to support the topic.

_____10. I take notes or outline when I read.

_____11. I vary my reading rate depending on my purpose and the complexity of the reading material.

_____12. I reread sections that I have difficulty understanding.

_____13. When graphs, charts, tables, and pictures are discussed, I take time to read and understand them.

_____14. I complete exercises or answer questions at the end of the chapters.

_____15. I continuously review what I read.

If you checked all or nearly all of these questions, then you have already established good reading strategies. If there are some statements that you did not check, read on and discover how to get more involved with your reading.

The rest of this chapter is divided into two sections. The first section discusses two important components of reading: the reading process and the characteristics of text. The second section teaches you specific strategies and techniques for improving your reading comprehension. It includes examples and exercises that provide an opportunity to apply these strategies and techniques.

Understanding the Reading Process

Reading is an extension of the way you learned the language. As a child, you learned to speak the language by first attaching meaning to groups of sounds that become words: _room._ Groups of words, or sentences, convey complete thoughts: *The room is large.* As sentences became longer and more complex, several ideas, concepts, or thoughts were communicated: *Because we were given a large room, our friends chose our room as the one in which to meet.* When you began to read, you associated visual symbols (letters) with sounds so you could understand the meaning of written language.

Let's examine skills and abilities that comprise the reading process. The skills include understanding

- sound/letter correspondences
- vocabulary
- sentences, paragraphs, and longer passages
- the need to vary your reading rate

Understanding How Sounds and Letters Correspond

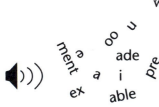

Written words are a series of sounds represented by letters. To read words, you must understand the relationship between sounds and letters, which is influenced by the sound patterns common in the English language. For example, an *e* at the end of a word is almost always silent, and the preceding vowel has a long vowel sound (or says its name) as in *made, recede, anticipate,* and *despite.* You can learn to pronounce words by using a dictionary that contains symbols for pronunciation. In some dictionaries, these symbols are explained in a key generally found at the bottom of each right-hand page.

Understanding Vocabulary

❑ Word Parts

Words often have several parts. These parts include word bases (roots) and affixes, which are both prefixes and suffixes. The root is the main part or base of the word. Prefixes and suffixes are word parts that have meaning. They are attached to either the beginning (prefix) or end (suffix) of a word. For example, in the words *prejudge* and *judgment, judge* is the base word, *pre* (meaning *in advance*) is the prefix, and *ment* (meaning *the result*) is the suffix.

In college you will need to learn the meanings of thousands of new words. One way to rapidly increase your vocabulary is to learn the meanings of word parts. Certain prefixes, roots, and suffixes are used repeatedly in the English language. For example, the word part *poly* means *many.* Knowing that, you are better prepared to decipher the meanings of words such as *polychrome, polygamist,* and *polyhedron.* In *Webster's Seventh New Collegiate Dictionary,* there are 123 words defined that begin with the word part *poly.*

Certain types of words that are very important for comprehension are referred to as qualifiers, conjunctions, and connectors.

❏ Qualifiers

Qualifying words modify the meaning of a statement and include such words as *always, never, sometimes, invariably, rarely,* and *probably.* Look carefully for qualifiers in multiple-choice or true/false exams because the inclusion of any one of them can totally change the meaning of a statement. For example, the statement "Professors are concerned with preparing interesting lectures for their students" is true, but the statement "Professors are *always* concerned with preparing interesting lectures for their students" is false.

❏ Conjunctions and Connectors

Conjunctions and connectors help you learn the relationship between ideas. Examples that express an alternate relationship between ideas are *or, otherwise, if not . . . then, either . . . or,* and *neither . . . nor.* "*Either* you lock your room, *or* you risk having your things stolen."

The concept of time is related by words such as *after, meanwhile, earlier,* and *soon.* "The professor gave the first exam *earlier* than the class expected."

Sometimes conjunctions and connectors provide transitions between ideas that have been presented and those that you are about to read. Some examples are *as a result, even though, however,* and *but.* "*Even though* she apologized, Bill vowed that he would never ask her out again."

❏ New Vocabulary

In each new subject you'll meet in college, you'll encounter vocabulary words specific to the subject matter. There are several ways to learn these new words.

- Prior to reading, scan the chapter for new words and define them.

- If the new vocabulary words are identified in the textbook either at the beginning or end of each chapter, take the time to look up their meanings.

- As you learned in the previous chapter, when the professor uses words in a lecture that are new to you, write them down and learn their meanings. They may reappear on the next exam.

- Photocopy the textbook's glossary and have it handy while reading the chapter.

Resources that can help you improve your ability to pronounce words and to improve your vocabulary are listed in Box 11.1.

Understanding Sentences, Paragraphs, and Longer Passages

Naturally, you cannot comprehend what you read by just knowing the meanings of words. You must also grasp the *relationship* between the words. And that requires getting involved with your reading! Initially, you have to determine the author's purpose and your purpose.

- Is the author trying to inform you or persuade you?

- Is the author presenting a lot of facts or an overview?

- Are you reading the material to get an overview or are there facts that you need to memorize for an exam?

Once you start reading, continue asking questions and start making predictions. If you do not understand something, ask yourself why. Propose several answers. Think about the way the new information relates to prior knowledge that you acquired in a previous chapter or lecture. Do new ideas expand, alter, or contradict old information? Is there information with which you disagree? The purpose of such questions is to stop periodically and think about the information and its relationship to material you have already learned.

Understanding the Need to Vary Your Reading Rate

The rate at which you read material depends on several factors: your specific purpose for reading, complexity of the sentences, difficulty level of the vocabulary, and subject matter.

Box 11.1

Resources for Improving Word Pronunciation and Vocabulary

• *Vowel Power I and II* are books that use innovative techniques to teach students to read multisyllabic words. Write to

Vowel Power I and II
Word Power Systems
P. O. Box 248H
Scarsdale, NY 10583

• The following materials help students develop their vocabularies through an understanding of suffixes and word roots.
Essential Suffixes (software)
Essential Word Roots Video (video or software)
Essential Roots Word Book
Essential Roots Work Book
C. Wilson Anderson, Jr., T. Elli Cross, and Joan Menche Stoner
Educators Publishing Service, Inc.
75 Moulton Street
Cambridge, MA 02138

• The *Word Attack Manual* is designed for students who have not developed adequate word-recognition skills.

Word Attack Manual
Josephine Rudd
Educators Publishing Service, Inc. (see address above)

• The following books will help college students increase their vocabularies.

Vocabulary Foundations for College Students
Harold Levine and Robert T. Levine
Amsco College Publications
315 Hudson Street
New York, NY 10013

Success with Words
Joan D. Carris
Peterson's Guides
Princeton, NJ 08543

Programmed College Vocabulary 3600
George W. Feinstein
Prentice Hall
Englewood Cliffs, NJ 07632

Regarding *purpose,* when you read a newspaper, magazine, or novel for enjoyment, you can increase your speed and, at times, skim the material. However, new concepts in your chemistry textbook that include complicated formulas may require several readings. You cannot equate reading a novel with reading a difficult textbook. You may be able to read 40 pages of a novel in an hour, but only 10 pages of chemistry text. *Complex sentences* and *unknown vocabulary* slow down your reading. Long sentences with several clauses and phrases are more difficult to understand because they often present several interrelated ideas. You may have to stop and reread, or divide complex sentences into shorter sentences. If you don't understand the meanings of some of the vocabulary, you need either to look up the meanings or take additional time to figure out the meanings by using the *context.*

Subject matter affects reading rate. Information that you are familiar with can be related to your prior knowledge (what you are reading makes sense and fits with previously learned information). But new information takes time to integrate into your thought patterns. You need additional time to think about the material, to try to figure out its connection with other ideas and concepts, or to develop questions for further explanation or clarification.

Understanding the Characteristics of Text

You understand or comprehend the meaning of information when it makes sense to you. Comprehension occurs by relating new ideas and concepts to information you already understand. If you do not understand or remember what you read, it is because you have not related the new information to your prior knowledge, or you have no prior knowledge about that subject.

One way of acquiring prior knowledge is to become familiar with the organization of your textbook. In fact, several studies on prior knowledge point out the importance of understanding text structure when subject matter is unfamiliar. In these situations, you can use your knowledge of the structure of the text to understand relationships between concepts (Roller, 1990). You are developing a framework, or a mental set, that will help you comprehend or make sense out of new information. Previewing the textbook also helps you form opinions about the information. You will get an idea of your back-

Sue Reads but Doesn't Comprehend

She looks at the syllabus, finds the reading assignment, opens the textbook, and *with no further preparation* she dutifully begins to read. Two hours later, Sue finishes reading the 30-page chapter, but she feels frustrated and nervous. She had difficulty understanding the information and did not remember anything she read. Sue saw words and sentences but did not grasp their meaning.

Sue's comprehension and memory of her reading assignment would have been significantly enhanced if she had had a general idea, some prior knowledge, of how the information fit within the context of the textbook or the course.

ground knowledge, level of interest, difficulty of the vocabulary, and the syntax. These are all factors to be considered to accomplish your purpose as effectively and efficiently as possible.

The Textbook

Let's consider the important features of textbooks, chapters, and paragraphs that you should preview. Textbooks have certain features that help you understand the author's purpose, the general and specific organization of the text, study aids (for example, questions and summaries), and additional sources of information. Before you start your assigned readings, take the time to learn the following features of your textbook.

1. The title is descriptive and provides information about the scope and purpose of the book.

2. The year of publication is indicated by the copyright date.

3. The preface or introduction gives an overall understanding of why the book was written. Often the preface describes for whom the book was written, scope or limitations, main points, focus, organization, and suggestions for studying.

4. The table of contents provides a chapter-by-chapter overview of the organization and content.

5. Additional sources used by the author are listed in the bibliography and may be cited in footnotes throughout the text.

6. A glossary is often included with meanings of specific terms.

Other features include an appendix, which provides supplementary information, and an index, which identifies specific pages on which a particular topic, event, or person was discussed. Authors and publishers devote considerable effort to designing a textbook with features that will enable you to strengthen your reading comprehension. Learn to use these features to your advantage.

Chapters

Chapter titles provide you clues to organization, point of view, and purpose. For example, the chapter title, "The Civil War: An Overview," tells you that the chapter is about the entire war, and it will be a general discussion. Often, chapter introductions provide either an overview, statement of objectives, or introductory explanation. Chapter subheadings are often in boldface and introduce specific points discussed under the chapter's topic. The conclusion provides a summary of the chapter or final thoughts. Words are usually in boldface or italics for emphasis or to identify new vocabulary. Charts, graphs, maps, and pictures present a clearer idea of some of the information presented. They are visual aids that point out comparisons and changing relationships. Often study aids such as vocabulary lists, questions, and exercises are included. These help in reviewing the main points of the chapter.

Paragraphs

You improve comprehension when you understand the specific organization of the paragraphs. Generally, individual paragraphs are devoted to one topic. That topic is represented by a main idea, which is a direct statement or implied idea about the topic. The main idea is usually the central or most important thought in the paragraph. It is supported with details that offer proof, explanation, reasons, or examples.

You improve your comprehension when you identify the overall plan of the paragraph. In most paragraphs, the main idea is the first sentence, but it also can be found in the middle or at the end. Sometimes, there is no main idea, but you must infer or derive its meaning from the details. Then you must ask yourself, "What is the one idea that the author discussed throughout the paragraph?" You will also find it helpful to understand the different ways by which supporting sentences relate to the main idea. These sentences might be descriptive or persuasive; they might present the details in chronological order or as a list of ideas. Sometimes the supporting details present relationships such as cause and effect or comparison and contrast.

In summary, you have learned skills that comprise the process of reading and you have learned how to understand the features of a textbook. What specific strategies can you develop that will make you a better reader?

Nine Strategies for Effective Reading

Several study systems have been developed to enhance comprehension, such as SQ3R (Survey-Question-Read-Recite-Review), POINT (Purpose-Overview-Interpret-Note-Test), and EARTH (Explore-Ask-Read-Tell-Harvest). These systems have many features in common. For example, they all include previewing, setting goals, reading, checking comprehension, and reviewing. Our goal is not to promote a specific study system, but to help you *understand, select,* and *apply* strategies that help improve your comprehension. *All* strategies do not have to be used for *all* types of reading. As a flexible reader, you will know which strategies are appropriate to accomplish *your* purpose for reading. Let's examine the following nine effective reading strategies.

- previewing
- taking your time
- interacting
- understanding visual aids
- rereading

- reciting

- taking notes

- answering questions and completing exercises

- reviewing

1. Previewing

By reading certain features of a textbook chapter, you establish your purpose, develop a mental outline or framework, and use prior knowledge. Begin by reading the title, subtitles, introduction, and first paragraph. Read the first and last sentences of each paragraph and the chapter summary. Ask yourself questions by turning titles and subheadings into questions. For instance, the title, "The Civil War: An Overview," becomes the question "What general information will I learn about the Civil War?"

When you preview, you use the skills of skimming and scanning. *Skimming* involves quickly glancing over a page to get the general idea. Reading the first and last sentences of each paragraph is effective because that is where you will most frequently find the main ideas. *Scanning* refers to the identification of specific facts or ideas. Typographical markers, such as words and phrases that are bold-faced, underlined, or italicized, help you quickly scan for key concepts and ideas.

2. Taking Your Time

Effective reading takes time. Difficult sections may need to be read *several* times. As indicated in the Chapter 5 discussion of time management, you may need to readjust your term schedule to accommodate courses that have heavy reading demands.

You may need to cross-reference with information in other chapters or in your lecture notes. Graphs, charts, and pictures are important visual aids but usually take time to understand. Completing exercises, answering questions, and taking notes also increase time needed to complete a reading assignment. There are no easy remedies or miracles for improving comprehension—just hard work. And that takes time! However, as you become a more effective reader, you will likely need a little less time to comprehend difficult concepts.

3. Interacting

There are several ways to interact with your textbook. Each involves stopping periodically and thinking about the material you read. One way is to stop and *summarize*. If you can encode (translate and organize) the information into your own words, you are comprehending. Also, you can ponder answers to questions that help you relate the material to prior knowledge. Questions you might ask include

- How does this information fit with what I already know?

- How and when can I use this information?

- Is this information consistent with other knowledge I have learned?

Writing in or *marking your textbook* is another way to interact. In fact, Nist and Simpson (1988) found that students who used this strategy not only performed better, but also decreased study time. It is generally recommended that between one-third to one-half of the reading material be marked. Marking includes

- circling words that you do not understand and will need to define

- placing question marks in the margin next to information you find confusing

- using asterisks or underlining to emphasize concepts

- drawing arrows to show the relationship between ideas

- writing notes to yourself or summary words that indicate your understanding

- categorizing information by noting ideas, facts, examples, and details

- writing key information on graphs and charts

- underlining or highlighting key concepts

Figure 11.1 is an example of a textbook passage that incorporates some of these marking techniques. Remember, however, marking is effective only if it is done thoughtfully. The mere act of moving a highlighter or circling a word will not aid comprehension.

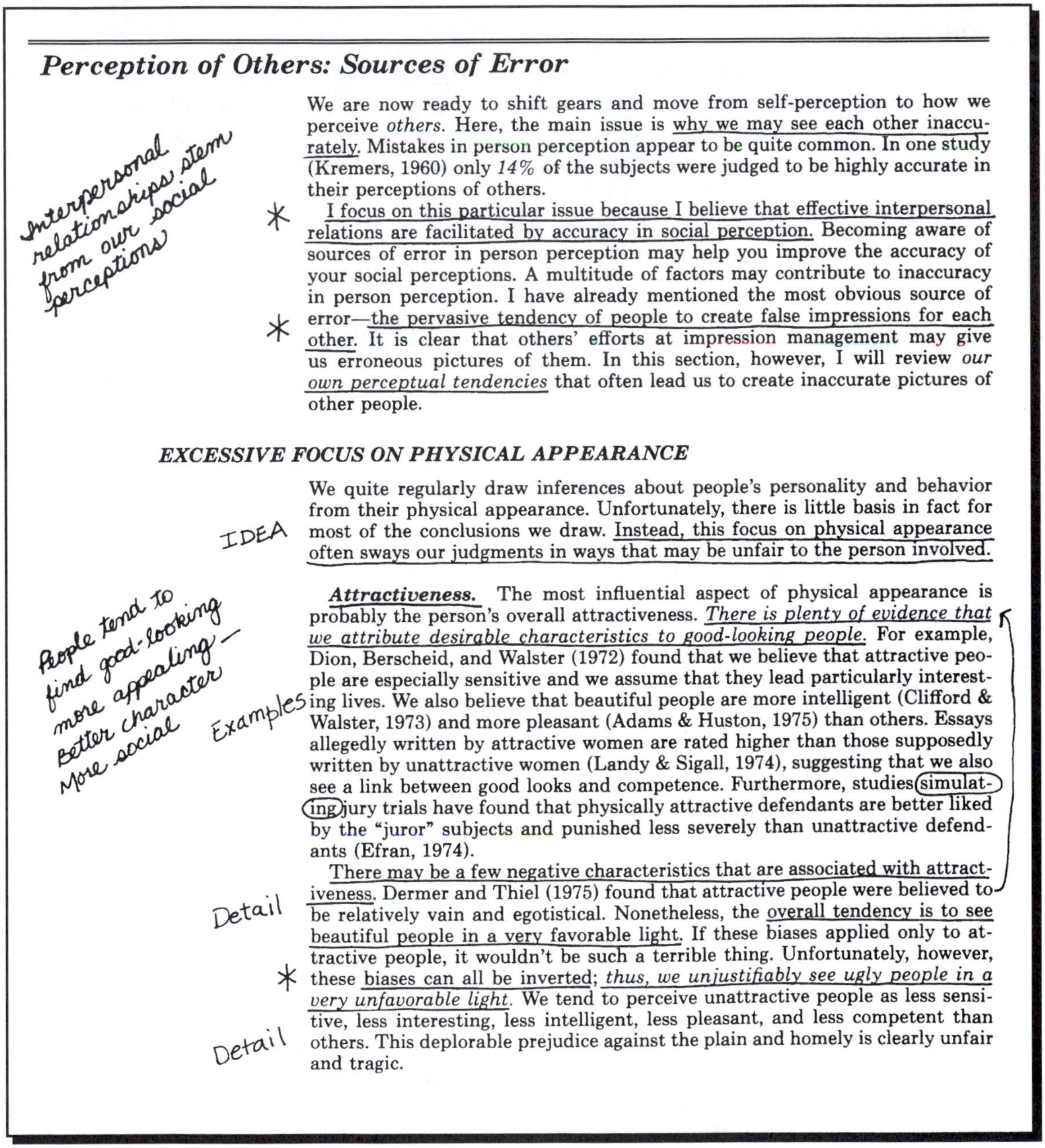

Perception of Others: Sources of Error

[handwritten: Interpersonal relationships stem from our social perceptions]

We are now ready to shift gears and move from self-perception to how we perceive *others*. Here, the main issue is <u>why we may see each other inaccurately</u>. Mistakes in person perception appear to be quite common. In one study (Kremers, 1960) only *14%* of the subjects were judged to be highly accurate in their perceptions of others.

[handwritten: ✱] <u>I focus on this particular issue because I believe that effective interpersonal relations are facilitated by accuracy in social perception.</u> Becoming aware of sources of error in person perception may help you improve the accuracy of your social perceptions. A multitude of factors may contribute to inaccuracy in person perception. I have already mentioned the most obvious source of error—<u>the pervasive tendency of people to create false impressions for each other.</u> *[handwritten: ✱]* It is clear that others' efforts at impression management may give us erroneous pictures of them. In this section, however, I will review *our own perceptual tendencies* that often lead us to create inaccurate pictures of other people.

EXCESSIVE FOCUS ON PHYSICAL APPEARANCE

[handwritten: IDEA]

We quite regularly draw inferences about people's personality and behavior from their physical appearance. Unfortunately, there is little basis in fact for most of the conclusions we draw. <u>Instead, this focus on physical appearance often sways our judgments in ways that may be unfair to the person involved.</u>

[handwritten: People tend to find good-looking more appealing — Better character More social]

Attractiveness. The most influential aspect of physical appearance is probably the person's overall attractiveness. *There is plenty of evidence that we attribute desirable characteristics to good-looking people.* For example, Dion, Berscheid, and Walster (1972) found that we believe that attractive people are especially sensitive and we assume that they lead particularly interesting lives. *[handwritten: Examples]* We also believe that beautiful people are more intelligent (Clifford & Walster, 1973) and more pleasant (Adams & Huston, 1975) than others. Essays allegedly written by attractive women are rated higher than those supposedly written by unattractive women (Landy & Sigall, 1974), suggesting that we also see a link between good looks and competence. Furthermore, studies (simulating) jury trials have found that physically attractive defendants are better liked by the "juror" subjects and punished less severely than unattractive defendants (Efran, 1974).

[handwritten: Detail] <u>There may be a few negative characteristics that are associated with attractiveness.</u> Dermer and Thiel (1975) found that attractive people were believed to be relatively vain and egotistical. Nonetheless, the <u>overall tendency is to see beautiful people in a very favorable light.</u> If these biases applied only to attractive people, it wouldn't be such a terrible thing. Unfortunately, however, *[handwritten: ✱]* these <u>biases can all be inverted</u>; *thus, we unjustifiably see ugly people in a very unfavorable light*. We tend to perceive unattractive people as less sensitive, less interesting, less intelligent, less pleasant, and less competent than others. This deplorable prejudice against the plain and homely is clearly unfair *[handwritten: Detail]* and tragic.

Figure 11.1 Marking Techniques [Source: From *Psychology Applied to Modern Life,* Second Edition, by W. Weiten, Brooks/ Cole Publishing, 1983.]

When you interact with a text, you apply your critical-reading skills. *Critical reading* is like critical thinking. It is an ongoing decision-making and problem-solving process that requires reasoning, logic, wisdom, imagination, and inference. Reading critically involves differentiating between fact and opinion. It includes examining the reliability, accuracy, and comprehensiveness of the material. You try to figure out the authors' less obvious purposes and make inferences from their tone, choice of words, or style.

Ask yourself what devices the author may be using to persuade you. When you read critically, you are not letting the author control your thinking. Instead, you are using his or her information to enhance your knowledge and goals.

4. Understanding Visual Aids

A visual aid provides a graphic representation to improve your comprehension of concepts. The author usually provides you with background information that you must grasp to make sense of the specific chart, table, graph, or picture. Begin by reading the title, captions of pictures, and headings and legends on charts, tables, and graphs. The legend includes words or numbers written at the side and bottom of the drawing and provides the units of measurement. For charts, tables, and graphs, determine what two or more factors are being compared; study them to understand their relationships. Then make a general statement explaining what trends or patterns are suggested. For example, in Figure 11.2, the percentage of drug use in 1978 is compared with use in 1969. The trend described is that all drug use increased, with the exception of marijuana; alcohol and marijuana are the drugs most used.

5. Rereading

Rereading is a widely used instructional strategy (Duffy & Roehler, 1982; Samuels, 1979). However, rereading may improve comprehension only quantitatively, not qualitatively. In other words, the amount of information retained increases but there is no improvement in understanding new relationships or reorganizing old information. Rereading is generally more effective when used with questions developed by the author. Questions can focus your attention on information or relationships considered critical to comprehension. Rereading can help you locate the information that answers the question. This information is then integrated into your existing thought patterns.

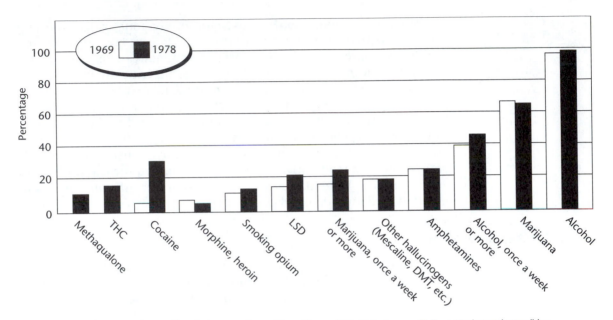

Figure 11.2 Interpreting a Graph [Source: From "Drug Use and Life-Style Among College Undergraduates," by H. G. Pope, Jr., M. Ionescu-Pioggia, and J. O. Cole. In *Archives of General Psychiatry, 38,* 588–591. Copyright © 1981 American Medical Association. Reprinted by permission.]

6. Reciting

Some people find that hearing themselves speak the information improves their comprehension. Reciting can occur in two ways. You can read aloud when you have difficulty understanding or concentrating. Or you can recite material in your own words to evaluate whether you are encoding and retaining information. If you are simply restating the material and cannot paraphrase it, then you are probably having trouble making connections and seeing relationships.

7. Taking Notes

Like reciting, taking notes enables you to become actively involved in reading by focusing your attention, evaluating the information, and expressing ideas in your own words. In fact, the advantage of taking notes rather than underlining alone is to force yourself to rephrase information and relate it to your prior knowledge.

Taking notes from your textbook uses the same skills as taking notes during lectures. As indicated in Chapter 10, you are "like a detective sifting thoughtfully through a barrage of evidence, searching for relevant cues and clues." In your textbook, such clues may include repeated words or the main ideas of paragraphs (which are usually found in the first or last sentences).

The format you use for taking notes on your reading is up to you. Many students prefer to outline, but not all text lends itself to formal outlines. Other students like to use a more flexible format that they can adapt to the material. In fact, some students report that they prefer to take notes on post-its and attach them to relevant pages.

Regardless of the format, you must preview and then read the information before going back to identify important points and facts. In addition, record the answers to questions you raised and the outcomes of predictions you made. Try to develop a consistent system for identifying the main ideas and supporting points. Most important, take notes that make sense to you, notes that are usable for study and review. To illustrate, examine the passage in Figure 11.3, then study Figure 11.4, which is one student's notes on that passage.

The organization and content of the notes in Figure 11.4 closely follow those of the text. The major sections and subsections are delineated by roman numerals, then uppercase letters, followed by arabic numbers and lowercase letters. The particular statements reflect the student's encoding, which follows the author's thinking closely. The outline contains a substantial amount of information. The student will not have trouble reviewing this outline for an exam.

Outlining a 30-page chapter this well may take considerable time. Yet when you outline thoughtfully, the time spent relative to the amount of material comprehended may be less than the time spent in several superficial rereadings.

8. Answering Questions and Completing Exercises

If the author includes questions or exercises, take advantage of these valuable study aids. They usually emphasize the important concepts and ideas. Questions that you cannot answer and exercises that you cannot complete identify information that you are not comprehending or remembering. When this happens, consider rereading or seeking help from your instructor or a tutor.

SELF-ESTEEM

SELF-ESTEEM. *A person's overall assessment of his or her personal adequacy or worth. The evaluative component of the self-concept.*

The term **self-esteem** refers to your global evaluation of your worth as a person (Hamachek, 1978). As mentioned earlier, this is a very important element of your self-concept.

Self-esteem is a somewhat messy concept to investigate, for a couple of reasons. First, there is some doubt about the validity of many measures of self-esteem. We tend to rely on verbal reports from subjects, which may obviously be biased. Wells and Marwell (1976) point out that, for many people, the "real" self-esteem that they feel and the level of self-esteem that they report on a questionnaire may be quite different. Second, in probing self-esteem it is often quite difficult to separate cause from effect. We have a fairly large volume of correlational data that tell us that certain behavioral characteristics are associated with positive or negative self-esteem. However, it is hard to tell whether these behavioral tendencies are the cause or the effect of a particular level of self-esteem. For instance, we know that people with a favorable self-concept are less willing than people with little self-esteem to accept negative feedback about themselves from others (Glenn & Janda, 1977). Unfortunately, we are not sure whether this distortive tendency leads to high self-esteem or whether high self-esteem leads to this distortive tendency. This problem in pinpointing causation should be kept in mind as we look at the determinants and effects of self-esteem.

IMPORTANCE OF SELF-ESTEEM

The importance of developing a positive attitude toward oneself can hardly be overestimated. A host of unfortunate behavioral tendencies are associated with poor self-esteem. Although it is difficult to distinguish cause from effect, it is clear that self-esteem is a very significant aspect of one's personality. To illustrate the enormous importance of self-esteem, I will review some of the behavioral characteristics that often accompany *low* self-esteem.

1. People with unfavorable self-concepts tend to develop more emotional problems than people with good self-esteem (Fitts, 1972; Howard & Kubis, 1964; Rosenberg, 1965). Among other things, they are more likely to report that they are troubled by anxiety, nervousness, insomnia, unhappiness, and psychosomatic symptoms.

2. There is also a relation between low self-esteem and relatively poor achievement. For instance, there is a correlation between low self-esteem and low grades in school (O'Malley & Bachman, 1979). This relatively poor achievement is probably due to the fact that people with low self-esteem set low goals for themselves (Purkey, 1970). They lack confidence and assume that they would not succeed even if they tried.

3. In social interactions, people with low self-esteem are often awkward, self-conscious, and especially vulnerable to rejection (Rosenberg, 1965). They have a particularly great need for acceptance from others, but they are often unable to pursue that social acceptance vigorously. Thus, they end up becoming socially "invisible." They rarely join formal groups and do not participate very actively in social encounters.

4. Because of their great need to be liked, people with unfavorable self-concepts tend to be quite susceptible to social influence (Wells & Marwell, 1976). They tend to be conforming, agreeable, and highly persuasible. They are often afraid to behave independently or assertively because they feel it might endanger their acceptance by others.

5. People who have a negative self-concept are also less likely than most to authentically like other people (Baron, 1974; Wylie, 1961). They tend to look

Figure 11.3 Passage on Self-Esteem [Source: From *Psychology Applied to Modern Life,* Second Edition, by W. Weiten, Brooks/Cole Publishing, 1983.]

for flaws in others and "tear them down." They do this because it allows them to feel a little better about themselves when they make their inevitable social comparisons. However, this also gives them a bias toward disliking others. They therefore tend to relate to others in negative ways, thereby courting rejection and compounding their problems.

DETERMINANTS OF SELF-ESTEEM

The foundations for high or low self-esteem appear to be laid down very early in life. There is evidence (Wattenberg & Clifford, 1964) that some children enter the first grade already possessing an unfavorable self-image.

Such an unfortunate circumstance so early in life would almost have to be attributable to parental feedback. Indeed, there is ample evidence that *parents have a marked influence on their children's self-esteem*. This became apparent in an extensive study of the antecedents of self-esteem in young boys conducted by Stanley Coopersmith (1967). He compared the child-rearing styles of parents of high- and low-self-esteem boys and found that the former (1) expressed more affection to their children, (2) were more interested in their children's activities, (3) were more accepting of their children, (4) used sound, consistent disciplinary procedures, and (5) had relatively high self-esteem themselves. In particular, it was parents' sincere *interest* in their children that seemed most strongly related to the development of a positive self-concept.

While parental feedback may be the crucial childhood determinant of self-esteem, it is clear that *children (and adults) make their own judgments about themselves as well*. Here the paramount issue is how they view their *achievements* in comparison to others. A history of failure in school is typically associated with a negative self-image (Glasser, 1969). Yet, success in an endeavor as simple as learning to swim can lead to enhanced self-esteem (Koocher, 1971). Thus, it is clear that our self-esteem may be augmented or diminished by our own observations of our successes and failures.

Of course, it should be mentioned that our definitions of success and failure are greatly influenced by others, especially parents and teachers. Some overly demanding parents and teachers employ unrealistically high standards and are virtually never satisfied with children's performance. Sometimes these unrealistic standards are an unfortunate by-product of good intentions; the parents and teachers simply want to push the children to high levels of achievement. However, this push for excellence sometimes backfires and leads children to apply unrealistically high standards in evaluating themselves. These unrealistic standards then cause the children to make largely unfavorable self-appraisals of their performance, thus lowering their self-esteem.

Perceptions of success and failure will also be influenced by the nature of one's *reference group*. Marsh and Parker (1984) found that preadolescents' self-esteem was affected by the quality of competition they faced in school. Children from schools in higher-socioeconomic-class areas with "high quality" competition were compared against children from schools in lower-class areas with "low quality" competition. In other words, children from a high-ability reference group were contrasted with children from a low-ability reference group. Interestingly, the children in the low-quality schools tended to display greater self-esteem than children of similar academic ability who were enrolled in the high-quality schools. Thus, the authors conclude that it might be beneficial to one's self-esteem to be "a large fish in a small pond." This finding that kids with similar talents vary in self-esteem, depending on their reference group, demonstrates the immense importance of social comparison processes in governing self-concept.

Figure 11.3 Passage on Self-Esteem *(continued)*

CHAPTER 6   Person Perception

Self-Esteem (pp. 217-220)
   I. Self-esteem refers to your overall evaluation of your
       self-worth and is an important element of your
       self-concept.
       A. Doubt exists about the validity of many measures
          of self-esteem.
          1. Rely on verbal reports that are often biased.
          2. Self-esteem reported can be very different from
             self-esteem that is felt.
       B. In probing positive and negative self-esteem, it is
          difficult to separate the cause from effect.
  II. Importance of self-esteem
       A. Behavioral characteristics that often accompany
          low self-esteem:
          1. Tend to develop more emotional problems
             a. Anxiety
             b. Nervousness
             c. Insomnia
             d. Unhappiness
             e. Psychosomatic symptoms
          2. Relationship exists between low self-esteem and
             poor achievement.
          3. Often are awkward, self-conscious, and vulnerable
             to rejection
             a. Great need for acceptance from others
             b. Does not participate actively in social encounters
          4. Susceptible to social influence
             a. Conforming
             b. Agreeable
             c. Highly personable
             d. Afraid to behave independently or assertively
          5. Less likely to authentically like other people

Figure 11.4   Student Outline of Self-Esteem Passage

III. Determinants of self-esteem
    A. The underlying basis for high or low self-esteem begins early in life.
        1. Parental influence is very important.
        2. Stanley Coopersmith study found that parents of children with high self-esteem did the following:
            a. Expressed more affection to their children
            b. Were more interested in their children's activities
            c. Were more accepting of their children
            d. Used sound, consistent disciplinary procedures
            e. Had relatively high self-esteem themselves
            f. Major characteristic was their strong interest in their children
    B. Children make their own judgment about themselves.
        1. View their achievements in comparison to others
        2. Unrealistic standards can cause poor self-appraisals of performance
    C. Perceptions of success and failure influenced by the reference group
        1. Marsh and Parker (M & P) found that self-esteem was affected by competition faced in school.
        2. M & P conclude that it might be beneficial to be a "large fish in a small pond." This finding demonstrates the immense importance of social comparison processes in governing self-concept.

Figure 11.4 Student Outline of Self-Esteem Passage (continued)

9. Reviewing

The importance of reviewing notes was stressed in the previous chapter. After you finish reading, review your notes and the chapter summary or conclusion. Try to focus on the entire chapter; take time to think about the material and its relationship to other readings and the lectures. Add new information to clarify existing knowledge. Make sure that your notes are legible enough to be helpful in future weeks when you prepare for exams. Finally, if you constantly return to the text to understand your notes, then your notes are not complete enough. Most important, make reviewing a regular part of studying.

In summary, the goal of this chapter has been to help you get involved with your reading, communicate with the author, and become a flexible reader who applies the most effective strategies at the appropriate times. By understanding the reading process and the characteristics of text material, you should be able to appreciate the importance and usefulness of the nine reading strategies. Finally, mastery of the reading strategies provides a solid foundation for strengthening memory. In fact, you will discover in the next chapter that the reading strategies and remembering strategies often overlap.

Connecting Reading to Your Career

How will reading skills help in your career? "I can't wait until I finish this chapter! I think that the book is rather dull and that the course is terribly boring. And neither has any relevance to my life. When will I ever need to know this information again?" Does this sound familiar? Unfortunately, this is a common reaction among college students to some of their readings and to certain courses.

Fortunately, the information that you have read in this chapter has tremendous relevance for your career. Recall the opening quotation: "Reading is to the mind what exercise is to the body." All the reading strategies presented in this chapter can help you improve your mind and enhance your job performance. During your career you will have to read reports, newsletters, journals, and books regularly to remain current in your field. However, you are not likely to have time to thoroughly read everything that comes across your desk. Therefore, you will need to use your previewing skills, such as skimming and scanning. For example, skimming the material will help you identify

Box 11.3

Reading Is His Business

When Jon enrolled in a study-skills course his sophomore year, he did not know what occupation in the business field he would enter, nor did he believe that reading would be especially important. On graduation, he was hired as a computer software sales representative in a major city where he works in a rapidly changing, highly competitive environment. To master the technological specifications of his company's products, many of which are upgraded regularly, Jon spends considerable time during his job and free time *reading* and mastering technical manuals and related materials. Similarly, when he is asked by customers and potential customers to compare his company's products with those of the competition's, Jon willingly *reads* his competitor's materials, often in the evenings and weekends. Jon's commitment to improve his reading speed and comprehension has contributed significantly to his success as a top-performing sales representative. In short, reading has become an essential part of his business. Many jobs require employees to remain current in their knowledge and skills by reading professional journals, bulletins, and similar materials. View reading not simply as a means to earning good grades, but as a skill that may be essential to advancement in your career and the enjoyment of your leisure time.

which information must later be read carefully. Scanning for new words will help you learn the jargon or particular language of your field. To improve your comprehension of important information in reports, journals, or training manuals, use the reading strategies that work best for you. If reading is exercise for the mind, why not start an exercise program while you are in college?

Action-Oriented Thought Starters

1. Develop a plan to increase your vocabulary. Using one of the resources listed in Box 11.1, identify a few words or word parts to learn each day. Consider making a card file with the word (or word part) written on one side, and the definition with the word used in a sentence on the other side. Try to incorporate the new words into your conversations and written assignments.

2. Using the following types of markings, mark the passage shown in Figure 11.5.

   a. Circle words that you do not understand and will need to define.

   b. Place question marks in the margin next to information you find confusing.

   c. Use asterisks or underlining to emphasize concepts.

   d. Draw arrows to show the relationship between ideas.

   e. Write notes to yourself or summary words that indicate your understanding.

   f. Categorize information by noting ideas, facts, examples, and details.

   g. Write key information on graphs and charts.

   After you marked the passage, compare it with the one marked by a student in Figure 11.6.

3. Photocopy one or two typical pages from your most difficult textbook, then review the nine strategies of effective reading described in the previous pages.

   a. Apply as many strategies as you can to comprehending the material on the pages you photocopied, including previewing, interacting, taking notes, and reviewing.

   b. Which strategies helped you most to understand the material?

   c. Which strategies are most difficult?

Other features. Our social perceptions are also affected by other aspects of physical appearance. For example, Lawson (1971) found that dark-haired men are viewed as more masculine and more intelligent than light-haired men. Greater virility, confidence, maturity, and courage are attributed to bearded than to clean-shaven men (Verinis & Roll, 1970). For women, the "dumb blonde" stereotype is not entirely mythical: Lawson (1971) found that blondes were seen as more beautiful and feminine but less intelligent and dependable. We also judge people differently when they wear glasses. People with eyeglasses are assumed to be relatively intelligent and reliable (Manz & Lueck, 1968).

Clothing is also a powerful determinant of our perceptions of others. Gibbins (1969) found that female subjects were willing to draw conclusions about a person's shyness, snobbishness, and morality on the basis of her or his mode of dress. There is also evidence (Bickman, 1971) that people may be treated more honestly when they are well dressed. In Bickman's clever study, a dime was repeatedly left in an obvious place in a public phone booth. When unsuspecting subjects pocketed the dime, an experimental confederate went into action. The confederate approached the subject and asked whether she or he had found the dime that the confederate claimed to have forgotten in the booth. The confederate's mode of dress was varied to convey either high social status (suit and tie) or low status (work clothes, lunch pail). Bickman found that when the confederates were well dressed, they got the dime back about twice as often as when they were more poorly dressed.

Actually, clothing may have some legitimacy as a determinant of our social perceptions. People have relatively little to say about such features of appearance as their attractiveness and hair color, but they *do* freely choose their clothes. Moreover, these choices may indeed reflect personality. For instance, Aiken (1963) found that women whose interest in clothing focused on decoration were relatively sociable, conforming, and nonintellectual. The fact is that people do use clothing to communicate to others how they wish to be seen. Hurlock (1974) points out that people may convey their sense of independence, their identification with some group, and their feelings of maturity or success by dressing in certain ways. Thus, clothing *may* be a legitimate source of information about a person; however, one should be cautious in interpreting these cues.

STEREOTYPES

STEREOTYPE. *A popular, usually oversimplified belief about some group of people; involves inaccurate overgeneralization.*

A **stereotype** is a widely shared, oversimplified belief about some group of people (Berkowitz, 1980). When we use stereotypes, we assume that people have certain characteristics because of their membership in some group. For example, we assume that Jews are shrewd or ambitious, that Blacks have athletic or musical ability, that Germans are methodical and efficient, that women are passive and conceited about their appearance, and that men are unemotional and domineering. Stereotyping is very similar (in a sense, identical) to the processes involved when we react to people on the basis of their physical appearance. In stereotyping, however, the reaction is based on membership in some group rather than physical qualities.

The most prevalent kinds of stereotypes are those based on sex and on membership in ethnic or occupational groups. Sex-role stereotypes, though in transition, remain pervasive in our society and are learned quite early in life (Williams, Bennett, & Best, 1975). Because of their great significance, I will focus on sex-role stereotypes in detail in a later chapter. Ethnic and racial stereotypes have also undergone some change but remain quite common (Karling, Coffman, & Walters, 1969). I shall discuss the contribution of stereotyping to racial prejudice in an upcoming portion of this chapter. Occupational stereotypes also exist, although they are obviously much less of a social problem. For example, people believe that accountants are conforming, executives are conservative, lawyers are manipulative, physicians are calm, artists are moody, and professors are radical (Beardslee & O'Dowd, 1962).

Figure 11.5 Passage on Person Perception [Source: From *Psychology Applied to Modern Life,* Second Edition, by W. Weiten, Brooks/Cole Publishing, 1983.]

Other features. Our social perceptions are also affected by other aspects of physical appearance. For example, Lawson (1971) found that dark-haired men are viewed as more masculine and more intelligent than light-haired men. Greater virility, confidence, maturity, and courage are attributed to bearded than to clean-shaven men (Verinis & Roll, 1970). For women, the "dumb blonde" stereotype is not entirely mythical: Lawson (1971) found that blondes were seen as more beautiful and feminine but less intelligent and dependable. We also judge people differently when they wear glasses. People with eyeglasses are assumed to be relatively intelligent and reliable (Manz & Lueck, 1968).

Clothing is also a powerful determinant of our perceptions of others. Gibbins (1969) found that female subjects were willing to draw conclusions about a person's shyness, snobbishness, and morality on the basis of her or his mode of dress. There is also evidence (Bickman, 1971) that people may be treated more honestly when they are well dressed. In Bickman's clever study, a dime was repeatedly left in an obvious place in a public phone booth. When unsuspecting subjects pocketed the dime, an experimental confederate went into action. The confederate approached the subject and asked whether she or he had found the dime that the confederate claimed to have forgotten in the booth. The confederate's mode of dress was varied to convey either high social status (suit and tie) or low status (work clothes, lunch pail). Bickman found that when the confederates were well dressed, they got the dime back about twice as often as when they were more poorly dressed.

Actually, clothing may have some legitimacy as a determinant of our social perceptions. People have relatively little to say about such features of appearance as their attractiveness and hair color, but they *do* freely choose their clothes. Moreover, these choices may indeed reflect personality. For instance, Aiken (1963) found that women whose interest in clothing focused on decoration were relatively sociable, conforming, and nonintellectual. The fact is that people do use clothing to communicate to others how they wish to be seen. Hurlock (1974) points out that people may convey their sense of independence, their identification with some group, and their feelings of maturity or success by dressing in certain ways. Thus, clothing *may* be a legitimate source of information about a person; however, one should be cautious in interpreting these cues.

STEREOTYPES

STEREOTYPE. *A popular, usually oversimplified belief about some group of people; involves inaccurate overgeneralization.*

A **stereotype** is a widely shared, oversimplified belief about some group of people (Berkowitz, 1980). When we use stereotypes, we assume that people have certain characteristics because of their membership in some group. For example, we assume that Jews are shrewd or ambitious, that Blacks have athletic or musical ability, that Germans are methodical and efficient, that women are passive and conceited about their appearance, and that men are unemotional and domineering. Stereotyping is very similar (in a sense, identical) to the processes involved when we react to people on the basis of their physical appearance. In stereotyping, however, the reaction is based on membership in some group rather than physical qualities.

The most prevalent kinds of stereotypes are those based on sex and on membership in ethnic or occupational groups. Sex-role stereotypes, though in transition, remain pervasive in our society and are learned quite early in life (Williams, Bennett, & Best, 1975). Because of their great significance, I will focus on sex-role stereotypes in detail in a later chapter. Ethnic and racial stereotypes have also undergone some change but remain quite common (Karling, Coffman, & Walters, 1969). I shall discuss the contribution of stereotyping to racial prejudice in an upcoming portion of this chapter. Occupational stereotypes also exist, although they are obviously much less of a social problem. For example, people believe that accountants are conforming, executives are conservative, lawyers are manipulative, physicians are calm, artists are moody, and professors are radical (Beardslee & O'Dowd, 1962).

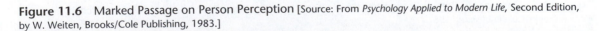

Figure 11.6 Marked Passage on Person Perception [Source: From *Psychology Applied to Modern Life*, Second Edition, by W. Weiten, Brooks/Cole Publishing, 1983.]

Handwritten annotations: Example · Examples · IDEA · IDEA · Examples? · Well-dressed people are treated better · IDEA · Examples · IDEA · Fact · Examples · There are 3 major categories of stereotypes: Sex, Ethnic Group, Occupational Group · IDEA

References and Recommended Readings

Duffy, G. G., & Roehler, L. R. (1982). The illusion of instruction. *Reading Research Quarterly, 17,* 438–445.

Estell, D., Sotchwell, M. L., & Wright, P. S. (1990). *Reading lists for college-bound students* (2nd ed.). New York: Macmillan.

Hennings, D. G. (1990). *Reading with meaning: Strategies for college success.* Englewood Cliffs, NJ: Prentice Hall.

Nist, S. L., & Simpson, M. L. (1988). The effectiveness and efficiency of training college students to annotate and underline text. In J. E. Readence & R. S. Baldwin (Eds.), *Dialogues in literacy research* (pp. 251–257). Chicago: National Reading Conference, Inc.

Roller, C. M. (1990). The interaction between knowledge and structure variables in the processing of expository prose. *Reading Research Quarterly, XXV/2,* 80–89.

Samuels, S. J. (1979). The method of repeated readings. *The Reading Teacher, 33,* 403–408.

CHAPTER 12

Remembering

Friendly Reminders

❏ Use Chapter 11 strategies such as previewing, summarizing, and marking as you read Chapter 12.

❏ Take notes on key topics of Chapter 12 using the page margins.

❏ Vary your reading speed to ensure that you understand the material you read.

"Memory is a net; one finds it full of fish when he takes it from the brook; but a dozen miles of water have run through it without sticking."

Oliver Wendell Holmes, Sr., (1809–1894),
American poet, novelist, physician

Do you remember the statistic mentioned in Chapter 10 about how much you forget 24 hours after learning it? Or did that fact pass like water through the net of your memory? Do we forget 25%, 40%, 50%, or 60%? What enables us to remember and what causes us to forget?

How Memory Works

Remembering is the active process of recalling something that you have already learned or experienced; *forgetting* is the failure to recall. *Memory* is our capacity to store, retain, and retrieve information. Without memory we are helpless; we are unable to call on those past experiences needed to contend with everyday demands. Daily we receive, process, retain, and discard an overwhelming amount of information: from the wakening sounds of our clock radio, to our classes, jobs, and social interactions, and through the media bombardment of our leisure time. Where does the information go? What do we do with it?

Memory Systems

According to the information-processing theory of remembering, there are three memory systems: sensory memory, short-term memory, and long-term memory. Information (input) received by our senses enters our *sensory memory* but remains only momentarily, about 3 seconds for auditory memory and a tenth of a second for visual memory (Wandersee, 1987). Typically, we *attend* to only a small fraction of the input; most goes unnoticed and disappears. For example, when you concentrate on your teacher's lecture, you seldom

The author gratefully acknowledges the assistance of Professor James Wandersee of Louisiana State University for his valuable suggestions in preparing the sections on the tree diagram, concept-map diagram, and concept-circle diagram and for reviewing the remainder of this chapter.

notice other visual stimuli or sounds, temperature, and odors unless they become strong enough to capture your attention.

Information that remains in our consciousness is transferred to *short-term memory,* where it lasts for about 30 seconds unless it is rehearsed. Short-term memory has a capacity for only seven to eight pieces of information at a time. Some researchers regard short-term memory as a scratch pad for a small amount of information held temporarily. We store information in short-term memory by grouping it into *chunks* and rehearsing it. For instance, would you more easily remember this phone number as 7085556642 or as (708) 555–6642?

Here's a typical example of how short-term memory operates. When a friend calls and asks you to meet her flight, you quickly write down the airline and flight number before an interruption causes you to forget it. You carry the note with you until the flight arrives, then discard it. If your friend takes the same flight often, chances are that your repeated rehearsal of the flight information will cause it to be transferred to long-term memory.

Long-term memory permits you to store vast amounts of information relatively undisturbed for periods lasting from a few minutes to a lifetime. Because of the central role that long-term memory takes in remembering the material we learn from our courses, we will devote the remainder of this chapter to strategies for long-term memory.

Why We Forget

According to Guy LeFrançois (1995), several theories have been proposed to explain the process of forgetting. Knowing the main point of each theory will help you understand why, as Thomas Fuller states, "We have all forgot [sic] more than we remember." According to the *fading theory,* we forget because the information is no longer used. Perhaps you learned to recite Lincoln's Gettysburg Address flawlessly in grade school. Could you recite it perfectly now?

The *distortion theory* maintains that forgetting occurs because information becomes misconstrued and twisted. Lincoln said, "Four score and seven years ago, our fathers brought forth on this continent a new nation, conceived in Liberty, and dedicated to the proposition that all men are created equal." However, several years after you learned it flawlessly, you might remember: "Four score and seventeen years ago our forefathers brought forth in this country a new nation conceived in justice and dedicated to the position that all people are equally created."

As you recall the occasions when you were forced to learn the Gettysburg Address, Hamlet's "To be, or not to be" soliloquy, or other verses, do you have pleasant or unpleasant memories? The *repression theory* proposes that many strong unpleasant memories are forced into the unconscious. Often, early experiences with math, English, or science (insert *your* least favorite subject here) generate anxiety and guilt, which you bury in your unconscious. As the French essayist Michel Montaigne said, "The memory represents to us not what we choose but what it pleases."

The *interference theory* holds that previous or subsequently learned information inhibits our ability to recall. For example, commands that you mastered for one word-processing computer program may interfere with learning a new program. Reading sociology prior to taking a psychology test may inhibit or distort our answers to the questions.

Our inability to recall information that we know that we "know" reflects the *retrieval-cue failure theory* of forgetting. The information is not lost because of decay, distortion, repression, or inhibition; it is simply not retrievable because the appropriate cues for recalling it are not available at the moment you need them. The key issue in remembering is whether or not you actually mastered the information as thoroughly as you believe. Each theory of forgetting explains some instances when we cannot remember. With this thumbnail summary of the three memory systems and the five theories of forgetting, you are ready to learn how to improve your ability to remember. As the title of the chapter indicates, our focus is on remembering: the *active process* of recalling something previously learned.

Strategies and Rules for Remembering

Using the work of Claire Weinstein and Richard Mayer (1986), Don Hamachek (1990) identified five strategies for improving long-term memory: affective, organizational, elaboration, comprehension, and rehearsal. Like a military strategy that generates a plan of action, these memory strategies suggest general action plans for strengthening memory: the eight rules of remembering.

Affective Strategies

Affective strategies are those mental and physical activities you perform to feel psychologically healthy and confident in your ability to succeed from day to day in college. They are the "take charge" skills that you were introduced to in Part One of this book, but they were not labeled as affective strategies. At first glance, affective strategies do not appear to be techniques for improving remembering, but collectively they reflect your attitudes, motives, and habits of learning.

Affective Strategies for Improving Long-term Memory

On the following lines, list five skills or activities that give you confidence in your ability to succeed. Cover the area below the lines now before continuing.

_____

_____

_____

_____

_____

Now compare your list with these familiar learning-how-to-learn skills.

- Establish your motives and monitor your goals for being in college.

- Manage stress effectively.

- Eat nutritiously; get sufficient sleep; exercise regularly.

- Learn to concentrate during study periods and class.

- Manage time to ensure a balance between work and leisure.

Although the first three skills may not influence remembering directly, combined they contribute to your health, morale, and overall ability to learn and remember. Add to these skills the enjoyment of learning, a positive mental attitude, and openness to new ideas and together they form the first rule of remembering. *Rule 1: Plan your day to promote your physical, motivational, and emotional needs.* Leonardo Da Vinci stated Rule 1 in these words: "Just as eating against one's will is injurious to health, so study without a liking for it spoils the memory, and it retains nothing it takes in."

Concentration, the fourth skill, has a direct link with long-term memory. Memory experts believe that when you *deliberately focus* your attention and energy on the subject matter, you increase your chances for remembering it. Studying with commitment to remember, in a quiet place at a regular time with specific study goals, enhances concentration. Concentration and motivation combine to form the second rule of remembering. *Rule 2: When you strive to remember, you can remember.*

❷

A sound time-management plan enables you to distribute study sessions over several days. For instance, when you prepare for an exam, allocate one- or two-hour study periods over a few days rather than a marathon session the night before the test. If you have job or family responsibilities, distributed study sessions are difficult to plan, but you should try. Distributing your study promotes learning for understanding and increases self-confidence. In contrast, cramming encourages rote memorization and generates anxiety. You may pass the test by cramming, but you will not understand or retain much of the information. Distributed study time is analogous to pouring liquid through a funnel. When you pour carefully, it passes through the funnel safely. When you pour too fast, spills occur that cannot be retrieved. *Rule 3: Plan, don't cram, your study time.*

❸

Organizational Strategies

In Chapter 6 you learned the value of organizing your physical and psychological environments. Organizational strategies of remembering are techniques that organize information to "highlight its hierarchical nature or the similarities and differences among the components being learned" (Hamachek, 1990, p. 202). *Hierarchical* means that a concept, fact, or idea can be arranged in order of rank or class to indicate its inclusiveness or relationship to other information. For example, notes that are taken in the outline format usually present information hierarchically. Textbook material is arranged hierarchically by section, chapter, topic, and subtopics. Information organized hierarchically helps you understand the similarities, differences, and relationships among facts and concepts which, in turn, facilitate remembering.

❏ Tree Diagrams

One way to organize information in a hierarchy is through a tree diagram. Study these nine words and sketch how you would organize them into hierarchical categories: peas, kiwi, corn, fruits, grapes, food, apples, potatoes, vegetables. Now compare your arrangement with that shown in Figure 12.1.

This tree diagram organized the nine terms hierarchically in three levels, with the most inclusive concept (food) at the top and the most specific concepts at the bottom. The diagram enables you to understand, connect, visualize, and remember the terms. You can *see* the organization immediately. Two additional organizational strategies that rely on visual representation are important to learn: concept maps and concept circles. Before examining each strategy, it is important that you understand what a *concept* is: a pattern of regularity among objects or events that we assign a label or a symbol. Thus, *chair* is the concept label for a single seat with a backrest and many different objects fit the pattern. *Rain* is an example of a concept based on an event rather than an object.

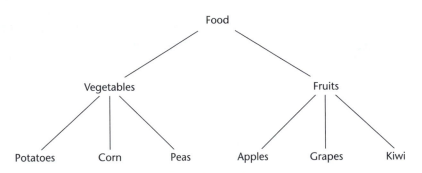

Figure 12.1   Tree Diagram of Food Categories

❑ **Concept Maps**

Concept mapping is an organizational strategy developed by Joseph Novak of Cornell University. Just as a road map of the United States aids your visual understanding of the relationship among the regions, states, and cities, a concept map visually represents the relationship among concepts that are related hierarchically.

To illustrate concept mapping, stop here and reread the previous section entitled "Memory Systems." Then recite or write what you have read before continuing.

If you were required to explain the three memory systems on an exam, would it be easier to remember the concepts as you recited or wrote them, or as they are mapped in Figure 12.2?

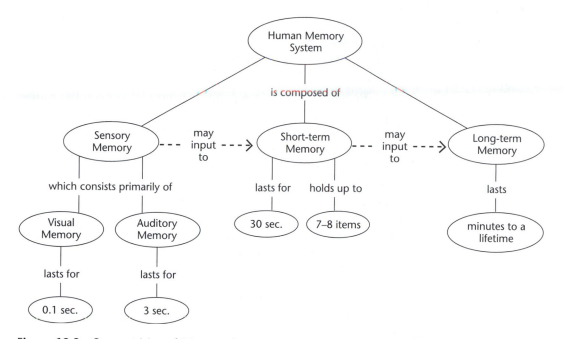

Figure 12.2 Concept Map of Memory System [Source: Adapted from "Drawing Concept Circles: A New Way to Teach and Test Students," by J. H. Wandersee, 1987, *Science Activities, 24*(4), p. 11. Copyright © 1987 J. H. Wandersee. Adapted by permission.]

Obviously, the visual map is easier to remember.

Figure 12.2 is an excellent example of how a concept map provides a clear and concise visual representation of hierarchically organized concepts. Creating concept maps requires time and practice, but it pays high dividends. It improves thinking and remembering and it can be used in many subjects. Transforming difficult concepts into a map or diagram is often fun. Following are procedures derived from Novak and Gowin's book *Learning How to Learn* (1984) that should enable you to construct your own concept maps. Be prepared to read and reread these procedures as you would the instructions for operating a new appliance.

1. *Premapping.* Before creating a concept map, spend several minutes to identify and rank-order the most important specific concepts contained in a particular section of the text or your notes. (Remember the definition of the term *concept*.) This premapping step lets you determine the crucial concepts, and it reduces the possibilities for misrepresenting the relationship among concepts.

If you place these concepts on separate "sticky" notes, you can arrange them in different ways until you are actually ready to draw your map.

2. *Organize the map.* Construct a concept map by locating the major concept at the top of the page and positioning subordinate concepts in levels below it according to their degree of specificity. Use circles or rectangles as shown in Figure 12.2 to enclose the concept labels. Place them on the map in a way that minimizes visual clutter.

3. *Enter key words.* Write the key words that connect the concepts directly on the linking line. For example, the words *is composed of* define the relationship between *Human Memory System* and each of the three  memory systems in Figure 12.2 and thus represents three propositions or assertions. Similarly, the words *may input to* connect sensory memory to short-term memory to long-term memory.

4. *Revise.* After constructing your concept map, you may discover problems or errors in the way you connected the concepts or in your choice of linking words, or the map may be cluttered and hard to read. You may discover that you need to add concepts for greater clarity. Revision is a normal part of the concept-mapping process and reflection helps you make meaning from the concepts you are studying. When you are finished, your concept map should be read from the top concept down to the end of each branch.

Occasionally, you will want to make cross-links across branches of your map. Use a broken line to indicate these and label them as before. You may use arrowheads to indicate the direction the cross-link is to be read.

For further information about concept mapping, consult Novak and Gowin (1984) or Novak and Wandersee (1990), which are cited in the References and Recommended Readings.

❏ Concept Circles

The concept-circle technique was invented by biologist James Wandersee (Wandersee, 1990). Like concept maps, concept circle diagrams are graphic representations of hierarchically ordered concepts designed to make information meaningful to students. The major differences between concept-circle diagrams and maps are these:

1. Concept-circle diagrams depict inclusive/exclusive relationships between five concepts or less and are simpler than concept maps.

2. Concept maps make the linkages between concepts more *explicit*.

3. Concept maps are visually and conceptually more complex.

The major advantages of the concept-circle diagram are ease of construction and visual effectiveness, especially when you wish to represent a small number of concepts in graphic form. To illustrate, you could remember the categories and subcategories of seed plants for your botany class by writing them on a sheet of paper and then rehearsing them. You could construct a concept map, or you could construct a concept-circle diagram like Professor Wandersee devised as an example for his students (see Figure 12.3).

Wandersee has developed several principles for constructing concept-circle diagrams, the most important of which are summarized below. Again, be ready to reread the principles to understand this technique.

1. Follow the format shown in Figure 12.3. Print the title of your diagram in the top portion of the page, print the concept label inside the largest circle (which here is drawn in the middle of the page) and write a short explanation of the diagram at the center bottom third of the page.

2. Draw smaller circles within the larger circle to represent subordinate concepts that are subsumed by (included within) a larger concept. Excluded concepts can be depicted by circles outside the main circle. Print concept names horizontally within the smaller circle (for example, see the *gymnosperms* and *angiosperms* circles).

3. Concepts that are independent (mutually exclusive) of each other are represented by circles that do not overlap. For example, *gymnosperms* are independent of *angiosperms; monocots* and *dicots* are mutually exclusive. Concepts that are not mutually exclusive are represented by overlapping circles.

4. The size of the circles represents the specificity of the concept. Larger circles are used for more general concepts; smaller circles for more specific concepts. For instance, *angiosperm* is a more

The Classification of Seed Plants

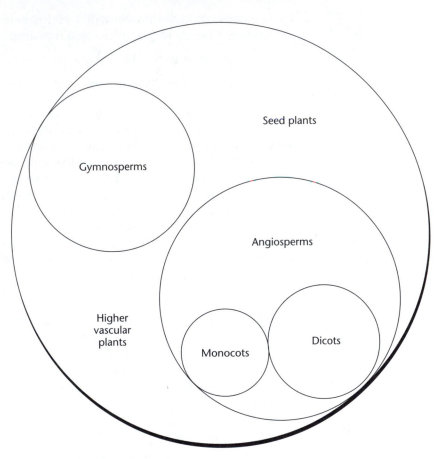

Explanation: Seed plants (higher vascular plants) are classified on the basis of their seed production and the number of seed leaves that they have.

Figure 12.3 Concept-Circle Diagram of Seed Plants [Source: Adapted from "Drawing Concept Circles: A New Way to Teach and Test Students," by J. H. Wandersee, 1987, *Science Activities, 24*(4), p. 16. Copyright © 1987 J. H. Wandersee. Adapted by permission.]

inclusive concept than *gymnosperm,* and there are more species of *dicots* than *monocots.*

5. Generally, you can color-code the circles with soft but contrasting colors to enhance your visual memory of the concept.

6. Empty, uncolored space around a concept implies that other concepts exist but are not included in this diagram. For example, there are other types of seed plants besides gymnosperms and angiosperms, but they are less important and consequently are omitted. Because the circle for seed plants does not include the now-extinct seed ferns, it would not be colored.

7. Because human memory works best when it is not overloaded, it is customary to limit the number of circles within a single diagram to no more than five.

Professor Wandersee's system contains additional rules for representing concepts that are related in time and number. For further information, see his 1987 article cited in the References and Recommended Readings. Although our illustration of concept circles is a topic in the natural sciences, the technique can be used in other disciplines. For example, you could create concept circles to represent

- categories of theories (for example, theories of personality can be subdivided into trait, psychoanalytic, social-learning, and humanistic theories; each theory can be further subdivided according to the principal theorists)

- categories of events by time (for example, 20th-century events can be subdivided into decades or categories of political, technological, and cultural events)

- the structure of government (for example, Congress is composed of members of the House and the Senate; committees are formed within each body)

Whew! Those organizational strategies are complicated! Or are they? Don't let the detailed, but necessary, steps we described for constructing concept-map and concept-circle diagrams discourage you from using these techniques. Be willing to reread each section. Work with a friend. After you construct a few diagrams, the process becomes easier. By then you are on your way to mastering a very valuable strategy for organizing information that will be useful in most of your courses for the rest of your college career, and beyond. The organizing strategies that you have been introduced to here can be reduced to the fourth rule of remembering. *Rule 4: Don't agonize. Organize information into outlines, tree diagrams, concept maps, and concept circles.*

Elaboration Strategies

Elaboration strategies are techniques for making connections among facts, concepts, and ideas. Connections make material meaningful to you and, consequently, facilitate recall from long-term memory. The most frequently used elaboration strategies are visual memory and imagery, mnemonics, summarizing, and questioning.

❑ Visual Memory and Imagery

Your introduction to concept maps and concept circles should convince you that a picture is worth a thousand words. Authors and publishers go to great lengths to represent information visually. To the extent that course material is presented in diagrams, maps, charts, tables, photographs, paintings, models, or cutaways, you have a distinct advantage for remembering it.

When important information is not presented visually, try to make it visual. Activate your visual memory and search for associations between the material you must learn and past experiences. For example, if you must remember characters from a 19th-century British novel, imagine them in the dress and hairstyles you have seen in films or paintings of that period. If you have traveled throughout the United States, you may easily imagine or recall Martin Luther King, Jr.'s Atlanta neighborhood, Willa Cather's Nebraska farmland, James Michener's Chesapeake Bay, or the differences between the Rocky Mountains and the Appalachian Mountains.

❑ Mnemonics

Mnemonic techniques are methods for connecting several concepts by a simple statement. Chances are that mnemonics helped you learn concepts such as

- the treble staff in the music scale: Every Good Boy Does Fine (E, G, B, D, and F notes)

- the Great Lakes: HOMES (Huron, Ontario, Michigan, Erie, and Superior)

- the color spectrum: ROY G. BIV (red, orange, yellow, green, blue, indigo and violet).

Box 12.1

Howard's Memories

Ever since Howard can remember, he has enjoyed traveling with his family. In cities, they visited historic sites, museums, aquariums, and architectural landmarks. When his family toured national parks, they learned about the geology, history, and ecology of the area. An older brother taught Howard to appreciate music, theater, and art. When Howard entered college, it was easy for him to connect many of his travel and cultural experiences to topics covered in his history, environmental biology, and fine arts courses. Because of Howard's earlier experiences, learning and remembering were often easy and fun for him.

Students who must learn the sequence of the 12 cranial nerves for a physiology course often associate the first letter of each word in a humorous sentence to the name of a cranial nerve.

On old Olympus's towering tops, a Finn and German viewed some hops.

Word	Cranial Nerve
On	Olfactory
Old	Optic
Olympus's	Oculomotor
Towering	Trochlear
Tops	Trigeminal
A	Abducens
Finn	Facial
And	Auditory vestibular
German	Glossopharyngeal
Viewed	Vagus
Some	Spinal accessory
Hops	Hypoglossal

Mnemonics may include rhymes such as "*i* before *e* except after *c*" and "Thirty days hath September, April, June, and November."

Mnemonic techniques make remembering fun. However, there are two drawbacks that often restrict their use. First, mnemonics are appropriate for the rote memory of names or simple concepts; they are less useful for understanding and remembering complex ideas. A mnemonic could help you *name* but not *explain* a series of ideas or concepts. Second, the time required to create new mnemonics can be considerable and may be better used by remembering the material another way.

❏ Summarizing

In the previous chapter, "Getting Involved with Your Reading," you learned that summarizing and questioning are strategies for improving reading. They also improve remembering by facilitating connections. Imagery creates meaningful connections among concepts visually; mnemonics creates meaningful connections through humor or rhyme. When you need to form connections among complex concepts, imagery and mnemonics may be difficult to use. Instead, make the material meaningful to you by summarizing abstract concepts into your own words with careful attention to their exact meanings. In the chapter on reading, you learned to pause at the end of each section in your text and summarize what you read. Such summaries connect the textbook's language to your language (encoding). Furthermore, summaries provide feedback, aid your comprehension, and organize main points for long-term memory. Knowing the main points may be sufficient for passing exams in some courses. However, when teachers want precise and comprehensive answers, summarizing is insufficient. It is only an *intermediate* step in the process of mastering information.

❏ Questioning

Questioning is an elaboration strategy that forces you to associate the information you need to know with significant issues. Return to the passage on self-esteem in Figure 11.3 (pages 222–223). Using cues contained in the author's statements, you could remember the main points by answering these questions:

- What does self-esteem refer to?

- What are some of the characteristics of people with low self-esteem?

- What are some of the factors that influence the development of self-esteem in children?

Finally, remember that the questions you create to form connections in your reading could reappear as test questions. Rule 5 summarizes the significance of elaboration strategies for long-term memory. *Rule 5: Create connections by using imagery, mnemonics, summarizing, and questioning.*

Comprehension-monitoring Strategies

Comprehension monitoring is a sophisticated term that can be reduced (perhaps oversimplified) to "What am I doing and how well am I doing it?" Essentially, comprehension-monitoring strategies for remembering include the answers to these questions:

- What are my specific goals for remembering this material?

- Are they being accomplished? Am I doing well what I am supposed to be doing?

- What adjustments in my study behavior must I make to achieve these goals?

Comprehension monitoring is a form of intellectual self-management. Curtis Miles (1991) argues that "students must become *conscious* managers of the tools and strategies they employ while thinking. Students must be trained to be aware of and reflect on their mental functioning as they evolve into increasingly thoughtful learners." When you monitor study behavior *while* you study, you are thinking about your thinking. Researchers call this activity *metacognition.* Metacognition, the essence of comprehension monitoring, is embedded in the sixth rule of remembering. *Rule 6: Think about your thinking: "Metacogitate."*

❏ Goals Revisited

Goals were mentioned earlier in this chapter. The goals that comprise the affective strategies of long-term memory are the short, intermediate, and long-range life goals first described in Chapter 3. However, goals that pertain to monitoring your comprehension are *study goals:* the specific objectives and strategies you establish before learning a particular unit of material. Study goals, first mentioned in Chapter 6, are important for long-term memory. For instance, when you spend an hour and a half preparing for a history examination, what specifically do you hope to accomplish?

- Do you expect to read one or two chapters in depth or review all chapters that will be on the exam?

- Do you plan to read the text and your notes together or separately?

- Are you trying to rote-memorize the material (fully aware that you won't *understand* much of it), or is your objective to understand it (fully aware that 90 minutes may not be sufficient)?

- Do you ask yourself which rules of remembering are best suited for remembering this material?

- How will you determine objectively when you have mastered the material?

- If this 90-minute study period is insufficient, where in your schedule will the additional time come from?

Asking yourself such questions helps you focus your time, energy, and intent to remember.

❏ Memorizing versus Understanding

Probably the most important question stated in the preceding example is the issue of memorizing versus understanding. If you are preparing for "factual" test questions, it is easy to memorize names and definitions and subsequently regurgitate them on an exam. Rote memory of essential facts and procedures is necessary in some stages of many courses. Rote memory and regurgitation can sometimes get you As.

However, at a later stage in a course, or in other courses of your academic program, you will be required to *compare, apply, analyze,* or *critically evaluate* ideas. Such higher-level Deep Strategy thinking demands that you comprehend the nature, significance, and implications of ideas. Memorizing facts is a first step in, not a substitute for, understanding ideas, concepts, and principles involved in higher-level thinking.

Finally, memorizing simply to pass an exam, with little concern for how the information fits into the subject matter or the discipline as a whole, is a waste of time in the long run. As a technique for remembering, memorizing is often specious (go ahead, look up the word in your dictionary). You can pass some exams by sheer memory, but it is unlikely that you will remember the material after the course is over, much less remember it for advanced courses. Research indicates that concepts that are comprehended are remembered longer than those that are rote-memorized. Yet the temptation is always present. Learning for understanding is time consuming and demanding; memorizing is quick and relatively painless. Ultimately, *you* must determine whether your goal in college is to obtain a degree (a sheet of paper that verifies the completion of graduation requirements) or an education (an investment in your future). *Rule 7: Make it your goal to comprehend, not to memorize.*

Rehearsal Strategies

Last but not least among the ways to strengthen long-term memory are the rehearsal strategies. *Rehearsal strategies* are techniques for repeating the material mentally, aloud, or in writing. *Repetition* is one of the most fundamental and powerful principles of learning and remembering. Repetition is one of the most fundamental and powerful principles of learning and remembering. Although you were introduced to certain rehearsal techniques in previous chapters, they are briefly repeated here because repetition is one of the most fundamental and powerful principles of learning and remembering.

Rehearsal techniques include

- mentally repeating material you learned during the review sessions, as recommended in Chapter 10

- reciting information aloud (also known as *shadowing*)

- copying information from books or notes

- selectively underlining material from books or notes

- writing notes from books or other notes

Simple information (names, dates, short lists, short formulas) can be rehearsed or recited. Complex information may require copying, underlining, or notetaking. Some authorities on memory maintain that the most powerful rule of remembering is simply **"Write it down!"**

When time permits, try to overlearn the material. *Overlearning* refers to continued rehearsal of information mastered previously. Overlearning tests your ability to recall information you learned by other rehearsal techniques. Furthermore, it provides feedback: Do you really know the material, or are you deceiving yourself? Reciting aloud is the most common method of overlearning.

Here are five additional suggestions for strengthening long-term memory.

1. Concentrate on the *meaning* of the information as you rehearse it. Reciting, copying, and underlining quickly become a meaningless, mechanical ritual unless you actively think about the material. Furthermore, rehearse when you are alert, motivated, and able to concentrate.

2. Schedule 10 minutes of rest for each 50 minutes of rehearsal. Taking a brisk walk during a break may be an effective way to relieve the stress that is created by intense mental activity.

3. Try to rehearse material before bedtime (assuming that you are somewhat alert) because sleep produces only minimal disruption of memory processes.

4. Some experts advise that you learn material in small amounts, one layer at a time. For example, divide each of the chapters you must know for an exam into several small sections. Learn the material from each section well, one section at a time, before proceeding to the next section. When you finish, connect the sections so that you understand the material as a whole.

5. Look for time pockets during your day. Use such times to rehearse from your texts, notes, or notecards.

A final dimension of rehearsal pertains to the frequency with which specific material is repeated within a course and from course to course. For example, students in a beginning level science or social science course are introduced to the topic of research or scientific method. Instructors usually stress fundamental research concepts throughout the course. When students enroll in subsequent courses, research concepts will likely be repeated or expanded. In fact, many programs require completion of a course in research methods.

According to memory researcher Harry Bahrick (Adler, 1991), people are likely to remember information "for decades as opposed to mere months when they learn the material over a longer period of time and build on and review the original material as they go along" (p. 10). When an instructor repeats key concepts throughout the course or administers cumulative exams, it is not necessarily a symptom of senility—it's a sign of good teaching. Similarly, you may have noticed that several concepts and recommendations are repeated in different chapters of this book. Remember *Rule 8: Rehearse! Rehearse! Rehearse! Then overlearn!*

In summary, remembering is an active process of storing, retaining, and retrieving information that was transferred from short-term memory to long-term memory. From five strategies, eight rules of remembering were derived. Our ability to remember is strengthened when we are healthy and motivated, strive to remember, distribute our study time, organize information, create connections, monitor our thinking, avoid memorizing, and rehearse.

Box 12.2

Remembering: Not for Tests Only

Information you learned months or years ago can be recalled or relearned *if* you can retrieve your course texts and notes. Unfortunately, too many students are quick to sell their textbooks and to dispose of their notes after a course is over. They may be desperate for money, filled with strong emotions about the course, or under the illusion that they can recall whatever they need to know. Given the amount of time and money invested, disposing of key course materials does not make sense in most circumstances. Learn from the mistakes of Vicky, John, and Linda.

- Vicky sold her marketing books to get money for a trip, but when asked a year later in her new job to develop a marketing strategy for a product, she didn't know what to do.

- When John completed a biology course during his freshman year, he thought it would be his last biology course so he sold his text and discarded his notes. When he changed his major from English to biology two years later, however, he had to buy the biology text again.

- Linda was so relieved when her statistics course was over that she sold the book and threw away her notes. She regretted her behavior three years later when she enrolled in a graduate program that required statistics during the first term.

In each case, the student committed considerable time and money to complete a college course successfully but then disposed of all tangible resources used to learn the subject matter. Should you treat your college education like a trip to McDonald's?

Remembering the five strategies and the eight rules derived from them can be overwhelming at first, especially if you tend to memorize. Consider this suggestion: When you read for *comprehension* (using suggestions from Chapter 11) and subsequently *review* these two approaches, focus on one approach at a time (*either* the five strategies *or* the eight rules). After you comprehend and master one approach, you can grasp the other relatively easily.

How Teachers Help You to Remember

This chapter could leave you with the impression that remembering is a skill you must develop on your own, outside of class.

WRONG!

Most of your teachers incorporate several strategies and rules for remembering during class. For example, one Spanish teacher uses several memory strategies. Students are taught to

- understand, not memorize, what they learn (comprehension-monitoring strategy)

- read and mentally outline material in advance of class (organizational strategy)

- use visual and auditory images when speaking a sentence such as "Maria opened the door and walked into the classroom." (elaboration strategy)

- generate new sentences by substituting different parts (different subjects, verbs, objects) and changing the statements into questions (elaboration strategies)

- repeat statements several times for each substitution individually and in a group, during class, and later in a language laboratory (rehearsal strategies)

Other examples of teachers' use of long-term memory strategies to help you remember include

- distributing an outline or previewing the major points of a lecture (organizational strategies)

- creating a diagram to explain a research design or a concept map to show the relationship among ideas (organizational strategy)

- showing slides, videotapes, motion pictures, or models (elaboration strategies)

- summarizing the major points of a lecture at the end of class (elaboration and rehearsal strategies)

- incorporating humor in a complex or dry subject (affective strategy)

- giving examples or citing applications of concepts (elaboration strategies)

In short, if you carefully observe the instructor's teaching techniques, you may discover a gold mine of long-term memory strategies. Oh yes, when you mine this gold you are simultaneously monitoring your comprehension: You are thinking about your thinking!

Connecting Remembering to Your Career

Whether you become a dentist or a drill-press operator, a technician or a teacher, a marketing manager or a magician, an accountant or an artist, strategies for remembering are essential. If your job will involve communicating with people, retrieving information, or coordinating several activities simultaneously (and most do), your capacity to process information *precisely* will often be stretched and stressed. The strategies and rules you learned in this chapter are oriented to the college classroom. Other memory techniques that you can learn can be found in the Higbee (1977) book listed in the References and Recommended Readings or in other sources.

Finally, you must regard the remembering skills that you develop as a means to an end, not an end in itself. The goal of remembering in college is to *understand and apply* knowledge, not simply to regurgitate it on an exam. Theologian and writer John Henry Newman spoke to this point when he said, "A great memory does not make a philosopher, any more than a dictionary can be called a grammar."

Action-Oriented Thought Starters

1. Spend a few minutes at the end of each day for one week and review the courses in which you are enrolled. Write down specific long-term memory strategies that your teachers are using to help you remember. Do your teachers' techniques help you master important ideas? You might perform this exercise alone or with a classmate.

2. What does Newman's statement at the end of the chapter mean to you? What are its implications for

   a. rote-memorizing versus understanding ideas?

   b. planning study periods?

   c. the guilt and anxiety we experience when we forget something important or struggle to remember new material (a special concern of many returning adult students)?

3. If you are like most college students who find the array of financial assistance programs confusing, you will wish that you had completed this exercise before entering college. Construct a tree diagram to show the relationship among the terms contained in the following description of financial aid programs.

   Students seeking financial assistance for college have a labyrinth of options to explore analogous to the proverbial rat finding its way through a maze. There are three major sources of assistance: the student's private funds, federal resources, and private resources.

   Since it is important for students to develop their own resources first, let's begin with them. Student resources include the money they have saved for college, the income they have earned from a job, and funds provided by parents and relatives.

   Because student sources are seldom sufficient, next consider the federal sources available such as Federal Pell grants, Campus-based programs, and Governmental Student Loans. By the way, a grant refers to a gift of money, like a scholarship. Aid from campus-based programs can be in the form of a job (Federal Work Study—FWS), a grant (Federal Supplemental Educational Opportunity Grant—SEOG), or a Federal Perkins loan. In addition, there are three types of loans: parent loan for undergraduates; Subsidized Stafford or Ford loan; and Unsubsidized Stafford or Ford loan.

Mind-boggling isn't it? And we still have the private sources, of which there are two. First, your college or university may provide financial assistance in the form of a job, grant, or a loan. Second, organizations such as businesses (for example, the place where a relative works) or not-for-profit organizations (local, state, or national) sometimes offer scholarships, loans, or jobs.

Isn't the world of financial assistance complicated and confusing? Simplify the preceding information into a tree diagram. It's not that complicated if you pay attention to the most important terms mentioned. Perhaps you will discover that you are eligible for a source of financial assistance that you never considered before. That alone could easily pay for this book and a few copies you may want to purchase for friends! When you finish with your tree diagram, compare it with the one shown in Figure 12.4. For purposes of instruction, Figure 12.4 is not a complete presentation of financial assistance programs and may contain information that changes.

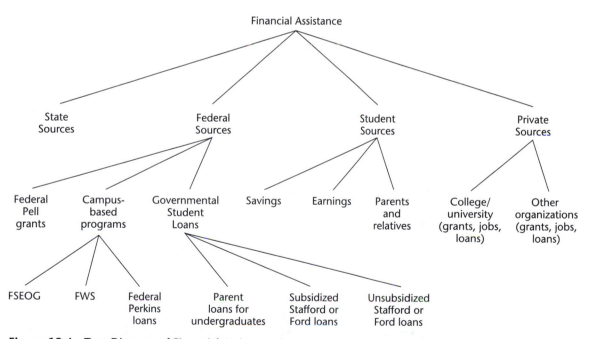

Figure 12.4 Tree Diagram of Financial Assistance Programs [Source: Based on data from the *Federal Student Aid Guide 1996–97,* published by the U.S. Department of Education.]

4. Use the five strategies of long-term remembering to help you remember material from this chapter.

   a. Describe those specific mental and physical activities (affective strategies) that are currently (now) helping or hindering you from remembering material from this chapter.

   b. Organize the topics covered in Chapter 12 by creating a tree diagram, concept map, and concept circle (choose any two). Compare the advantages and limitations of the two organizational strategies you used.

   c. Create a mnemonic from the first letter of each of the five strategies for long-term remembering. Describe how you would use any one of the remaining elaboration strategies to remember the section Elaboration Strategies.

   d. Write questions that would describe how you would monitor your comprehension of the section How Memory Works.

   e. Use a rehearsal strategy to remember the material presented in the section of the chapter you found most difficult.

   f. The previous chapter on reading emphasized knowing the meanings of prefixes and suffixes. The term *metacognition* was used in the section Comprehension-monitoring Strategies. What does *meta* mean? What does *cognition* mean? In your own words, define metacognition. How many other words in the dictionary begin with meta?

References and Recommended Readings

Adler, T. (1991, February). Cumulative learning aids memory. *APA Monitor,* 10.

Hamachek, D. (1990). *Psychology in teaching learning and growth* (4th ed.). Boston, MA: Allyn and Bacon.

Higbee, K. L. (1977). *Your Memory: How it works and how to improve it.* Englewood Cliffs, NJ: Prentice Hall.

LeFrançois, G. R. (1995). *Theories of human learning: Kro's Report* (3rd ed.). Pacific Grove, CA: Brooks/Cole.

Miles, C. (1991). The fourth "R": Instructional strategies for thoughtful learning. *Journal of Developmental Education, 15,* 36.

"A mistake in judgment isn't fatal, but too much anxiety about judgment is."
—Pauline Kael (1919–),
film critic, author

On the first day of my study-skills course, I ask students what they hope to learn. The topic most frequently named is test taking. The response is not surprising considering the role that testing occupies in a person's life, beginning with elementary school and continuing through the licensing of professionals. An often-quoted but unknown cynic once said that there are only two certainties in life: death and taxes. As a student, would you agree that a third certainty is being tested?

Evaluation: The Third Certainty of Life

Being tested means being evaluated. To evaluate, according to *Webster's New World Dictionary and Thesaurus* (Agnes, 1996), is to judge the value or worth of. As infants, our growth was monitored by our parents. Throughout school our intellectual, social, and emotional worth was continuously judged inside and outside the classroom. Our emotions were conditioned to being evaluated, especially when we delivered our first speech, sweated through standardized achievement tests, or waited anxiously to be chosen for a softball game.

College-bound students worry about being good enough to be accepted by their favorite college; new college graduates worry about being good enough to be hired by their favorite company. Evaluation is also an inherent part of establishing relationships: Are they going to let me in the group? Does she like me?

Evaluation for Better or for Worse: Five Insights

If testing and evaluation is an inevitable fact of life, then why not develop a positive attitude toward it? No one expects you to *like* being tested. But there are insights you can gain about the process of evaluation that will benefit you during and after college. Let's examine five of them.

1. The *purpose* of evaluation is to enable an expert to obtain, interpret, and communicate information (data) about yourself to you.

Whether the expert is a teacher, counselor, advisor, or employer, evaluation is intended to help you. For example, test scores of your writing, math, and study skills enable your advisor to place you in the proper courses. Data regarding your occupational interests enable a career counselor to advise you about vocational choices. Performance measures on tests and assignments enable an instructor to judge your progress and assign a grade. Knowledge of your skills and work experience guides an employer's selection decision.

2. Data obtained by an expert permits an *objective evaluation* of your performance. Although each of us is capable of accurate self-assessment on some activities, our ignorance and biases are often obstacles to an objective judgment. Can you imagine an Olympic-bound athlete training without a coach? Or a student preparing for a profession without formal instruction and assessment? Evaluation is a process of comparing your performance with an objective standard so that you can improve.

3. Testing and evaluation are designed to *measure representative samples* of your knowledge, not everything that you have learned. In fact, *test* is often defined as a sample of a person's knowledge. Time and circumstances do not permit teachers to assess everything you know. Consequently, all of the hours that you spend reading, writing, thinking, and discussing are represented by (and reduced to) your responses to a particular set of test questions administered by the teacher during a particular class period. As all students and instructors know, what you actually learn or accomplish may not be accurately reflected by the evaluation process.

4. All forms of evaluation, including the most sophisticated, are open to a certain amount of *error:* error in sampling or selecting information from the material presented and error in interpreting what you learned. Counselors, teachers, and employers who truly understand the evaluation process are aware of error and strive to minimize it. Remember, evaluation at its best is usually an imperfect process.

5. Everyone, including you, is an *evaluator* of something or someone. For instance, when you visited prospective colleges you judged them using criteria such as quality of programs, cost, faculty, and campus atmosphere. As consumers we evaluate the products we purchase. You choose friends carefully and compare their attitudes and behavior to your standards. When you interview for a job, you carefully assess your potential employer. As a supervisor or manager, you will regularly evaluate the performance of subordinates. As a

specialist in a technical field, you will be asked for recommendations about products, services, or procedures. Each of us carefully screens the person with whom we choose to spend our life. Learn what you can about the process of evaluation so that, when you are in the position of judging the worth of others, you are a fair and competent judge.

Like it or not, evaluation *is* a fact of life. If you understand these five insights, you can approach those countless tests as opportunities to learn, not simply as aversive experiences. Finally, if an open attitude toward evaluation motivates your study behavior, you are likely to become a more successful learner.

Test-taking Tips: A Time Perspective

Tests may take several forms, including

- using pencil and paper
- conducting an experiment
- choreographing or performing a dance
- giving an oral report
- designing and constructing an object
- painting a picture
- analyzing a film, play, or field experience

Because pencil-and-paper tests are the most common form, the rest of the chapter is devoted to developing successful test-taking skills. One way to learn testing skills is to group them according to time: before, during, and after an examination.

Before an Exam

Preparation is the key to any successful evaluation. If you persistently practice most (no one is perfect!) of the learning skills described in earlier chapters, you already know the essentials of preparing for exams. To evaluate your test-preparation skills, complete the following exercise.

Learning Skills Revisited

Circle the number on the scale that best describes the extent to which you actually practice the learning skill. Numbers below the scale represent the percentage of time you practice the skill *when it can be performed.* The number in parentheses next to the item denotes the chapter in which the topic was presented.

To what extent do you	% =	Almost Always 90–100	Often 60–89	Sometimes 40–59	Seldom 10–9	Almost Never 0–9
1. mark the pages you read in your text? (11)		4	3	2	1	0
2. schedule test-preparation time on your weekly assignment sheet? (5)		4	3	2	1	0
3. prepare for tests in a regular study place? (6)		4	3	2	1	0
4. strive to understand and manage your stress? (8)		4	3	2	1	0
5. choose carefully with whom you study? (7)		4	3	2	1	0
6. distribute your study time before an exam? (12)		4	3	2	1	0
7. eat and sleep properly the night before an exam? (8)		4	3	2	1	0
8. listen attentively and objectively to the instructor? (9)		4	3	2	1	0
9. ask the teacher about the type of test to be given? (9, 10)		4	3	2	1	0
10. review your notes the day you wrote them? (10)		4	3	2	1	0
11. organize the material into diagrams? (12)		4	3	2	1	0
12. view tests as learning opportunities, not aversions? (13)		4	3	2	1	0

Compute your score on this scale by adding the numerical values of your responses and comparing that value to the following scale. Return to the chapter in which the topic was taken if you are unclear of its significance.

42 to 48 = A. Excellent! You have mastered key learning skills that help you prepare for exams.

30 to 41 = B. Good work. You have developed many good skills. Keep it up!

18 to 29 = C. Average. You have started to develop some important skills, but there is much more that you can do. Renew your commitment.

0 to 17 = D. Below average. If this is the first chapter that you have read in this book, don't worry. If you read previous chapters, you may need to review such topics as motivation and goal setting.

In addition to the techniques mentioned here, there are other steps you should follow to prepare for exams.

❑ 1. Review Past Tests

When an instructor returns an exam, it becomes part of the public domain. *Sometimes* it is helpful to review past tests, especially if the professor follows a consistent format. Search for clues in the topics covered, the wording and weight (point value) of items, and the depth of knowledge required for a correct answer. These clues may provide insights into the instructor's thought processes. However, do not assume that you will encounter the same or even similar questions; this strategy can backfire. For instance, a student named Al heard that the teacher's first test always consists of matching and short-answer essay questions. He obtained an old copy of an exam and studied it. However, dissatisfied with the test format and suspicious that his tests had circulated widely, the instructor prepared a long-answer essay exam. Unprepared for the long-answer essay questions, Al earned a D on the exam. He used old tests more cautiously in the future. The moral of this story is that old exams should be treated as a supplement to, not a substitute for, studying.

❑ 2. Simulate the Test

When time permits write test questions, easy and hard, that you think the teacher may ask. Next, answer those questions within the time period that will be allowed on the exam. If possible, complete the simulated exam in the classroom where the course is held. Finally, compare your answers with the information contained in the text and your notes. Test simulation can help some test-anxious students relax by experiencing a "test" under less threatening conditions.

❏ 3. Carefully Plan the Final Hours

The checklist you completed above demonstrates that your time-management skills dramatically influence your ability to prepare for and succeed on an exam. All exams should be marked on your appointment calendar well in advance. Your weekly work list should list several additional hours for exam preparations. The items on your daily DO-list should be kept to a minimum before an exam. If you have difficulty with specific material, you should have scheduled an appointment with the instructor or course tutor. For the efficient time manager, preparing for a test does not necessarily create anxiety.

How much time should you spend studying? The answer depends on several factors, including the effectiveness of your study habits, your ability to *understand* (not memorize) the material, the amount and difficulty of the material, and the instructor's expectations. In preparation for your first test in a course, *spend several hours more than you think is necessary*. If you "ace" the exam, congratulate yourself on your persistence. If you do not perform as well as you expected, plan to increase your time, but also obtain feedback about the quality of your efforts. In either situation, log the hours you spend preparing for a test on your weekly work list and adjust your next exam schedule accordingly.

On the night before an exam, conduct a thorough final review of your notes and text material before you go to bed. But don't become overstimulated because sleep is one of your best friends the night before a test. Calm down a half hour before bedtime with soft lighting, light reading, meditating, throwing darts, or anything that relaxes the mind and the body.

Managing peer pressure is one of the most difficult skills students must master to survive in college. Your ability to deal with peers can be tested to its limits before an exam. A group study session could be an effective means of *supplementing* your individual efforts, *if* you read in advance and follow the advice contained in Chapter 17 (pp. 358–360). *Always* avoid the "panic-peddlers." Panic-peddlers are highly anxious students who believe that improbable questions (e.g., Name the exact date Haydn completed his 78th symphony) will comprise the whole test. You learned from Chapter 8 that this style of distorted thinking, catastrophizing, will increase your stress. Also, avoid the "leeches" who know very little but want to know everything you know ("Uh, I didn't take notes the past 2 weeks, would you have a *few minutes* to explain something to me?") Compounding the problem is that the panic-peddler or the leech could be your friend or your roommate. Anticipate those moments when you must be diplomatically assertive with peers. If you live at home, you may experience additional concerns before exams: Who will prepare the meals, perform the chores, and take care of the kids while you study for your test? Try to negotiate several days in advance for rearranging responsibilities, quiet times, and quiet places to study. The night before an exam need not precipitate unmanageable anxiety if you previously organized your time, your environment, and your mind. In fact, you could experience the confidence and competence to allow yourself a *short* break for a *short* conversation over a *small* snack the night before a test.

On the day of an exam, try to conduct another review of the material before you leave for school or work or during your breaks. Be nice to your brain (if you want it to work well for you) and eat nutritious meals.

Carry extra pens, pencils, and paper and arrive 2 or 3 minutes before class begins. If you must arrive earlier, do not talk about the test; you do not want the panic-peddler to begin his or her list of unlikely questions. Conversely, do not arrive just as class begins because the teacher may start the exam early. Do nothing to increase your anxiety level.

Students often review their notes up to the point when the instructor distributes the exam. Some students benefit from this practice, but others do not. Try to assess (metacogitate) whether last-minute reviewing helps or hinders your test performance. Finally, do not sit near close friends or distractions, or in a position that would be conducive to cheating.

What should you do if you must miss an exam because of sickness or an emergency? If the instructor has a policy on makeup exams (an excellent question to pose on the first day of class), you may know what to do when such occasions arise. If a genuine emergency or an incapacitating illness keeps you from an exam, call the teacher *as soon as you know that you cannot attend.* Professors differ in their beliefs and practices regarding missing and making up exams. They can advise you about the consequences of completing an exam while sick or highly stressed and the options for taking a makeup exam. In any event, be quick to contact the instructor, be diplomatic, and be honest.

❏ **4. How to Cram for an Exam**

The space above was left blank because cramming can easily become a bad habit, perhaps an addiction. Cramming may get you a passing grade but it does not promote learning. However, if an emergency prevents you from reviewing the material in a timely manner, page through Chapters 12 (remembering) and 13 (this chapter) before you cram your review.

During an Exam

There are several steps you can take during an exam to improve your score.

❏ **1. Become Calm**

The most important rule to follow when you receive the test is to be calm and take charge of yourself. Take a couple of deep breaths and exhale slowly to relax. *Focus on the exam,* not on your classmates or on your feelings about the exam. Be confident. If you read and reviewed the material properly and practiced your learning strategies, then you may be better prepared than most students. Besides, a test is a test is a test; it's not the end of the world!

However, if you did not prepare properly (for whatever reasons), you have a legitimate reason for feeling anxious. You cannot change the situation now, but you can resolve to be better prepared for the next test. Besides remaining calm, there are several other procedures for succeeding on exams. Those that pertain especially to essay and multiple-choice tests are discussed in a later section.

❏ **2. Survey the Exam**

When you receive the test, listen for special instructions from your instructor. If you become confused about the wording of an item or the instructions *after* the test begins, go to the teacher for clarification.

Just as you might page through your favorite magazine before reading it, survey your exam and answer these questions.

• How many items are there? Do I have all the pages to the test? Ask the teacher if you are in doubt; occasionally a staple loses its grip on the last page.

- Which items seem easy to answer? Which seem hard?

- Will answering the easier items facilitate responding to the difficult items? Sometimes it does.

- Is there a pattern to the items? (For example, are the topics mixed together or in the order presented in class?)

- Are point values (weights) shown for each item so that I can spend more time with the heavily weighted items?

- If there are different parts to the test, which part should I do first? Usually, it is beneficial to answer multiple-choice items before essay questions.

❏ 3. Track Your TPI (Time Per Item)

Always carry a watch to a test; ask about the time available. From the total time available, deduct a few minutes for surveying the exam and a few minutes for editing and proofreading your answers. Divide the remaining time by the number of items to obtain your average time per item. Remember that heavily weighted items require more time than the average TPI.

In your first pass through the exam, answer the easy questions. Then recalculate your TPI and answer the difficult items. Finally, allow time to reread, verify, and edit your answers. Periodically, check the time to pace your work, but don't let clock-watching interrupt your thinking.

❏ 4. Avoid Social Pressures

Although the test is *your* test, designed to evaluate what *you* learned to calculate *your* grade, you may be tempted to cave in to social pressures. Do the following *don't*s.

1. Don't worry about who finishes the test before you. The first person out the door may receive an A (having mastered the material), or an F (having capitulated to poor preparation), or any other grade. The order in which students leave should have no bearing on your work as long as you are tracking your TPI.

2. Don't rush through the test in order to leave with a friend. True friends will wait or make contact later. Think of what you will gain and lose by completing the exam prematurely.

3. Don't cheat. When you are tempted to cheat, remember the words of former first lady Betty Ford: "Don't compromise yourself. You are all you've got." You may rationalize righteously that cheating is common on college campuses, but it remains unethical behavior. Do you really want your unethical behavior to serve as a precedent for future decisions you will make under stressful conditions? Seek counseling if you cheat frequently; cheating is usually a sign of low self-esteem and inability to manage stress, as well as ignorance of the material. If you see others cheat, don't hesitate to tell them how unfair that behavior is. Without identifying the cheaters, don't hesitate to inform the instructor after class. Talk to the department chairperson or an academic dean about the instructor who consistently permits cheating.

Feedback: After the Exam

The Spanish philosopher George Santayana said, "Those who cannot remember the past are condemned to repeat it." *Providing* feedback is an essential component of the evaluation process. *Using* feedback is essential to learning; it is the foundation of self-regulated behavior, and it can have a powerful effect on your test-taking skills.

❑ Conduct a Posttest Debriefing Session

Immediately after an exam your feelings often dominate your thinking. However, take charge of your emotions and conduct a debriefing session. For best results, complete Part 1 of the following Posttest Debriefing Survey; complete Part 2 when the test is returned.

Posttest Debriefing Survey
Part 1: Immediately After the Exam

1. In what ways (list them) was the examination similar to and different from the way the instructor said it would be?

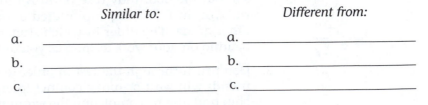

	Similar to:		Different from:
a.	_____	a.	_____
b.	_____	b.	_____
c.	_____	c.	_____

2. In regard to my preparation,

    a. what did I do correctly?

    b. what should I have done but didn't?

Part 2: When the Exam Is Returned

1. Approximately what percentage of the exam required me to

    a. rote-memorize facts? _____%

    b. comprehend concepts? _____%

    c. apply or demonstrate concepts? _____%

    d. analyze or evaluate concepts _____%

                             Total = 100 %

2. About what percent of the exam questions were drawn from

    a. class notes? _____%

    b. the text/readings? _____%

    c. both sources used together? _____%

                             Total = 100 %

3. What did I learn about

    a. my learning skills (Chapters 2 through 12)?

    b. preparing for the exam?

    c. taking the exam?

4. *Specifically,* what should I do differently the next time?

    a. _____

    b. _____

    c. _____

    d. _____

❑ Analyze Your Performance

When an instructor returns your graded test, take charge of your emotions, take responsibility for your performance, *and* take notes. Take notes on how answers were scored and how grades were distributed. The extent of the instructor's feedback may range from an in-depth review of the whole test to comments on the most frequently missed items, an invitation to look at a scoring key after class, or simple advice that you look up the answers in your textbook. If you need more feedback than the instructor is willing to provide at that time, remain after class or make an appointment to discuss your answers. Before the day is over you should complete Part 2 of the Posttest Debriefing Survey.

If your performance was better than expected, congratulate yourself, but save the Posttest Debriefing Survey for the next test. If you were disappointed, review the Posttest Debriefing Survey again, in depth. Additionally, review your time-management plan to determine whether the time you spent in preparation was sufficient and of high quality. Finally, review the graded exam and perform the following error analysis to classify and analyze your mistakes.

Error Analysis

Below are several reasons for making mistakes on tests. Enter the test item number next to the reason(s) that best explain why you made the error.

Item no.
1. I *did not study* the material pertaining to this question because

    _____a. I did not take time to read the assignments.

    _____b. it did not seem important enough to know.

    _____c. it was too difficult (I avoided it).

    _____d. I did not take notes on it.

2. I *studied the material,* but

    _____a. I did not understand it.

    _____b. I was distracted or fatigued at the time.

    _____c. not as thoroughly as I should have.

    _____d. I tried to memorize, not understand it.

3. I *knew and understood* the material before the test, but

    _____a. I "read into" and misinterpreted the items.

_____b. the questions were stated differently from the way I studied the material (too much memorizing?).

_____c. I was too anxious.

_____d. I was not mentally alert at the time.

When you classify your mistakes in the preceding categories, you take an important step toward improving your test-taking skills. In short, diagnosis suggests the treatment.

- Category 1 represents *attitude* errors and may reflect a lack of motivation and goals, inadequate listening and notetaking, or time-management problems.

- Category 2, *study* errors, may be caused by problems occurring *during the learning and review process.* Reread the main points in Chapters 11 and 12 and the section in Chapter 6 on concentration.

- Category 3 errors occurred *during the examination,* even though you knew the material in advance. Ask your instructor for advice about a and b, a counselor or advisor about c, and check your schedule and commitments regarding d.

The "treatments" prescribed above for these test-taking problems should be regarded as incomplete, general guidelines. Student characteristics and situations are too diverse to provide more detailed advice. However, with the help of your instructor or advisor, you may learn more about your test-taking behavior. Most important, become involved with the feedback process and search for ways to improve.

A student named Renita studied hard for her first general psychology test and was shocked to receive a D. After regaining her composure, she asked to review the key for the 60-item multiple-choice test. Her professor instructed Renita to use feedback strategies similar to those shown on pages 268–271. Renita reread each incorrect question and assigned it to one of the three major categories shown above. Most of her 24 incorrect answers fell into Categories 1–a (didn't understand), 2–c (thoroughness), and 2–d (excessive memorization). On the second examination Renita's grade soared to a high B and remained at that level for the rest of the course.

❏ Getting Help

If your car or television set breaks down, do you ignore the problem? If your study efforts break down, *can* you ignore the problem? If your analysis of errors does not sufficiently reveal the reasons for unsatisfactory test performance, make an appointment with your instructor. Prepare your questions in advance so that your time is spent efficiently. Ask to take notes during your meeting. As you review the exam, pay as close attention to the instructor's comments on the questions as you do to the correct answers. Chances are the instructor's thought processes will be reflected in subsequent tests. If you need additional help, ask whether tutorial services are available either through the department or through the institution's learning resource center. Be persistent in trying to learn how you can improve.

❏ Facing Failure

Poor or failing grades make you feel discouraged and depressed, especially if you worked hard to succeed. Your self-esteem drops and you feel like a failure. How do you deal with this situation?

1. Review the specific feedback you have received in all of your courses. Commend yourself on your successes. Ask why you are experiencing difficulty with a particular course. Is the material more difficult than other courses? Are your attitude and work habits appropriate? Is there "bad chemistry" between you and the instructor? Are there particular circumstances regarding the class (time of day, preceding events) that affect your performance? Most students have at least one area of academic weakness—their Achilles' heel—so if your frustration is centered on one course, persist. You may have to be content with a less-than-satisfactory (to you) grade. If you are doing poorly in other courses, recognize the danger. Review your goals and motivation. Consult your academic advisor or college counselor. Get help before it is too late.

2. Distinguish between being a failure and failing a test. Failing a test means only that you did not satisfactorily answer certain questions on a particular exam given by an instructor on a particular day in one of your college courses. To reiterate an earlier remark: A test is a test is a test. It's not the end of the world. Do not generalize (another style of distorted thinking) from one or two failing grades on tests to anticipating a lifetime of failures. If you were to fail all of your courses in college, you still would not be a failure. Life consists of far more than taking tests, in spite of our assertion that taking tests is the third fact of life! As a former student once said, "Failure is not fatal. Ask yourself what you can learn from the experience." Thomas

Edison stated this idea another way: "I have never had failures, only ways that didn't work."

3. If I have failed to convince you of the difference between failing a test and being a failure, then talk to an expert on the subject of failure—the college counselor, who has probably talked to innumerable students who *thought* they were failures.

❏ Remarks on Test Anxiety

Almost everyone experiences anxiety about tests. Anxiety is a normal part of our everyday behavior. A small amount of anxiety about an examination can motivate you to do your best. It is normal to worry and wonder about the specific items, the teacher's reactions to your answers, and the grade you will receive. Nearly all students worry about such issues; some students worry too much. Excessive worry before and during an examination distracts you from your task. Excessive worry after an examination is useless and destructive. If you become very anxious about examinations, but obtain satisfactory grades, be pleased with your successes and seek resources that will help you manage your anxiety. If test anxiety is so strong that it is the cause of low grades, in spite of your sound study habits, then you need help.

Unfortunately, test anxiety is a highly complex phenomenon that is affected by the student's past experiences, the material presented, and several situational factors. Because of its complexity, researchers cannot yet agree on specific guidelines for reducing test anxiety. However, they agree that good study habits are often the best frontline defense. In addition, test-anxious students should consult the college's counseling services, where trained counselors can work individually or in small groups with test-anxious students.

Test Formats

Tests are often classified as either objective or essay. Students often assume that essay exams are subjective—that is, that they are scored without objective criteria. However, many instructors use objective (though not necessarily quantitative) criteria to score essay exams.

A more useful way to group exams is according to the presence or absence of the correct answer in the test item. Items such as multiple choice and matching, which display the correct answer somewhere in the item, are called *recognition* tests. They require a student to master the material to a level where the correct answer can be recognized and discriminated from incorrect answers. In contrast, essay and problem questions that require you to recall, reconstruct, and express your knowledge in writing, are *retrieval* tests. Fill-in-the-blank and short-answer essay questions require recall but require little reconstruction or expression of ideas in writing.

Recognition Tests

❑ Multiple Choice

Some students believe that multiple-choice tests can measure only rote memory and that essay tests always measure higher-level thinking. In fact, depending on how test items are written, either multiple-choice or essay questions may measure rote memory or higher-level learning.

There are several steps you can take to strengthen your proficiency in multiple-choice tests. Earlier you learned that you should answer easy items first, then return and respond to difficult items. Here are other test-taking tips that you can practice.

1. Change an answer only if you are reasonably sure that it is wrong. When the corrected exam is returned, review the answers you changed to verify your decision. According to Mark Shatz and John Best (1987), if a student "has a fairly clear and logical reason for changing answers, then the odds are good that answer changing will produce a wrong-to-right change" (p. 242). However, if you are unsure of the correct answer, it may be better to leave it unchanged.

2. If you are allowed to mark on the exam, underline or circle key words in the stem (statement) of the item. For example, mark all negative words (*not, no*) and prefixes where *not* is implied (*in-, un-,* and *non-*). Items containing negatives usually require more thought; they often *appear* to be "trick" questions.

3. Mark words that qualify the statement. You learned in Chapter 11 that qualifiers change the meaning of a word. Qualifiers include terms such as *always, often, sometimes, generally, occasionally, never,* and *probably*. Beware of universal qualifiers such as *never, always, must,* and *absolutely*, for they denote no exceptions. If you wrote

down these words when you first heard them in class, you can deal with qualifiers confidently.

4. Read each test item part by part and each of the answers (options) completely. Accept the items at their face value; avoid "reading in" meanings that are not there.

5. When the item is in the form of a question (*How many provinces are there in Canada?*), or when the answer is at the end of the item (*The number of provinces in Canada is _____.*), cover the options before you read them. In other words, when possible try to answer the question *before* reading the options.

6. Cross out incorrect options. Usually one or two options in a multiple-choice question are quickly recognized as incorrect by the student who prepared for the test. After the obvious incorrect options are eliminated, the item seems like a true/false statement with only two options.

7. When you are forced to guess, follow these guidelines for good guessing.

   a. Choose the longest, most complete answer.

   b. Choose the middle value in a series of numbers.

   c. Choose the middle option.

   d. If two options are similar to each other in sentence structure and different from the others, chances are that one of the similar options is correct.

   e. Read the complete statement with each of the options in it and look for grammatical errors or inconsistencies that may signal an incorrect answer.

❏ True/False

The first three suggestions for answering multiple-choice items also apply to true/false tests. Pay very close attention to negatives and qualifiers; they are a common trap in true/false items. Furthermore, look for statements where one part may be true and another part false. For instance, here is a true/false statement: As a representative of the baroque composers, Beethoven's music had significant impact on later composers of classical music. The second part of this statement is true, but the first part is false. (Beethoven was not a baroque-period composer.)

❑ **Matching**

When you respond to a matching test

1. first, read *all* of the items in *each* column

2. next, match all pairs that you *know* you know

3. cross out items that you have used

4. reread items and match the remaining pairs

5. check your answers

Retrieval Tests

Retrieval tests challenge you to

- recall information from memory

- reconstruct that information

- express your thoughts in a clear, organized manner within the time limits

Retrieval tests vary in their demands. At one extreme, a fill-in-the-blank item may require recall of only one or two words. At the other extreme, a long-answer essay question may require several pages of facts, concepts, and critical thinking woven together. Between the two extremes lie essay questions, the length and requirements of which vary from teacher to teacher. Following are several suggestions for answering a variety of essay questions.

1. Survey the test as suggested earlier.

2. Answer the easier questions first. However, to conserve time, do not "overanswer" the easy items by including more information than needed for a high score. Next, check the time remaining and begin to answer the more difficult items. Sometimes information you provided in the easier items will facilitate your answers to difficult items.

3. Underline key words in the item, especially verbs. Verbs direct you to perform a specific operation with the information that you are retrieving. Ann Stephanie Stano (1981) grouped many common verbs used in essay exams according to the six levels of thinking in the Bloom Taxonomy of Educational Objectives as shown in Figure 13.1. The Bloom Taxonomy will be explained in Chapter 14, "Becoming an

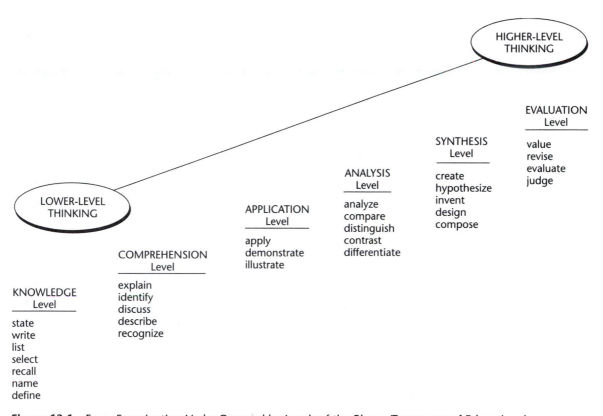

Figure 13.1 Essay Examination Verbs Grouped by Levels of the Bloom Taxonomy of Educational Objectives [Source: Adapted from *A Study of the Relationship Between Teaching Techniques and Students' Achievement on High Cognitive Level Questions Asking Skills,* by Ann Stephanie Stano, S.S.J., Ph.D., 1981. Unpublished doctoral dissertation, University of Chicago. Adapted with permission.]

Independent Thinker." As you study Figure 13.1 from the lower to higher levels of thinking, notice that the verbs make progressively greater demands on your ability to retrieve, reconstruct, and express the required information. For example, if your instructor was going to ask about the causes of the Civil War, consider how different your answers would be to these questions.

- *List* the causes of the Civil War. (knowledge level)

- *Discuss* the causes of the Civil War. (comprehension level)

- *Analyze* the causes of the Civil War (analysis level) *and evaluate* (evaluation level) whether or not the war was justified.

Did you notice that in the last sentence the conjunction *and* was italicized? Italicizing *and* was important because it is a signal that there are two specific operations you must perform to properly answer this item: *analyze the causes of the Civil War,* and *evaluate whether or not the war was justified.* Here is a second example: *Summarize Maslow's concept of the hierarchy of needs and evaluate its strengths and weaknesses.*

On a test, you should underline the two verbs (*summarize, evaluate*) and the two conjunctions (*and, and*). This question is divided into two main parts; the second part is further subdivided, requiring a total of three parts: *summarize* Maslow's concept; *evaluate* its strengths; and *evaluate* its weaknesses. Also, you could have underlined *strengths* and *weaknesses* for added emphasis. Underlining key terms is an important habit to develop because one of the most common errors students make on essay exams is misreading the verb.

4. Outline your answer to a long-essay question on your test sheet or on scrap paper (if the teacher permits) *before* you write it. Outlining takes time but it can save time—the time it takes to reorganize and rewrite a hastily composed and incorrect answer.

5. Be concise but complete. This statement seems like an oxymoron (go ahead, look up the definition), but it is not. Once again, you can grasp the meaning of this suggestion by doing the following *don't*s.

- Don't rewrite the question in your answer. The teacher *knows* what the item is.

- Don't pad your answer with flowery language; it is not a substitute for knowledge.

- Don't circumvent the question by omitting the core ideas or by mentioning them briefly in your last sentence.

- Don't be general or superficial in your answer. If all that you know is reduced to a few phrases, then you may need to practice listening, note-taking, and reading skills. Typically, main points must be supported by details or specific evidence that reflects your understanding of the issue.

- Don't ignore the ideas that your teacher spoke of most enthusiastically.

- Don't repeat earlier statements using slightly different terms. Some teachers are quickly irritated by such writing defects and are equally quick to assign low grades to answers that contain them.

- Don't convince yourself that yours is probably the first test this naive teacher ever scored.

6. Write like a professional, as if your answers were to be posted on the bulletin board. Many teachers award higher scores, intentionally or unintentionally, to neatly written papers than to slovenly papers. Consequently, it pays you to

- write or print legibly
- use blue or black ink
- create indented paragraphs to separate the major components of your answer
- skip lines between paragraphs and between answers
- begin answers to long essay questions at the top of a new sheet so that the instructor can score answers separately
- respond to multipart questions by clearly labeling each part of your answer with each part of the question
- use good grammar, punctuation, and spelling
- leave margins on all four sides
- proofread your answers during the last few minutes of class

7. Attempting to answer all questions is better than overanswering some items and leaving others blank. To illustrate, you will probably earn more points by giving three-fourths of an answer to ten questions than to fully answer or overanswer seven questions and leave three blank. Do not hesitate to seek your instructor's policy on this issue.

In summary, if you view test taking as part of the pervasive process of evaluation, tests can serve as opportunities to learn. The best way to prepare for an exam and the best defense against test anxiety is to keep practicing the suggestions offered in previous chapters. After the exam begins, survey the test, keep track of your time, and avoid social pressures. Be aware that some test-taking tips are common to recognition and retrieval tests, but that others are specific to the test format. Finally, remember that getting and using feedback is the secret to improving future test scores.

Connecting Evaluation to Your Career

Chapter 13 views evaluation as a fact of life, not just a fact of student life. After graduation the evaluation process continues when we seek employment, work toward promotion, manage subordinates, and establish relationships. Your skills for taking recognition and retrieval tests can be used when you participate in your organization's training programs, attend graduate or professional school, or take tests for licensure or certification that are required in many professions. In these situations proper preparations will be essential: goal setting; managing time and stress; and concentration, listening, note-taking, and reading skills. Most important, learning to solicit, use, and value constructive feedback will help you continue to learn, mature, and achieve your goals.

Action-Oriented Thought Starters

1. Review your old essay tests and make a list of the verbs contained in the questions.

    a. Which verbs were used most often? At which level do they fit on the Stano scale in Figure 13.1?

    b. Look up the definition of those verbs in your dictionary and compare the dictionary definitions to the way your teachers use them. In what ways are they the same or different?

2. Review your old multiple-choice and true/false tests. Underline and make a list of all verbs, conjunctions, negative words, and qualifiers. Consult the list when you prepare for the next exam.

References and Recommended Readings

Agnes, M. (Ed.) (1996). *Webster's New World Dictionary and Thesaurus.* New York: Simon & Schuster, Inc.

Kesselman-Turkel, J., & Peterson, F. (1981). *Test taking strategies.* Chicago: Contemporary Books.

Shatz, M. A., & Best, J. B. (1987). Students' reasons for changing answers on objective tests. *Teaching of Psychology, 14,* 241–242.

Stano, A. S. (1981). *A study of the relationship between teaching techniques and students' achievement on high cognitive level questions asking skills.* Unpublished doctoral dissertation, University of Chicago.

CHAPTER 14

Becoming an Independent Thinker

Jane S. Halonen
Alverno College

Friendly Reminder

❏ As you read the chapter, make it your goal to apply at least three of the five strategies for remembering.

❏ Preview Chapter 14 using the Preview Checklist on page 11, and use the Deep strategies on page 9.

❏ As you read major ideas, anticipate how they could be translated into exam questions at the knowledge and comprehension Bloom levels.

"Nothing in education is so astonishing as the amount of ignorance it accumulates in the form of inert facts."

—Henry Adams (1838–1918),
American historian and author

You have just invested a great deal of time in prior chapters learning the study skills that will make you a successful student over the next few years. You will spend countless hours in college reading and studying a variety of disciplines. A virtual parade of instructors with diverging teaching styles establishes expectations of your academic performance. You have learned from studying this text the importance of doing everything your professors require in a thorough and timely manner. Now, Henry Adams's remark implies that your education could merely expose you to a large amount of "inert facts."

Were you a little surprised when you read the quotation? At first glance, his statement suggests your pursuit of a college education may not lead to a desirable end. However, careful reading of the quotation will clarify the problem. Facts don't necessarily lead to ignorance; it is the accumulation of *inert* facts that causes the problem.

Your reaction to this statement represents a typical cycle of critical thinking. First, you start out with a knowledge base that includes a set of beliefs and a storehouse of facts that arm you to deal with the world. Then, something—an idea, a comment, a statement like Adams's—jars you. It doesn't fit with your expectation about how the world operates. To resolve this discrepancy between your own perspective and the new information you have encountered, you must either revise how you think or muster additional argument through thought, research, or more careful scrutiny to reject the new information. The discrepancy-based approach to explain critical thinking is explained in more detail elsewhere (Halonen, 1995). However, this example sets the stage for a discussion about the importance of developing critical-thinking abilities.

Nearly every college includes in its catalog a mission statement that identifies as a fundamental goal of the liberal arts education helping students to develop independent thinking and good critical judgment. To the beginning student, this can seem like a paradox (go ahead, look up the word in your dictionary). How can you become independent in your thinking if you are merely following the expectations of the people who wrote the catalog? Is there some kind of magical transformation in thinking skills? Some research (Perry, 1970) suggests that the parade of professors and projects helps students through specific stages of cognitive growth as they progress in developing their critical-thinking skills.

The purpose of this chapter is to promote developing critical-thinking skills, not only to prevent the accumulation of inert facts, but also to improve the quality of your learning and decision making in practical matters. First, we will explore how different kinds of thinking demands emerge in college classes. The work of Benjamin Bloom and his colleagues (Bloom, Englehart, Furst, and Krathwohl, 1956) will provide a framework to explore different elements of critical thinking. Then we will look at Marcia Baxter Magolda's stages of cognitive development as a map of where you might expect your own college career to take you in the development of complex thinking. We'll provide a summary of the attitudes that seem to be most consistent with effective critical thinking. We'll conclude with a list of recommendations and examples that may help you develop your ability to think independently. These tips for improving critical thinking should also help improve your academic performance in your undergraduate classes.

The Academic Disciplines: A Source of Evolving Knowledge and Skills

When you begin college, you cross the threshold with many years of educational and life experiences behind you. You have developed your own personal theories about how life works. You have formed values about what is important in life and where you want to invest your energies. You have developed many beliefs about the kinds of gains you can derive from attending college. And you are likely to make some assumptions about the educational experience ahead of you.

One of the most burdensome beliefs often held by the beginning student is the tendency to see the academic challenge of college as a relatively simple matter of information storage. Students with this belief see their texts as so many pages of material to be memorized and regurgitated at test time. One of my students once referred to this process as the "bulimic" model of education. (Unfortunately, this belief will be reinforced by many professors who won't require much from the student other than memorization.) Such students tend to regard education as a fairly static process. That is, the academic discipline is perceived as complete and stable, to be mastered by rote-memorization. With this outlook, college courses can be a fairly unstimulating experience.

In fact, most academic disciplines are quite dynamic. Truths in one decade may be cast aside for new truths in the next. Although new students may be tempted to see a discipline as unchanging, most disciplines show relentless growth. Looking at a set of introductory texts from any discipline over a span of about 30 years illustrates this principle. For one thing, the size and weight of introductory texts expand over time. The expansion of introductory texts reflects only a portion of the actual growth of knowledge in each discipline.

The expansion of knowledge or information comes from people like you who have decided during college that contributing to the knowledge base of a discipline is worthwhile and exciting. They obtain advanced degrees and contribute to the discipline through professional-level academic critical thinking. Your instructors will often be people who have committed themselves to the growth of the discipline through their own research. To help you learn, they will be sharing the concepts, frameworks for thinking, and, sometimes, theories that help to communicate how their discipline is best understood. In this process, they will challenge you to demonstrate a variety of cognitive skills.

The Bloom Taxonomy of Educational Objectives

One framework for the development of thinking skills is the Bloom taxonomy, to which you were introduced in the previous chapter. Benjamin Bloom and his colleagues have suggested that cognitive abilities can be organized into a taxonomy (a hierarchy) of six skills that reflect the variable complexity of professor's demands. These stages are illustrated in Figure 14.1 and discussed in the following sections.

Knowledge and Memorization

At the foundation of the taxonomy is the *knowledge* level, which is reflected in the skill of *memorization*. Certainly, content retention is an important part of nearly every college course. As indicated in Chapter 12, disciplines have basic information that must be memorized for

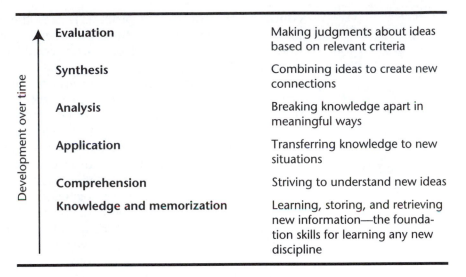

Figure 14.1 Bloom's Taxonomy of Educational Objectives

students to progress in their studies. For instance, all students of human anatomy must memorize the names of the 206 bones in the body as standard learning in this field. However, memorization is not the most appropriate way to meet *all* the challenges that college offers.

Many students believe they should memorize page for page assigned course readings as a way to survive the challenges of testing. Unfortunately, this strategy represents the worst of accumulating inert facts. One conclusion from research on the memorization of nonsense syllables is that humans are capable of committing to memory connections that don't even make sense! This kind of learning is demonstrated in its worst form when students cram for exams. You stuff your memory full of details to pass an exam. Unfortunately, memorized connections between ideas, especially those achieved during cramming, tend to be quite fragile. You cannot assume memorized ideas are learned ideas. Meaningful learning depends on much more.

Comprehension

In contrast to simple memorization strategies, comprehension emphasizes *understanding* the material you are trying to learn. In this category of Bloom's taxonomy, you will become more focused in "getting" what the author or speaker is trying to say. One example of comprehension skills is the process of doing research on a topic. After you locate a relevant resource, your challenge is to read, interpret, and paraphrase the author's key ideas in a form that can be used in your own work. You must understand the author's thinking and communicate your own understanding in your own words to demonstrate your comprehension.

The reading skills described in Chapter 11 help you more effectively understand the key ideas and the nuances being presented. Once you *really* understand the material, you will find the ideas much easier to remember. But that's just the start.

Application

The third skill in Bloom's taxonomy is application. When you apply what you understood in your coursework, you *transfer* your new knowledge to different situations. In this skill, you can begin to involve yourself more fully by trying to link the examples you study to experiences in your own life. For instance, you may be asked to identify an experience you had that is similar to that of the main character in a short story assigned for English class. Your ability to see a parallel between the example in the text and the experience in your own life is the thinking skill of application.

Analysis

Analysis requires you to take an example or problem and break it apart in meaningful ways. Analysis is a fundamental critical-thinking skill in nearly every discipline. In physics, you may need to identify the component parts of a problem relating weight and gravity. In history, you may have to discuss assumptions and inferences in a famous speech. In psychology, you may have to outline the significant concepts you learned in a case study on abnormal behavior. By breaking apart the case, you narrow it down to symptoms that can be linked to key diagnostic concepts in the course. All these examples have in common relating the problem's pieces to the whole.

Synthesis

In the fifth category you combine different ideas to create a new whole. Synthesizing requires you to survey your existing knowledge base—now enriched by experiences gained in your classes—and create new combinations of these ideas. You generate *creative* solutions. For example, you may collaborate with a group to develop new strategies about managing ecological challenges based on the discussions and readings related to the course.

Evaluation

Evaluation is the final category in Bloom's taxonomy. In this skill you must use your personal judgment about an issue after grappling with the quality and relevance of the available evidence of "facts." You may be asked to evaluate whether a painting is aesthetically pleasing or to determine whether a social policy is adequate in providing aid and assistance to poor people. You may be asked to judge how well each of three procedures in chemistry will produce a desired outcome.

In some instances of evaluation, the professor may not provide the criteria by which a judgment is to be made. Part of your critical-thinking task may be to generate your own standards for decision making. In evaluation, you must reach a conclusion using criteria based on your interpretation of the evidence.

As you may have noticed, Bloom's taxonomy generally increases in complexity and the amount of personal involvement needed as you move from one level to the next. The higher-order cognitive skills presume mastery of basic content, but also require greater independence from the thinker. As you pursue specialized content in your major and minor areas of study, your professors will make higher-order demands on you. Part of the reason that course work seems more challenging as you progress in your major is that the kinds of thinking required will be of a higher order.

The kinds of thinking skills required in college vary from class to class. In some courses your learning will be tested using multiple-choice examination questions. Unless the instructor is a very skilled test-item writer, most items will favor items at the lower levels of Bloom's taxonomy (memorization and comprehension). However, when appropriate, most college instructors prefer assignments that require higher-order cognitive skills because they encourage the integration of the discipline's ways of thinking with your own.

To assist you in determining the kind of critical thinking required in a class, return to the list of essay test verbs contained in Figure 13.1 (page 277).

Understanding Growth in Reasoning Abilities: Baxter Magolda's Stages of Cognitive Development

We can also look at your changing ability to think critically in another way. Many researchers have suggested that students demonstrate stages in their development of good critical-thinking skills. Focusing on his male students at Harvard, William Perry (1970) was one of the first researchers to observe the systematic changes in attitudes and reasoning abilities that students undergo as a result of their college experience. Perry proposed that their growth in cognitive development was based primarily on how his students related to authority figures. Subsequently, many researchers believed that Perry's approach didn't quite do justice to the array of experiences that college students reported in their changing skills.

More recently, Marcia Baxter Magolda (1992) conducted a comprehensive study of her male and female students' development over a 5-year period. Her intensive interviews suggested another strategy to characterize how students change. She agreed with Perry that students change in how they related to authority. However, as their own distinctive voices emerge, students also change in how they perceive the value of their peers and how they perceive the nature of knowledge itself. The following sections describe each of these stages, which are illustrated in Figure 14.2.

Absolute Knowing

According to Baxter Magolda, most beginning students regard knowledge as a commodity that is delivered by an instructor. They tend to listen passively and record any information that they think will help them secure success in the required course performances. They feel frustrated by activities that distract from this one-way transaction. For example, they resent their peers who respond to an instructor with questions or comments. They don't see peers as contributing to their own cognitive development but will participate in class discussions if the environment feels safe.

Beginning students treat knowledge as absolute. For the Absolute Knower, the world is neatly organized into tidy categories, such as *wrong versus right, good versus evil.* Consistent with Perry's original observations, Absolute Knowers view the instructor as an authority not

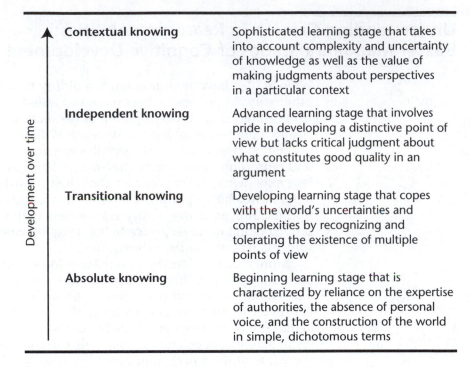

Contextual knowing	Sophisticated learning stage that takes into account complexity and uncertainty of knowledge as well as the value of making judgments about perspectives in a particular context
Independent knowing	Advanced learning stage that involves pride in developing a distinctive point of view but lacks critical judgment about what constitutes good quality in an argument
Transitional knowing	Developing learning stage that copes with the world's uncertainties and complexities by recognizing and tolerating the existence of multiple points of view
Absolute knowing	Beginning learning stage that is characterized by reliance on the expertise of authorities, the absence of personal voice, and the construction of the world in simple, dichotomous terms

Development over time

Figure 14.2   Baxter Magolda's Stages of Cognitive Development

to be challenged. Printed matter is equally unchallengeable. For example, I once asked a psychology student to criticize a research design in her textbook. She declined to do it, stating emphatically, "How can I do that? The guy who put the textbook together thought it was pretty good or he wouldn't have put it in the book!" Absolute Knowers cannot make independent judgments about ideas that have already been evaluated by the experts in the field.

Unfortunately, people who think in absolute terms often relinquish their own responsibility as critical thinkers; they defer to those who appear to be wise or more authoritative. Absolute Knowers have no personal voice or opinion; they are satisfied to repeat what the experts say. They prefer teachers who provide a straightforward, uncluttered atmosphere in which they can muster this well-defined expertise.

Transitional Knowing

When most students inevitably discover that authorities can be fallible, the stage is set to help them move from Absolute Knowing into Transitional Knowing. The introduction of conflicting and contradictory ideas ushers in new possibilities about how the world works, including how much in the world is still uncertain. Transitional Knowers believe that some aspects of knowledge are fixed and certain but other aspects may be in flux.

In Baxter Magolda's second stage, students focus less on acquiring knowledge and more on understanding knowledge. They are no longer satisfied with merely recording information; they are driven to make sense of the material and their experiences. Exposure to uncertainty fuels greater interest in finding out what others think as a way of enriching their own understanding. They begin to enjoy lively exchanges with their peers and applications of course concepts because both approaches enhance how they learn. Applications will be most valuable when they produce meaningful learning. For example, applications that are linked to future career objectives may provide an especially strong motivation to learn.

Transitional Knowers no longer rely solely on an authority figure to dictate the best resolution or to chase away ambiguities. Even though Transitional Knowers might prefer to rely on an authority's wisdom, they tolerate many situations in which faith in expertise is no longer satisfying. They expect authorities and peers to be helpful resources in developing their individual viewpoint, so they relish the opportunity to share their opinions with others. They begin to assume more responsibility for critically analyzing the ideas in any perspective under scrutiny.

Students in this stage also begin to accept complexity in most ideas they encounter. Dichotomies, such as *good versus evil* and even *right versus wrong*, no longer seem so easy to apply to most problems. Transitional Knowers recognize that many ideas and perspectives can be relevant to any problem. They start to expect that ideas, problems, and issues will be messy. They develop some patience for answers that aren't quick in coming and learn to tolerate messy, real-life problems better as well.

Illustrations of transitional knowing exist in many of your courses. For example, in your science courses, you find conflicting theories that purport to explain the same phenomenon. In your humanities courses, you discover that critics of works of literature disagree on the quality of a work. You find wildly different opinions and levels of enthusiasm in a class for the same project or the same work. Although this absence of agreement may be initially unsettling, Transitional Knowers begin to take some pleasure in complexity.

Independent Knowing

"Everything is relative" for the Independent Knower, according to Baxter Magolda. The Independent Knower experiences far greater uncertainty in life and study than the Transitional Knower. The array of opinions on controversial topics in any class reinforces the uncertainty of knowledge. Independent Knowers are receptive to the opinions of others, but begin to place greater value on their own constructions of reality. They assume responsibility for critical thinking and enjoy feeling validated in their beliefs by class discussion. The Independent Knower appreciates classrooms that can support a vivid exchange of ideas among equals.

The quality of thinking apparent in any position is not a particular concern for the Independent Knower. The exchange of intelligent opinions generates sufficient excitement that the independent learner may be satisfied by a full range of opinions. Each student tends to promote his or her individual belief rather than critically analyze where the flaws of the argument might weaken its credibility or validity.

As you can probably predict, not all college students progress to the independent knowing stage in the short span of an undergraduate career. However, the relativistic approach encourages a stronger development of voice and a greater respect for well-articulated arguments from their peers.

Contextual Knowing

In this final stage of reasoning, learners no longer honor all beliefs but recognize that some ideas can be judged as better than others *relative to a particular context or situation*. Although Contextual Knowers construct a particular point of view, they purposefully take into account the situational factors that influence the topics they study. They require evidence to make a persuasive argument.

The Contextual Knower integrates ideas across resources in a context-sensitive manner. For example, as they evaluate a particular theory, they try to remember to incorporate influences from the historical context in which the theory developed. Or they purposefully think through the intellectual context that may prompt a critic to develop a set of criticisms. The primary objective for the Contextual Knower is developing intellectually sound arguments that appropriately reflect contextual factors.

Academic relationships also change for the Contextual Knower. The relationship between student and teacher becomes two-way. The Contextual Knower values peers to the extent that they can produce well-developed arguments supported with evidence. According to Baxter Magolda, few students reach this stage of cognitive complexity during their college years. Baxter Magolda suggested that as few as 2 percent of the population she studied reached the sophistication of contextual knowing by the time they graduated.

Applying Bloom and Baxter Magolda: Executing Course Assignments

One secret of success in college is to understand and follow your instructor's directions on course assignments. Students vary in how they manage directions, depending on their developmental stage (Baxter Magolda) and their cognitive skills (Bloom). For example, how might students in each of Baxter Magolda's stages deal with a history term paper with limited direction by their teacher?

Absolute Knowers will ask the instructor questions that reflect their dependence on the instructor. Their questions are designed to remove any ambiguity from the assignment so they can complete it properly. "How long do you want it?" asks the Absolute Knower, struggling to meet what he or she perceives to be the exacting, but unexpressed, standards of the instructor.

Ironically, instructors can sometimes hear this question in a negative manner. Instructors can be annoyed to have their assignments reduced to a 500-word template (go ahead, look up the word in the dictionary) for success. They believe the project's intellectual requirements should dictate its length. The instructor's standard response, "As long as it takes," accurately reflects the belief of the instructor but will be distinctly unhelpful to the Absolute Knower. The Absolute Knower would not find much help in the interpretations of their peers either, because their peers are not experts at understanding what the history teacher demands.

The Absolute Knower is most comfortable demonstrating skills that would be considered lower-level skills in Bloom's taxonomy. They define the task as reporting relevant historical content, emphasizing *memorizing* skills. Their resulting projects will look more like historical reporting than historical thinking. Absolute Knowers tend to be more concerned with the appearance of their work than they are with the content of their work, so their comprehension of the concepts may be quite limited.

In contrast, the Transitional Knower would be less preoccupied with establishing the proper *format* of the work and would emphasize the relevant *content* involved in producing the assignment. Any historical essay will uncover conflicts in interpretation and challenges that require the essay writer to acknowledge multiple viewpoints. The student might ask the instructor, "Which perspectives need to be represented in this work?"

There is likely to be little representation of Bloom's higher-order thinking skills in the finished product of the Transitional Knower. Students in this state still emphasize reporting ideas, but they are more likely to expect and report conflicting views in their written work. The conflicts encourage more development in Bloom's levels of *comprehension* and *application* in order to address the discomfort students encounter when experts don't agree. Peers would not yet be seen as a resource in helping to resolve questions about effective completion of the assignment.

Independent Knowers are less interested in getting definitive clarification of directions from the instructor. They treat the assignment as an opportunity to relate how much they know and what they think about the topic. For the Independent Knower, proud of developing an intellectual voice, success may be defined by how exhaustive they have been in capturing the diverse perspectives involved in the assignment. In Bloom's terminology, they are likely to show *analysis* and *synthesis* as they begin to make connections among the perspectives they report, but they may not show much in the manner of evaluative judgments. They are not entirely confident in expressing their own opinions and may show little attention to establishing the quality of their arguments.

The Contextual Knower sees the absence of direction as an opportunity to create an even more meaningful exercise. Because this student has become intellectually committed to education or to the specific major, the process of completing an assignment is as rewarding as the final product. Using Bloom's terminology, Contextual Knowers incorporate *evaluation*. They show concern with the development of

effective arguments and even welcome the opportunity to create their own criteria for judging the quality of what they have created.

Contextual Knowers who seek clarification from the instructor would ask whether the approach is "in the ballpark." For example, the Contextual Knower might ask, "I plan to approach the project in this manner. Is that consistent with what you are expecting?" The Contextual Knower might also seek out the opinion of other peers whose work has been valuable, to enrich the process of completing the assignment.

Can you review your own style of relating to professors and their requirements to determine which of Bloom's cognitive skills shape the quality of your work? Can you identify which of Baxter Magolda's developmental stages best characterizes your approach to your classes? No matter how you describe your achievements to date, the challenges that lie ahead in your academic career are likely to foster your growing independence as a good critical thinker.

Developing the Attitudes of Good Critical Thinking

As you think about all the changes that lie ahead, you may be eager to develop Bloom's taxonomy skills and move through Baxter Magolda's stages as quickly as possible. Some educators believe there are specific attitudes that facilitate a critical approach. The following list (Appleby, 1997) summarizes the attitudes that characterize an intellectually responsible critical thinker.

1. We must define terms and issues clearly before we can meaningfully discuss them.

2. We need to acknowledge that there are many different points of view for every major issue.

3. We must analyze carefully and understand completely the assumptions of a theory, tradition, or belief before we can accept or reject it.

4. We should investigate all sides of an argument in an unbiased manner before reaching a conclusion.

5. We should show healthy skepticism, especially when confronted with slanted, selective, prejudiced, or self-justifying information.

6. We must make every effort to understand the perspectives of those with whom we disagree.

7. We should disagree in an agreeable manner in order to produce constructive discussions, not arguments.

8. Those with whom we agree are not always right and those with whom we disagree are not always wrong.

9. We must look beyond obvious, commonsense, or traditional answers to complex human problems because solutions are rarely simplistic or dogmatic.

10. We should recognize that it is acceptable, and often highly desirable, to change our beliefs, values, or behaviors if presented with sufficient evidence or logical justification to do so.

Thinking about applying these principles to everything you read, see, and hear may be frustrating. In fact, critical thinkers are selective in where and how they apply their skills. No one thinks critically all the time, but the joy of learning in college rests partly in discovering and refining critical-thinking skills in many contexts. The more quickly you recognize your own responsibility for understanding and evaluating the ideas put before you by your instructors, the more you will gain from your college education.

Improving Your Critical-thinking Skills

Seven Related Activities

You can do some specific activities early in your academic career to facilitate independence of thought. Here are some recommendations to enhance your critical-thinking abilities.

❏ 1. Prepare Course Assignments Critically

You need to organize the course material to maximize your learning experience with new ideas. Many professors recommend outlining key ideas or making concept maps to reinforce the basic process of *knowledge* and *memorization*. Then ask yourself questions that enhance your understanding and reflect higher levels of Bloom's taxonomy:

- Which concepts don't make sense yet? (*comprehension*)

- Where have I seen these ideas in operation? (*application*)

- What additional meaning could these concepts have for me? (*analysis*)

- How do these concepts relate to each other? (*synthesis*)

- Do I agree that the ideas seem truthful? Adequate? Pleasing? (*evaluation*)

You may want to ask practical questions about the learning process to enhance your performance and satisfaction with what you are learning:

- How might instructors translate these course experiences into test questions or assignments? (*analysis*)

- How does what I am learning fit with my own developing worldview? (*evaluation*)

❏ 2. Identify What Kinds of Cognitive Skills Work in Different Contexts

Lecture

Even in classes that are primarily lecture oriented, instructors expect you to be more than a passive recorder of what they say. They expect *you* to identify key ideas and comprehend them. However, some instructors encourage even greater involvement to enhance your learning: They encourage discussing the concepts as a way to improve comprehension and recall. Student examples or questions often demonstrate application, analysis, and synthesis of course concepts. Some instructors solicit a student's personal experiences to clarify content. Other instructors might find personal disclosures a distraction, or at least would prefer to hear students' illustrations in a short discussion after class.

Discussion

Size up the type of discussion the instructor prefers. How does the professor respond when questions are asked? Does the professor ask follow-up questions? Does she make a point of elaborating on the course concept that was being discussed? Or does she quickly return to the plan for the day? Does her body language (averted eyes, nervous gestures) signify that the questions are unwelcome? Even in those classes where discussion may not be encouraged, don't let that deter you from thinking privately to elaborate the meaning of the course content.

Tests

Another opportunity for you to communicate with your instructors is testing. As suggested in the previous chapter, review past tests to identify what kinds of thinking the test items measure. Decode the level of complexity your instructors use in their tests. Successful decoding can guide how you study. If the questions use words such as *identify* and *name,* then spend your preparation time memorizing the most important concepts. If the items ask you to *compare* and *contrast,* then use your time to analyze the relationships between course concepts.

Projects

Project work is another avenue for communication between you and the professor. Projects tend to add more complex cognitive demands basic to academic work. You will be able to learn a lot about the professor's expectations if you can examine projects done by previous students. In addition, the following questions may help you clarify the nature of the work required.

- Do your project instructions help you to identify the kinds of thinking you are required to do?

- How much personal interpretation does the instructor prefer? How much personal interpretation is permitted within the discipline?

- Are you being asked to analyze and synthesize existing ideas or should you develop some new perspective?

- Should you confine your resources to the discipline or can you cite ideas from many different disciplines?

❏ 3. Expect Variation in Your Critical-thinking Skills

Good critical thinking varies in how hard it is and how long it takes. Some critical thinking can happen in a moment. Other critical thinking can take years. Sometimes critical thinking is subtle. We make so many judgments using inference and analysis during the day that it may be hard to consider these examples of critical thinking. All of us do an enormous amount of critical thinking to function on a day-to-day basis. We may adapt a recipe based on ingredients we have. We

may navigate to a new place from a poor map. One of our most beloved (and sometimes accurate) academic stereotypes, the absentminded professor, suggests that professors are not always very effective in practical kinds of critical thinking—an example of how critical-thinking ability can vary.

One of the major challenges of college is learning how to do the critical thinking your college courses will require. You may also notice that you have a lot of natural talent in some kinds of critical thinking and may not be as effective in other areas. For example, one of my students was surprised that she found it hard to relate ideas in the humanities and easy to connect ideas in social science. Identifying those areas in which critical thinking is easier and more fun may be helpful in selecting your academic major and preparing for your career.

Even really effective critical thinkers are not effective all the time, so don't be too disappointed by the errors you make as you learn. When something goes wrong, the discrepancy can be quite obvious and inconvenient. But it can also be a powerful incentive to learn more to prevent similar critical-thinking lapses in the future.

❏ 4. Think of the Disciplines as Dynamic

The academic disciplines have evolved through decades of critical thinking—and they will continue to evolve. Artists will continue to produce challenging rearrangements of reality. Scientists will continue to redefine theories to explain the world. Ten years from now, the discipline may be quite different from what you study today. There is room in the discipline for criticism. In fact, all disciplines develop from critical discourse. Most instructors will enjoy your attempts to work with course material in an interactive and critical way. Just as your own personal theories are modifiable, so are the theories of the discipline. Expect that the disciplines will continue to flourish, just as you expect your own cognitive growth to continue to thrive through college and beyond.

Make an Appointment with Your Professor

Most professors enjoy talking informally to their students about the discipline. Ask for a 15- to 30-minute appointment as part of your own intellectual development. Tell him that you want to explore how people in the discipline think. Ask your teacher about his personal experiences: "What drew you to the discipline? How have you seen the discipline change since you studied it at the undergraduate level?

What changes can you predict in the next 10 years? Would you have done anything differently in planning your studies? Given my interest in a specialized area of chemistry, would you have any recommendations for me?" Such requests from students are rare, so professors generally enjoy the opportunity to talk about their own experiences. If you get rejected, move on to another professor.

Read Current New Magazines

Many popular news magazines are divided into sections that correspond with the disciplines you are studying. Read some issues completely—even sections you are less interested in—as a way of seeing how different fields communicate about the world. Reading the sections most closely aligned with your major will give you a head start in making meaningful associations in your course work.

❑ 5. Think About How the Disciplines Relate

All kinds of connections exist among course experiences that you will have in college. Look for those connections. Think about how the skills that you are learning in one course are similar to or different from the skills that you are learning in another.

- How does observation of human behavior in the lab compare to observation of human behavior in novels?

- How do the patterns you learn about in physics compare to the patterns you learn about in music appreciation?

- How does cultural context affect how we think about human nature in all the disciplines?

All disciplines tend to have distinctive ways of executing critical thinking. Sometimes the differences can be reflected along a continuum of objectivity/subjectivity. In the former case, objective standards will require that you work from observable evidence in developing your argument. Personal experience as evidence is often discounted in some disciplines. In other areas, subjective interpretations are honored. In these contexts, you will be encouraged to use your personal interpretations to enhance your understanding of the works you study.

These are just a few of many possible suggestions for making effective connections. Such considerations can help you develop good analytic habits that will serve you well as you progress to the more intense demands of higher-order cognitive projects. You may also find that keeping a journal as described in Chapter 6 is helpful in developing these abilities.

❏ 6. Practice a Critical Attitude

Thinking critically is relatively easy when a huge discrepancy exists between how you expect the world to function and how it actually does. The trick in developing your own critical-thinking skills is to develop an attitude of expecting and actively looking for things not to fit together. If you expect to see something imperfect, you will more routinely challenge yourself to think in analytic and evaluative ways to understand the problem at hand. As you make progress in a selected course, you will notice that your ability to find discrepancies in what you study will improve. You will be able to handle increasingly subtle discrepancies. You may even be able to identify and resolve problems that escape the attention of others.

Authorities are fallible humans, incomplete and biased. Sometimes a beginner's fresh eye on a problem can spot an invalid assumption or a new way of looking at things that can make an important breakthrough. Sometimes, complex conclusions can be built on erroneous assumptions. Questioning underlying assumptions is an especially productive way of thinking critically.

But what about when you think your professor is wrong? Teachers can make mistakes. When you think a professor is mistaken, should you challenge him or her in class? This is tricky, but the answer is yes.

What appears to you to be mistake may, in fact, be a problem of communication. The professor may simply not have communicated the concept. Your question will help clarify the point, not just for you, but for your classmates as well. You might ask the professor, "Could you expand on that last idea? I'm not certain I understand what you mean." This will courteously encourage the professor to add more details to the explanation.

If the problem is not one of clarity but accuracy, then the challenge is even more difficult. If you believe that the professor welcomes intellectual discussion as part of class activities, then being straightforward is an effective challenge. You might first repeat or paraphrase to the professor the idea you find problematic (for example, "I think you are saying that . . . Is that correct?") to establish the professor's position. Then explain your problem with that position ("I disagree with that idea. It *seems* to me that we could look at this in a different way . . ."). It is wise to challenge persons in authority tentatively because most of us respond defensively if we believe we are under attack.

If the instructor realizes that you are questioning because you want to understand, then he or she will probably be enthusiastic about your challenge. Professors will feel gratified that the course is generating such good critical thinking, even if it requires them to revise their positions. Most professors delight in students who ask questions because they perceive these students as more serious about their education. If you don't believe a professor would welcome this kind of challenge, then it's probably a better idea to see him or her after class.

❏ 7. Expect a More Difficult Path

Henry Ford once commented, "Thinking is the hardest work there is, which is the probable reason why so few engage in it." Life can be more comfortable when we see the world more simply. When our existing beliefs are challenged, we may be confronted with some painful realities about abandoning ways of thinking that made the world safe and comfortable. As we learn to tolerate the absence of answers and move away from a more certain existence, we may feel the full weight of our own responsibility in developing our best selves.

As you become more responsible and independent in your college studies, you may find your enthusiasm for learning is not popular with your peers. Often passive participation norms predominate in college courses. Sometimes instructors may not reinforce your enthusiasm. It may be taxing to feel as though you're in a minority of people who truly care about the quality of their educational experience. But don't despair. Happily, effective critical thinking is its own reward. You do not have to be reinforced by others. There is joy in discovering a new connection, in understanding something that you didn't understand before. As your critical thinking improves, you engage in more self-evaluation and use objective and personal criteria to determine your satisfaction in thinking tasks. After all, your professors won't be following you around the rest of your life evaluating your effectiveness. Developing and maintaining your own standards helps you maintain a strong cognitive self-view.

Connecting Independent Thinking to Your Career

In Chapter 3 you learned how to establish and monitor short-term, intermediate, and long-range goals. Chances are that the goals you set for yourself include careers where higher levels of thinking are prerequisite to *entry*-level positions. You may see yourself in 5 to 10 years as a skilled professional responsible for making or contributing to decisions that daily affect your life and those of others in your organization. Will you have the intellectual resources to make decisions, solve problems, and develop new perspectives? Will you be able to comprehend, apply, analyze, synthesize, and evaluate information? Will you be able to think independently and contextually?

Did you learn from this chapter that your stage of thinking is primarily at Bloom's knowledge (memorization) or comprehension levels? Or that you are primarily at Baxter Magolda's stage of absolute knowing? If you are new to college, don't be surprised or depressed by this discovery; most of your peers are at similar levels. Baxter Magolda has shown that cognitive growth is often accelerated by the experiences of college. In the workplace it is accelerated in situations in which employees learn through direct experience, function independently, utilize various resources, collaborate with peers, and make subjective decisions (Baxter Magolda, 1994). This chapter has introduced you to concepts and tools that can facilitate your intellectual development so that you may enter your career as an independent thinker, not just a college graduate overwhelmed by inert facts.

Action-Oriented Thought Starters

1. One way to sharpen your critical-thinking skills is to take the opposite stance of whatever you are hearing or reading. This practice is sometimes called *playing devil's advocate*. Scholars will sometimes propose this position as a way of introducing threatening ideas into a discussion without taking complete ownership of the idea.

   When you play devil's advocate, pay careful attention to the ideas presented with the objective of finding holes in the argument. You must first assume that there is something wrong in the presentation. You may want to apply the following criteria to the presentation.

- Are the ideas accurate?

- Is the presentation complete?

- Is the presentation well structured?

- Is the presentation timely?

- Who wouldn't agree with the perspective being presented?

- How could the presentation be improved?

If the presentation seems to meet the criteria, you may decide that the arguments and ideas are intellectually satisfying. However, you will have concluded this on the basis of *your own* critical thinking.

2. "Owning a Magic Wand" is an exercise in creative thinking. One of the greatest obstacles to creativity is the assumption that things should stay as they are. We often get "stuck" in accepting ideas as they are presented because we may not give ourselves permission to play with ideas as a way of opening ourselves up to new connections.

Assume you own a magic wand that allows you to change ideas and objects in new and interesting ways. As you examine a new idea, what would happen if you

- could change the time frame?

- make some aspects larger (or smaller)?

- could change to a new location?

- had to get along without the idea?

- looked at the idea like an alien might?

- mailed the whole thing to your mother?

This simple new perspective may allow you to adopt a more playful attitude toward the ideas you are being asked to review. A playful approach in combining new ideas is the start of many new great inventions and works of art or science. It may all start with play.

References and Recommended Readings

Appleby, D. C. (1997). *The handbook of psychology.* New York: Addison-Wesley Longman, Inc.

Baxter Magolda, M. B. (1992). *Knowing and reasoning in college.* San Francisco: Jossey-Bass.

Baxter Magolda, M. B. (1994). Post-college experiences and epistemology. *The Review of Higher Education, 18*(1), 25–44.

Bloom, B. S., Englehart, M. D., Furst, E. J., & Krathwohl, D. R. (1956). *Taxonomy of educational objectives: Cognitive domain.* New York: David McKay.

Halonen, J. (Ed.). (1995). *Teaching critical thinking in psychology* (2nd ed.). Milwaukee, WI: Alverno Publications.

Halpern, D. (1996). *Thought and knowledge: An introduction to critical thinking* (3rd ed.). Mohwah, NJ: Erlbaum.

Perkins, D. N. (1981). *The mind's best work.* Cambridge, MA: Harvard University.

Perry, W. (1970). *Forms in intellectual and ethical development in the college years: A scheme.* New York: Holt, Rinehart, and Winston.

Von Oech, R. (1990). *A whack on the side of the head: How you can be more creative.* New York: Warner Books.

CHAPTER 15

Improving Oral Communication Skills (A Short Course in Public Speaking)

Nancy F. Krippel
Barat College

Friendly Reminders

❑ As you read, ask how your instructor could test your knowledge of this material at the knowledge, comprehension, and application levels of Bloom's taxonomy.

❑ As you read, summarize, mark important concepts, and take notes; use an organizational strategy (e.g., concept map) to remember key concepts.

❑ *You* choose a friendly reminder to yourself.

*"He gave man speech, and speech created thought,
Which is the measure of the universe."*

—Percy Bysshe Shelley (1792–1822),
English Romantic poet

Public Speaking: The Communication Model

You may believe that you already know enough about oral communication. After all, you talk to your friends, argue with parents and siblings—what more is there to communicating? The next two chapters answer that question and delineate the basic components of communicating. In this chapter, you will discover that presenting yourself and your ideas either to a group of people or to one person, in front of a class or in an interview, requires that you consider more than just *what* you have to say. You must consider *how* you say it and to *whom* you are saying it. These three basic parts of any speaking engagement comprise the three factors of the communication model:

- the speech or message factor (what you say)

- the audience or receiver factor (to whom you are saying it)

- the speaker (communicator) or sender factor (how it is said)

You were introduced to this model in Chapter 9. In Chapter 16, "A Primer on Interpersonal Skills," the model is the framework for understanding interpersonal and group skills. Each factor is important in creating a successful speaking encounter.

The Speaker

First, you as the speaker must be aware of yourself. You are, after all, on stage during a presentation. How you look and how you sound directly influence how your audience receives the content of your presentation. If you make a presentation in cut-off jeans or sweats, you feel differently about yourself and the material than you do if you are dressed in a professional manner. Sloppy attire indicates to both you and the audience sloppy thought and content. This, of course, does not mean that you must wear a cocktail dress or a dinner jacket, but it does mean neat and "nice" clothes. Consider how you judge people by the way they look—so will your audience judge you by the way you look. You want to project an image of sincerity, credibility, and interest in your topic and your audience. In part, you will accomplish this by the way you look.

However, you also need to consider how you sound to the audience. When you are preparing an essay, you have to attend to the minutiae of writing: where the commas go, how to spell *separate,* and so on. When you are preparing a speech, you need to attend to another set of concerns: how your voice sounds and the image you project. The force and range of your voice, for example, are important aspects of oral communication. If the audience cannot hear you, the content of the speech will be lost. If you speak in a monotone, the audience may grow bored with your message.

If your grammar is incorrect, the audience will lose faith in you. And the vocabulary of the speech must be appropriate to the occasion. Listeners expect and deserve to hear a vocabulary they can understand. Consider carefully the points you wish to emphasize: all light and no shadows (or the reverse) make for a dull speech.

The Audience

The audience, too, is a vital part of the process of creating a good speech. You must consider your listeners: Who are they? What are their age, race, gender, and educational level? What do they need to know? If you do not consider the makeup of your audience *before* you begin to write your speech, you may well write the wrong speech. However, adapting your speech to the needs of your audience isn't just another restriction on you as the speaker. Ask yourself questions such as: In what aspects of my subject are these particular listeners most likely to be interested? What examples can I use to make the content clearer and more interesting to this audience? Taking the audience into account does not mean that your interest and inclinations are not important. They are, and the choices you make should reflect you and your personality.

The Speech

The third component of oral communication is the speech itself. You deliver a speech to have an effect on a particular audience. The effects vary from situation to situation. Your basic purpose is, of course, to receive a satisfactory grade. However, you must always have another overriding purpose: to inform, entertain, or persuade your audience, rather than merely fulfilling your instructor's requirement.

An effective speech has four qualities.

- It is appropriate to the occasion and the audience.
- It is credible.
- It is clear.
- It is interesting.

These qualities, as aims, guide your choice of subject and preparation. They help to create a good speech, which will in turn achieve the desired goals of developing a skill and earning a good grade. Think of your speech as a unified strategy aimed at achieving a specific effect within a given time limit. You must decide what to use, where to use it, and why to use it.

The Three Components of a Speech

Like an essay, a speech divides neatly into three main components: introduction, body, and conclusion. In other words, tell your audience what you are going to say. Say it. Then remind them what you said. To help you understand the differences among these components, they are described within the context of a hypothetical speech.

The Introduction

The introduction orients your audience and tells them what the speech is about. The introduction should include a statement of purpose, a specific focus, and a manageable thesis. Usually you will want to lead up to your statement of purpose and thesis with a remark that establishes your credibility and gains audience interest: a striking example, a short story, or a brief summary of your qualifications on the subject.

To illustrate, let's say that your instructor's assignment requires you to describe some activity or process you know well. You decide on the topic of changing a bicycle tire. Your audience is a group of your peers, most of whom own bicycles and most of whom are on limited budgets. Thus, you can stress the money-saving aspects of knowing how to change a flat tire rather than depending on the local bike shop.

You might begin by telling your audience how, as the oldest sibling in your family, it fell to you to keep the family bikes in good repair. In high school you completed a physical education class on outdoor education that included a section on biking. Since then, you have saved yourself and your family hundreds of dollars by handling the bike repairs yourself.

Such remarks enable you to establish your credibility, demonstrate the importance of the topic, and gain the interest of your audience.

The Body

In the introduction of your speech, you told the audience what you intend to accomplish; in the body, you actually accomplish it. Divide the subject into main sections, each supported with examples and details. For instance, changing a bicycle tire can be reduced to three major steps: removing the tire, fixing it or replacing it, and putting it back on the bike. Each step requires that you explain and expand your points to make your audience "see" the process. With this topic, you would follow a chronological organization of the steps (First . . ., Second . . ., Third . . .) rather than rambling around relating bits and pieces of changing the tire. Move smoothly from the beginning to the end of your remarks. Also, incorporate transitional statements so that your listeners always know where they are: "Now that you have the tire off the bike . . ."

The Conclusion

Finally, you arrive at what is probably the most difficult part of the speech: the conclusion. A well-crafted conclusion should make the audience feel that you are ending your speech smoothly and that you are in control, rather than just running out of things to say and rushing back to your seat. Perhaps you have seen movies, read books, or heard speeches that simply stop rather than end. You want to leave your audience with a sense of completion (an ending), so a planned conclusion benefits both the speaker and the audience. A strong final sentence allows you to leave the stage with some semblance of grace and dignity.

Typically, a conclusion contains a summary of main points, provides a tie-in to your introduction, or offers a suggestion on how the audience might use the information. Never raise new ideas that rightly belong in the body of the speech. For example, in the tire-changing speech, you might refer to the opening story about the usefulness of this skill. Not only is the skill helpful to students on a limited budget, but also when some of the audience members have families of their own. Always prepare a strong final sentence; never go out with a whimper—end with a bang!

Preparing the Presentation

The previous sections introduced you to the communication model and the three components of a speech. This section presents specific steps for preparing your presentation.

First Things: Topic, Purpose, Thesis

The first two elements to consider when you prepare your speech are topic and purpose. They really cannot be separated.

❏ Topic and Purpose

The topic of your speech must fit the occasion (the assignment) and engage the audience. The purpose determines the way you narrow a broad subject down to a workable topic and the types of details and examples you include to make your point. Again, let's illustrate these concepts with a hypothetical case. You are enrolled in an education course and the instructor requires that each student prepare a 15-minute oral presentation on some aspect of education. That is a very broad but common assignment from a college teacher. You know the general subject, but you must create a topic out of it.

Where do you begin? One of the articles you read for the course discussed the importance of preschool education and mentions the Montessori method, which mildly interests you. To narrow the topic further, you decide to prepare your presentation on the Montessori method of preschool education.

You have chosen a topic. Now you must decide on a purpose. Broadly speaking, you have three choices regarding general purpose: to inform, to persuade, or to solve a problem. If the assignment does not clearly indicate the purpose of your presentation, ask your instructor for clarification. You may decide that *persuading* your audience to choose a Montessori school will not work because most of them do not have children. You want, instead, to *inform* these teachers-to-be about the basic premises of the Montessori method. Although Maria Montessori, the originator of the method, is a fascinating woman, you have only 15 minutes. You choose to skip all biographical and historical information. Instead, you concentrate on the way the method strives to allow the children to learn at their own pace and within their scope of interest.

❏ Thesis

You have a topic and a purpose—what next? You begin to gather material (research the topic) by reading about the Montessori method in original sources, textbooks, or journals. In addition, you may want to observe a Montessori school. You interview the director of your local school and perhaps talk with some parents. Once you have all your information, you formulate a thesis statement or controlling idea. You will use this thesis as your primary organizational tool; it determines what information you present and guides the flow of that information. Based on your research, you develop the following thesis: "By dividing the classroom into three distinct units, the Montessori method encourages children to develop as individuals."

The Middle Thing: An Outline

Now that you have your thesis, you need to organize the material. The single best way to organize a speech is by constructing an outline. Some students live in fear of the dreaded outline, but, particularly in oral communication, the outline offers the easiest and the best way to organize your thoughts. An outline prevents you from writing out a speech verbatim and then trying to reproduce it in front of the class. Never try to memorize a speech; the result is stilted and totally without spontaneity. Table 15.1 shows the general structure of an outline that you can use for preparing a speech.

The thesis for the Montessori speech provides you with a clear organizational pattern: the three classroom units. Each unit becomes a main heading in your outline. You fill in the subheadings with details from your research and specific examples from those observations that support your thesis that the students develop as individuals. Let your audience "see" specific children doing what they do in the classroom.

The Beginning and the End

Once you have the body of the speech outlined, you need to construct your introduction and the conclusion. First, plan to introduce yourself: "Good morning, I am _____ and today I am going

Table 15.1   A Sample Outline for Preparing a Speech

Title of Topic
- I.   Introduction
  - A.   your name
  - B.   attention-getter
  - C.   orient audience
  - D.   thesis
- II.   Body
  - A.   first main point
    - 1.   details
    - 2.   specific example
    - 3.   transition
  - B.   second main point
    - 1.   details
    - 2.   specific example
    - 3.   transition
  - C.   third main point
    - 1.   details
    - 2.   specific example
    - 3.   transition
- III.   Conclusion
  - A.   summarize
  - B.   "tie it up"
  - C.   exit line

to . . ." Although introducing yourself to the class may seem silly, it is nonetheless a good way to begin. Next, get your audience's attention, perhaps with an anecdote that reveals your topic. Then you might include background information to orient your audience. Keep it brief and to the point. Finally, present your thesis. At this point the audience should know exactly what you are going to talk about and what the point of your speech is.

Once you have prepared the introduction to your speech, you are ready to craft your conclusion. As indicated earlier, the conclusion is extremely important. It is what the audience is most likely to remember because it is the last thing they hear. The longer the speech, the more important it is for you to summarize your main points. Restate, but do not repeat verbatim, your thesis. End your talk with a strong final statement, something that ties the conclusion to the introduction. For example, if in the introduction you named a specific child in the Montessori school you visited, then give the audience a final glimpse of that same child in your conclusion.

The Notecard

When you have completed your outline and have a sense of your introduction and conclusion, you begin the real work of giving a speech. First, transfer a short version of your outline to a *single* notecard (4 × 6-inch or 5 × 7-inch); you may use both front and back. Limit your card to single-word memory prompts; do not write out complete sentences, unless it is a direct quote. Why only one card? Because a surefire way to foul up a presentation is to lose your place in a myriad of notecards.

Rehearsal Time

Once you have your notecard ready, begin to rehearse. A rule of thumb for preparation is for every minute of speaking, you should spend one hour preparing. So for a 15-minute speech, you would prepare 15 hours. About one half the time is spent gathering material, creating the outline, and crafting the introduction and the conclusion. The other half (7 to 8 hours) is spent *rehearsing* the presentation. Never write out the speech; always practice from your notecard. When you rehearse, do it aloud. Saying the speech in your head does not work very well; you cannot get a good sense of the time it takes and you do not hear the message. Although some people like to rehearse in front of a mirror, this practice can make you self-conscious of how you look while you are speaking.

Box 15.1

Les Learns Ludicrously

Les was a compulsive student who decided, in spite of instructions to the contrary, to write as much of his speech as he could on 3 x 5 notecards. The results of his labor were ten neatly written cards, but insufficient practice time. As he stood at the podium waiting to begin, he nervously shuffled the cards. You guessed it; when Les began to speak, he could not find the first card. He stopped for 2 or 3 minutes and anxiously rearranged his pile of cards. Neither he nor the audience was able to ignore the rocky start of his speech. All of his hard work researching and writing the speech were for naught. So unless you develop a foolproof method to stay calm, stick to one card.

If you are a commuter, practice the speech aloud in the car as you drive to and from school or work. People in the other cars may think you are crazy, but you could pretend to be speaking to a child on the seat next to you. Persuade a friend to be a guinea pig and ask for advice on improving your presentation. If you fail to capture a practice audience, saying the speech aloud to yourself helps you to hear the awkward spots. It is not possible to overrehearse as long as you do not try to memorize the presentation. Each time you practice, it will be slightly different from the last time. The change is good because neither you nor your speech will grow stale.

The Moment of Truth

You have chosen your topic, gathered your material, created a thesis, written an outline, crafted an impressive introduction and a tight conclusion, practiced until you are blue in the face, and the big day is finally here.

Remember to dress for the occasion and bring your notecard to class. The teacher calls your name; here we go! First, remove your chewing gum. The audience will appreciate not having to listen to you through a wad of bubble gum. Next, do not take anything to the podium with you except your notecard (unless you are using a visual aid, which I will discuss in the next section). Leave your pen, paper clip, notebook, everything at your desk. Remove any large rings or bracelets that may hit the podium and distract the audience.

Place your notecard as high up on the podium as you can, so that you don't have to bend your head down to see it (otherwise the audience is looking at the top of your head). Put your feet flat on the floor. Relax your knees, take a deep breath, look at the audience, smile, and go for it! You're ready: you look terrific; you know the material; you're interested in your topic. Don't worry about your hands; they will take care of themselves. Keep smiling and looking at the whole audience. Do not choose some poor classmate in the front row to stare at, no matter how attractive that person is. Spread your eye contact around the room. If you fail to look at the people in the audience, they will neither look at nor listen to you.

Before you know it, you've finished your talk and returned to your desk to the sound of applause. Now that wasn't so bad, was it? And the next time it will be even easier. As long as you are at ease with your material (that means you have rehearsed and rehearsed and rehearsed the presentation), no bout with public speaking will ever get the better of you. You will always come out a winner.

Visual Aids

Depending on the topic and the course, you may need to incorporate visual aids into the talk. A visual aid is anything you use to enhance your verbal presentation of material: a picture that shows, a chart or graph that clarifies, or a model that demonstrates.

For instance, Susan's marketing teacher requires each student to "create" a product and then "sell" it to the class. Susan decides to create a can of spray paint that contains the three primary colors: red, yellow, and blue. She takes an ordinary can of paint and makes a new label for it. Although she can't make the can hold three colors, she creates a dummy label and presents the spray can to the class as her visual aid. Being able to see the can helps the audience to visualize the product she is selling.

The problem with visual aids lies in the fact that sometimes they seem to take on a life of their own at the precise moment when the speaker attempts to use them, like the perfectly trained dog that refuses to obey the simplest command for guests. Therefore, to use visual aids effectively, follow a few simple guidelines:

1. Always plan in advance exactly how to use the aid. Leave nothing to chance. Make sure you know how to operate any machine you may be using. For example, if you are going to use an overhead projector, know how to operate it and how to place transparencies correctly. Check the location of the wall outlet in the room. Does the furniture need rearranging? Do you need an extension cord or an adapter? Often it is the minor thing that throws you into a state of confusion, ruining an otherwise excellent presentation.

2. Speak to the audience, not to the visual aid. If you are using a graph, chart, or map, place it on an easel and face the audience while you point to the graph. Never turn your back to the audience.

3. Make sure that the aid is large enough for the audience to see clearly, but also small enough for you to handle easily. A ring is

too small to be a good visual aid, and an automobile tire is too large and unwieldy. If you use a hand-held model or object, do not hold it directly in front of your face.

4. Remember Murphy's Law: If anything can go wrong, it will!

5. Let the visual aid supplement your speech; it should never be more important than your speech. It is, after all, an aid, not a speech. Choose an aid that is suited to your abilities and skills. Remain calm and take adequate time to set up for a demonstration. Don't rush or let the silence stampede you. On the other hand, avoid the aid that takes too much time to set up; it will put both you and the audience on edge. Introduce the aid at the appropriate moment and put it aside when you finish with it. Don't ever compete with the aid. Keep it simple, large but not unwieldy, and clearly legible. A chart should be presented in heavy contrast, in color, and in sufficient light.

6. Finally, *always* rehearse with the aid. It should be as familiar to you as the content of the speech. A visual aid can make a presentation more effective; the proper use adds interest and variety to a speech.

Box 15.2

Murphy's Law in Action

Jane must give a demonstration for her speech class; she decides to demonstrate how to give a baby a bath. She is a mother of two and has given innumerable baths to her children, so she thinks that bathing will be the perfect choice. Jane brings the necessary equipment to class and one of her daughter's plastic baby dolls to substitute for the real thing. Everything is going smoothly until she takes the plastic doll out of the soapy bath water. Unlike a human baby, the doll's plastic skin is extremely slippery after being soaped. When Jane pulls the doll from the water, it slips out of her hands and falls head first, skidding across the floor and finally coming to rest at the feet of Jane's teacher. The audience, Jane, and even the teacher are laughing so hard that poor Jane never really gets the speech back on track.

Final Note

This chapter is not meant to substitute for a course on public speaking. It's only intended to provide you with the most basic concepts and recommendations so that you can prepare and present a speech in class or speak to a group of your peers without having a nervous breakdown. Though many of us live in abject terror of facing an audience, I recommend that you complete a speech course because the only way to master the art of public speaking is to do it—over and over and over again. You will never fully eliminate nervous tension, nor should you. However, with practice you can make that nervous tension work for you rather than against you.

Connecting Public Speaking to Your Career

At the beginning of this chapter, I said that you may think you know a lot about public speaking. You speak to each other and converse on a wide variety of topics. Yet arguing the merits of a particular movie with a group of friends over lunch is quite different from presenting a technical report to a group of associates in a business setting. Most careers require you to perfect your verbal skills in either group settings or one-on-one situations. The ability to organize your thoughts and create a concise, coherent presentation of ideas and facts is an essential skill for anyone in business and industry, in science and technology, or in art and academe. Whether you seek a career in advertising or scientific research, you will be required to present yourself and your ideas to your associates. Along with competence in written communication, competence in oral communication stands as one of the most valuable skills you will carry from college to career.

Action-Oriented Thought Starters

1. Attend a lecture at your college and evaluate the speaker using the criteria described in this chapter.

   a. What would you do differently?

   b. What did the speaker do well that you could incorporate into your preparations?

2. Make a list of the trouble spots in your oral communications. Select at least one deficiency and work to eliminate it from your next presentation. Monitor your progress through the self-contract or journal techniques described in Chapter 6.

3. Attend a movie and then attempt to persuade a friend to see it, based on your opinion. If you succeed, ask your friend to identify those aspects of your persuasive remarks that were most and least effective.

References and Recommended Readings

Aristotle. (1984). *Rhetoric and poetics of Aristotle.* New York: Random House/Modern Library College Edition.

Beebe, S., & Beebe, S. (1994). *Public speaking: An audience centered approach* (2nd ed.). Englewood Cliffs, NJ: Prentice Hall.

PART THREE

Learning from Groups

CHAPTER 16

A Primer on Interpersonal Skills

Merikay Kimball
Psychotherapist in Private Practice

Friendly Reminders

❑ Read to comprehend: previews, summarize, take notes, mark, review. Note that Figure 16.1 is a type of concept map to aid remembering.

❑ Check your level of intrinsic motivation; relate Chapter 16 concepts to your short-term, intermediate, and long-range goals.

❑ *You* choose a reminder.

"The spoken word belongs half to the one who speaks and half to the one who hears."

—Anonymous

Group living and learning starts early for most of us. We begin life as a member of a family learning to interact according to the communication rules of our parents. These rules continue to be refined and defined by the many additional groups we join as we grow and develop.

It is no surprise that groups are an inescapable reality of the college experience. Whether you join a team, committee, residence-hall board, or study group, or are a student in class, or work with others in your job, you are part of a group. In these settings you are likely to be asked to solve problems, plan, debate, offer ideas, resolve conflicts, support, and interact within the group. In short, the groups you belong to are another classroom, another opportunity to learn how to learn. Your encounters with groups become infinitely easier when you understand the fundamental principles and tools for communicating.

In the previous chapter, you learned the fundamentals of communicating through a prepared speech. This chapter introduces you to concepts and skills that *empower* you to communicate *interpersonally* during those countless everyday occasions when you interact with others. From Chapters 17 and 18 you can gain insights and skills for operating successfully in the six common group settings you encounter in college: classrooms, study groups, residence situations, campus organizations, your job setting, and the college as a whole. Learning to become an effective member of a group is one of the most crucial learning-how-to-learn skills that marks an educated person.

Interpersonal Communications and the Communication Model

It has been said that you cannot *not* communicate. For example, when you enter a classroom for the first time, you begin receiving and sending messages, even when you are not speaking. You form impressions of your fellow classmates by the way they speak, act, and look. Similarly, their spoken and unspoken messages affect the way you think, feel, and behave. We can understand the process of interpersonal communication by referring to the communication model described in Chapter 15.

Figure 16.1 represents this model as it applies to interpersonal communication. The most important point to note about Figure 16.1, and a major difference between public speaking and interpersonal communication, is that interpersonal communication is an *interactive* (back and forth) process between a sender and a receiver. The message of the sender is carried verbally and nonverbally. The receiver, in turn, uses feedback (also verbal and nonverbal) not only to complete the communication loop, but also to clarify and/or confirm the speaker's words. Because communication is interactive, ultimately both sender and receiver engage in message sending and feedback as they interact.

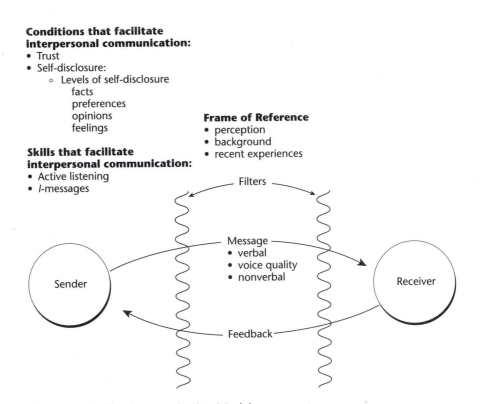

Conditions that facilitate interpersonal communication:
• Trust
• Self-disclosure:
    ○ Levels of self-disclosure
        facts
        preferences
        opinions
        feelings

Frame of Reference
• perception
• background
• recent experiences

Skills that facilitate interpersonal communication:
• Active listening
• *I*-messages

Filters

Message
• verbal
• voice quality
• nonverbal

Sender

Receiver

Feedback

Figure 16.1 The Communication Model

The Sender

Every communication contains information. You, the sender, may want to tell another student about an assignment given when he was sick or out of town, or you may express your heartfelt feelings about the death of a loved one. Whether you disclose facts or feelings, your message contains information that defines your relationship, information that is transmitted through your spoken words, voice quality, and nonverbal cues that you emit. Let's examine the role of these three message characteristics.

❏ Spoken Words: The Verbal Component

The particular words and phrases you choose contribute significantly to the *meaning* of your message. Meanings may denote or connote. The *denotative* meaning of a word is the accepted or dictionary definition, the objective description of the word. The *connotative* meaning is based on your personal or subjective experience with the word. Connotations may reflect, for example, gender-, job-, family-, or ethnic-related issues or emotional reactions to past experiences.

For instance, the word *soldier* denotes a person who serves in an army. Until the 1991 Gulf War, *soldier* generally connoted men only, even though women had served for several decades. Because women fought, died, and were captured during the Gulf War, the term *soldier* now connotes men and women. Similarly, *homemaker* denotes a person who cares for or manages a home. In past decades *homemaker* connoted a housewife; now the term includes men. In short, words are symbols for people, places, and things that you experience in your daily life. How individuals "think" about words, denotatively or connotatively, explains the variety of meanings that group members may have for a particular word as a symbol.

How do the denotative and connotative meanings of words apply to the college setting? Consider the following typical situation. At your study group meeting, someone mentions the name of your instructor. Mike raves about the teacher's stimulating lectures and praises his ability to present endless options for exploration. Karin is less enthusiastic; she complains that the instructor is too abstract and skips around rather than lectures sequentially. Finally, Martha, a re-entry adult attempting to balance college and job demands, expresses frustration with her inability to negotiate time away from class for job-related travel. As a student in the same class, you are faced with the task of sorting through the connotative meanings that have been assigned this instructor.

Similarly, ask a group of freshmen their attitudes toward taking a required science course (or any specific subject) and the responses are likely to range from excitement to horror. Their past experiences with a subject that denotes a specific body of information determine the connotation they assign to words.

The following exercise will show you how to distinguish between denotative and connotative meanings. Your attitudes are partially determined by your ability to distinguish denotations from connotations. Consider the different meanings you would assign to the following terms. When you think about the connotation of a term below, *define* and reflect on its meaning based on your experiences; don't simply write down the first word that comes to mind.

The term(s):	denotes	but connotes
final exam	_____	_____
cultural events	_____	_____
a relationship	_____	_____
campus security	_____	_____
pledge week	_____	_____
quiet time	_____	_____
education	_____	_____
dean of students	_____	_____
math	_____	_____
party	_____	_____
alone	_____	_____

Are there differences between the denotative and connotative meanings of these terms? If so, how do you account for these differences?

❏ Voice Quality

Your voice quality delivers the message. It provides emotional "color" and, like marking an important passage in a textbook, voice characteristics "underline" your words. Similarly, your articulation (go ahead, look it up), fluency, and rate of speaking can tell the listener about your emotional state, educational level, ethnic background, and, sometimes, personality traits.

The impact of your voice can be considerable. Words delivered in a voice that trembles communicate far different meanings from words spoken with firmness. Words spoken rapidly in a high pitch are connotatively different from words spoken calmly and slowly.

Try to become aware of your voice qualities as you speak to others. If possible, record (video or audio) a conversation. When you play back the tape, listen for the characteristics of voice quality in your own and your peers' statements.

❏ Nonverbal Communication

What is not said, but communicated nonverbally, can be as important as your words. According to some experts, about 80% of the message in interpersonal communication is carried nonverbally. What you wear (appearance), how you stand (posture), and your facial expression have an impact on your message.

When members of a group dynamics class were asked for their first impressions of fellow students, they reported appearance as the most important factor. In an end-of-semester activity designed to compare first impressions of a person with actual experience, one student humorously reported mistaking a fellow student for the instructor on the first day because she was dressed in a suit and wore high heels! On the other hand, the instructor was mistaken for a student because she dressed more casually in slacks and sweater. As such instances are common on campus and in some work settings, it pays to study the dress habits of the group you are joining.

Posture can regulate the flow of communication. A case in point, Baird and Schubert (1974) report that leaders give more positive head nods and use more gestures than nonleaders. Generally, uncrossed arms and legs, unbuttoned coats or jackets, and general openness in posture signal a relaxed communication style. Students who slouch in their chairs with folded arms and eyes fixed on the classroom clock communicate a message that is very different from those who sit upright, take notes, and maintain eye contact with the instructor. Many teachers infer the specific attitudes and motives of their students by observing posture; so do employers, friends, and loved ones.

Facial expression communicates feelings and attitudes. For example, Dale Leathers's research suggests that the face can communicate evaluative judgments through pleasant or unpleasant expressions (Leathers, 1976). The face can send messages about our level of interest in a conversation. Facial expression can inform us about the amount of control a person has over his feelings. Finally, our eyes and mouth often communicate feelings that influence the receiver's perception of our message.

Take time to observe the influence of appearance, facial expression, and posture on messages communicated by your professors, in television shows, films, or plays. Better yet, enroll in an acting course if those aspects of communication interest you. However, remember the warning given in Chapter 9, to resist simplistic interpretations to nonverbal cues.

The Receiver

Despite your efforts to choose words carefully, speak clearly, and support them with appropriate nonverbal behaviors, the message you send often is not the message received. Your words, voice characteristics, and nonverbal messages are *filtered* through the perceptions, background, and recent experiences of the listener. Together these interrelated factors form the receiver's *frame of reference.* The message-filtering system is represented in Figure 16.1 by the vertical wavy lines. Note in the figure that the sender also filters the message through his frame of reference.

❏ Frame of Reference

Perception refers to the way you organize, interpret, and evaluate your sensory experiences. Perception is a highly selective process: We select-in information that we want to hear and we select-out less important or threatening information. Perception is influenced by our past (background) and recent experiences with the person, object, or subject.

For example, if you attend a talk about drug problems, your judgment about the speaker and the message is influenced by your frame of reference for "drug problems." Your frame of reference will include selective perceptions about the topic, which are, in turn, dependent on your background experiences. If you grew up in an environment characterized by heavy drug usage, you will attach a different meaning to the phrase *drug problem* than someone who grew up in a drug-free environment.

Your perceptions of drug problems will also depend on your recent experiences with articles you read, drug users you know, and your own experiences (or lack of experiences) with drugs. If 30 persons hear the talk, there will be 30 different (from slightly to radically different) frames of references—we *are* unique.

Similarly, the frame of reference you bring to a class discussion, a club meeting, your job, a hallway conversation, or any other group event is likely to differ, at least a little, from your peers. No wonder it is sometimes said that meanings are in people, not in words. According to one anonymous source, "clear communication grows out of a meeting of minds, instead of just an exchange of words."

When individuals meet over a period of time, a group frame of reference often develops. People who frequently share experiences develop an overlap of experience. The sharing allows group members to develop similar meanings when they communicate. A group frame of reference may develop in any group, be it athletic teams, clubs, support groups, roommates, or fellow employees.

Feedback: The Corrective Factor

But people do not always agree. Differences in perception inevitably occur during interactive communication that often lead to conflict. These differences are best combated through the *feedback* process, which is represented by the bottom arrow in Figure 16.1. As listener (receiver), you can control a speaker's (sender's) subsequent messages by correcting or clarifying it. Your feedback completes the message loop and provides the sender an opportunity to restate or clarify his or her remarks, if they were distorted by your frame of reference.

You have seen the term *feedback* used so often throughout this book that its meanings should be clarified. In Chapter 3, "Setting and Monitoring Goals," you learned that *obtaining feedback* was an essential step to reaching your goals; it helps you monitor your progress. In Chapter 6, "G.O.: Get Organized," two methods of obtaining feedback were described and recommended: self-contracting and journal writing. In Chapter 13, "Evaluation and Test-taking Tips," you were advised to obtain feedback about your exams in order to improve. In the development of interpersonal skills, feedback provides the speaker with a "reading" (measurement) about her message and behavior. Through feedback we can learn to see ourselves as others see us.

Feedback is a term borrowed from technology. For example, early rockets sent signals back from space to a steering mechanism that monitored those signals and adjusted the course of the rocket. Similarly, members of a group may be viewed as a steering mechanism sending signals to individual members that enable them to determine whether their communication is "on target" or requires adjustment.

When you provide feedback to another person, you are engaged in a verbal and nonverbal process that lets that person know what you have observed or inferred about his or her message and behavior. Your method of delivering that feedback is especially important because you want to minimize defensiveness. If an individual cannot accept your message because he is defensive, the feedback is useless. Feedback must be provided so that the person receiving it can "hear" or understand it objectively (and with minimal distortion), then choose to use or not use the feedback.

Two Skills for Interpersonal Communication

As Figure 16.1 indicates, you enter the communication process with an option to speak (to share facts, preferences, opinions, and feelings), as well as the option to listen and respond to the information shared. Your skills in each option determine your level of comfort and effectiveness in the group. The goal of this section is to introduce you to two major skills or tools of interpersonal communication: *I*-messages and active listening, skills you can use for message sending and feedback.

I-Messages versus *You*-Messages

The words you choose and the manner in which you deliver them influence how people respond. They affect the climate of trust and self-disclosure in your group. Imagine for a minute that a member of your class continually interrupts when you attempt to speak.

It would be easy to lash out and put the person in his place with an emphatic *you*-message: "You think you are the only one who knows anything! Why don't you give some of the rest of us a chance to speak?" If you lashed out, he would feel attacked; he might respond defensively. Messages that begin with the word *you* normally place the listener on alert. *You*-messages produce defensive comments especially if they precede words such as *always* and *never* ("You always . . ." or "You never . . .").

So how do you respond to the classmate who interrupts frequently? Clearly he annoys you and monopolizes the group interaction. How can you respond in a way that expresses what you want to say while minimizing the likelihood of a defensive comment? Communication experts believe that substituting the word *I* for the word *you* often resolves the problem. When you say "I" you assume responsibility for *your* feelings, wants, and needs and no one else's. There are three parts to an *I*-message:

- how you feel
- what has happened (the specific behavior of the other person)
- how that behavior affects you specifically

Following is an example of how you might address the interrupter in the preceding example:

"I FEEL irritated [your feeling] WHEN YOU interrupt me [the specific behavior] BECAUSE I cannot finish my sentence [its specific effect on you]."

Note that it is appropriate to start an *I*-message with either the *feeling* or the *behavior*. For example, you could just as easily have said, "When you interrupt me, I feel irritated, because I cannot finish my sentence."

Like any skill, responding with *I*-messages requires practice. Spend a few minutes now and practice changing *you*-messages to *I*-messages by completing the exercise below.

Changing *You*-Messages to *I*-Messages

Rewrite the following *you*-messages as *I*-messages using the three-part format described previously: I FEEL . . . [your feeling] WHEN YOU . . . [specific behavior] BECAUSE . . . [its effect].

1. "You never listen to me!"

2. "Why can't you ever meet me on time?"

3. "You're acting like a baby."

4. "You drive me crazy!"

5. "All you think about is yourself."

6. "You make me so angry!"

7. Enter the *you*-message that *you* use most often and rewrite it to an *I*-message:
   "You" . . .

Now compare your first six statements with suggested answers at the end of this chapter.

Become aware of those emotion-arousing occasions when *you*-messages want to burst forth from your mouth. Be patient with yourself, but be persistent as you attempt to substitute *I*-messages for *you*-messages. Remember, you are learning a *skill* and skill building demands patience, practice, and persistence.

I-messages have several advantages.

1. *I*-messages reduce defensiveness because they do not contain evaluations or putdowns. Labels such as *irresponsible, lazy,* and *poor attitude* are eliminated when we use *I*-messages.

2. *I*-messages encourage you to be honest with your feelings and to drop the masks that you may be hiding behind.

3. *I*-messages help you identify the behavior of the person to whom you are speaking and the consequences that behavior has on you.

4. When spoken correctly, *I*-messages invite the listener to *explore* his or her behavior; *I*-messages do not demand change.

5. *I*-messages define the limits we place on the other person, such as, "I will not continue being interrupted."

Think of *I*-messages as assertiveness—standing up for yourself. Assertiveness has several advantages. First, an assertive person steers a middle course between doing nothing (passivity) and doing too much (aggressiveness). Second, an assertive individual communicates in a way that respects the rights of everyone in the group. Finally, an assertive person is one who acts, but in a responsible manner.

Active Listening: Listening to Understand

How you listen and what you choose to hear also affect the communication process. Listening as a member of a group differs from listening as a student in a lecture class. As a group member you do not listen to take notes or to receive a grade. Instead, you seek to *understand* the speaker's message so that information can be exchanged, problems solved, plans developed, or support rendered.

Unfortunately, listening to understand someone is sometimes a low priority. Why is this so? Either we do not know how to listen (as indicated in Chapter 9) or we are not motivated at a particular time. Furthermore, as members of a group we bring differing values, viewpoints, and opinions to any group experience.

❏ Listening to Yourself Lets You Listen to Others

The emotional and intellectual barriers discussed in Chapter 9 also create barriers to active listening. When listening is most necessary, it is often most difficult to put aside our own concerns and be understanding! For instance, when a teacher explains why your paper received a D, you may be so controlled by your emotions that you do not listen to the critique. When the hall resident assistant explains that your radio is much too loud, you may become so angry at being criticized that you fail to listen to the warning. What can you do when you become defensive or resentful of the views of the speaker? Stop listening to the speaker and start listening to yourself, as the case of Barbara illustrates.

Barbara joined a group actively involved in exploring ways to address the rise of acquaintance rape on campus. At one meeting she felt herself becoming angry and defensive as she listened to Dan. Dan was questioning the validity of some victims' accusations and wondered whether the rights of the accused had also been violated. Angrily, Barbara claimed that Dan was attempting to minimize the problem by "protecting" the rights of men, when everyone in the group knew that men were the problem.

Angered by this outburst, Dan left the meeting immediately. However, with the help of another group member, Barbara was able to *step back* from this exchange. She began to understand the meaning of this episode for her and why she had been unable to listen actively. *Listening to herself* enabled Barbara to understand that her angry response had much to do with the fact that her sister had been date raped on another college campus. The anger Barbara expressed toward Dan was really linked to the fact that her sister's attacker was never prosecuted.

As this example illustrates, listening to one's self is often a prerequisite to listening to others. Barbara's experience with date rape had triggered feelings that blocked her attempts to listen with understanding. Had she been able to listen to herself first and share her feelings with Dan and other group members, the discussion would not have ended prematurely.

As you learn how to listen actively, recognize that this skill is limited by your ability to listen to yourself. If Barbara had been able to listen actively instead of defensively, she would have tried to grasp the facts and feelings contained in Dan's message. As the listener, she would have attempted to put herself in Dan's place, trying to share his feelings. As an active listener, she would have responded in a way that let Dan know that she appreciated both the feeling and content contained in his message.

❏ Active-listening Responses

Your options for active listening are more varied than *I*-messages. However, the focus of an active-listening response includes the feeling ("You FEEL . . .") and content ("BECAUSE . . .") components of the message. Returning to the example above, Barbara would demonstrate active listening to Dan by saying, "It sounds like YOU FEEL resentful BECAUSE you believe men are often blamed unfairly in date-rape cases."

Verbal efforts to listen actively are aimed at *paraphrasing* the speaker's message. They go beyond the feeling and content components by using phrases that keep the communications options open for the person speaking.

- "It sounds like you are saying . . ."

- "I'm wondering if you mean . . ."

- "In other words . . ."

- "Tell me more about . . ."

Avoid closed-end questions that begin with phrases such as "Did he . . .?", "Should you . . .?", "Could it be . . .?", "Have you . . .?", "Are . . .?", and "Is . . .?" Closed-end questions *demand* a yes or no answer from the receiver.

At the nonverbal level you can give cues to the speaker that show you are attempting to listen actively. Referred to as *attending behaviors,* these cues include

- sitting or standing directly opposite the person speaking

- establishing eye contact

- leaning slightly forward to convey interest

- maintaining a relaxed posture

❏ The Active-listening Attitude

Active listening is a skill that communicates your acceptance of the speaker's remarks and increases interpersonal trust among group members. Your verbal and nonverbal efforts are helped further by the attitudes you bring to your active-listening efforts.

1. You must want to hear what the person has to say. This means that you are willing to take the time to listen. If you do not have sufficient time or motivation when the issue is first mentioned, schedule time to discuss it.

2. You must be able to accept the person, no matter how much the opinions, values, and feelings expressed differ from your own. To "accept" means that you acknowledge that he is entitled to his own views; acceptance does not imply agreement with those views. An attitude of acceptance takes time to develop and involves giving up your *you shoulds.*

3. As a corollary (go ahead, look up the definition) to the previous remark, remember that your goal is to understand, not judge!

Giving Feedback with *I*-Messages

You will be pleased to know that when you want to give a member of your group feedback, you can rely on *I*-messages and active listening to accomplish this task. Because *I*-messages focus on the behavior of the other person, you can remain objective as you feed back your reactions.

For example, Tom continually arrives late for a student government meeting and disrupts the committee reports. You begin to speak when he enters the room, drops his notebook, and tries to slide quietly into his chair. You may be inclined to shoot him a look that nonverbally communicates your displeasure or verbally label him as rude! However, you know that he will have a better chance of changing his behavior with feedback that does not place him on the defensive. You communicate an *I*-message to Tom: "Tom, I really FEEL annoyed when you continually show up late for our meeting BECAUSE I feel that what I have to say is unimportant to you." By providing feedback that focuses on his behavior—that is, " . . .when you continually show up late . . ."—you have identified a specific behavior that can be changed.

Giving Feedback with Active Listening

Active listening provides the speaker with feedback because, when used properly, it expresses your understanding of the speaker's words. When you translate what you hear into your own words and then feed it back to the speaker, you are engaged in a *mutual-feedback* process. The speaker either accepts or corrects what you paraphrased (fed back).

Remember, learning when and how to use *I*-messages and active listening is a complex skill. Your first attempts are usually clumsy and riddled with mistakes. With practice, you receive the feedback from yourself and others that leads to proficiency and confidence. To help you gain that confidence, perform the exercises included in Action-Oriented Thought Starters at the end of the chapter.

Conditions for Developing Interpersonal Communication

The communication model is a framework for understanding the give-and-take of human interaction. What actually happens between two people, however, depends to a large extent on two conditions or factors in the psychological climate of the situation: self-disclosure and trust. Like the sunlight and moisture required for the growth of plant life, self-disclosure and trust are the nutrients for interactive communication. Self-disclosure influences the growth of trust; trust regulates the level of self-disclosure.

Self-disclosure

The level of self-disclosure (the willingness to reveal one's self to another) between two people may range from superficial to intimate. Research indicates that self-disclosure moves through four levels as individuals get to know each other; Figure 16.1 depicts these levels as characteristics of the sender. When you become acquainted with someone, you are likely to begin by disclosing *facts,* then move on to disclosing *preferences* and *opinions,* and, finally, your *feelings.* All four levels could be expressed on one occasion or spread across several occasions. At the fact level, you share your name and other demographic information. Shared preferences include the persons, places, and things that you like and dislike. Your opinions reflect your beliefs, impressions, and evaluations. Finally, your feelings serve to deepen the self-disclosure process and add the emotional component to the communication.

Personal feelings shared at the getting-acquainted phase of group development often cause discomfort for group members. For example, you have joined a study group for your accounting class. On the day of the first meeting, the last member of your group arrives late, appears distraught, and launches into a detailed description of a fight she had with her boyfriend. Her communication focuses on the feeling level and leaves many members of the group feeling awkward and uncertain how to respond. The strong feeling expression of one group member is inappropriate and premature. It might take several meetings of the study group before group members feel comfortable about responding to such feelings.

❏ Guidelines for Self-disclosure

Ask yourself the following questions as guidelines for self-disclosure. Then determine an appropriate level for you individually or as a group member.

- Is the receiver of your message important to you? In other words, is this an ongoing relationship that justifies deeper levels of self-disclosure?

- Is the amount and level of self-disclosure appropriate? High levels of risk cause anxiety; low levels of risk are not stimulating.

- Is the risk relevant to the situation at hand?

- Is the self-disclosure reciprocated by the other person?

If you can answer yes to all or nearly all these questions, higher levels of self-disclosure may be appropriate.

Trust

Trust is the second condition that nurtures interactive communication. The development of trust depends on the balance and reciprocation of self-disclosure between receiver and sender. Group members who sit silently and offer little to the communication effort inhibit the flow of conversation. Because they fail to disclose at any level, they are treated with suspicion by other members. It is difficult to know where they stand in the group or where the group stands with them.

Equally detrimental to nurturing trust in a group are those who attempt to evaluate, control, or manipulate others. Such behaviors produce defensiveness and, therefore, an imbalance of self-disclosure in group members.

As a case in point, a student fund-raising group for the child-care department of a community college met to brainstorm ideas that would accomplish their goal. Brainstorming is a problem-solving technique in which creative ideas are offered freely and judgment about their merits is withheld until all ideas are identified. The fund-raising ideas were barely presented before Jane, a longtime member, began to criticize them. Disclosures by other group members declined and enthusiasm for the project quickly dwindled until the group leader took Jane aside. The leader explained to Jane that her premature judgments had created defensiveness among other members and all but shut down its cooperative efforts.

❏ Guidelines for Creating Self-disclosure and Trust

Self-disclosure and trust tend to flourish in groups that work hard to create a communication climate that supports open discussion while minimizing defensiveness. The following guidelines facilitate a supportive climate for self-disclosure and trust in a group.

1. Speak only for yourself; you do not *know* how others think or feel until you ask them. For instance, if you tell me why I said something or why I feel a certain way, I will feel defensive because you are attempting to speak for me.

2. Make sure that you know what the other person means, denotatively and connotatively, before agreeing or disagreeing. Ask for an explanation or clarification if you are uncertain.

3. Do not ignore any communications from group members that are contributed seriously. If members speak, they need to know the effect of their remarks on other members in the group. If you ignore their remarks, they will wonder whether they have been heard or understood.

In short, successful interpersonal communication requires individuals to create and nurture a climate that supports self-disclosure and mutual trust.

Connecting Interpersonal Skills to Your Career and Life

Since the first edition of *Learning Skills for College and Career* was published, the world of work has changed dramatically. Downsizing (layoffs), restructuring, and reorganization have narrowed the job market and created stiff competition for first-time job seekers. However, graduates with good communication skills often have an edge to landing a job.

The job interview is often the first place where your communication skills are under scrutiny. In this arena, your nonverbal skills are as important as the spoken word. Your appearance—how you dress, how you walk, your eye contact and handshake—all tell the potential employer something about your confidence and competence. A brief review of attending behaviors (p. 335) should prepare you for this all-important aspect of job search. Your verbal communication skills are also being assessed, in person and on the phone. They reflect your ability to clearly convey your expertise, as well as listen to and understand what a potential employer might be looking for in the job interview. Before you interview for a job, even that unexciting part-time job you desperately need to pay bills, contact your college's career planning office for advice.

If you think that getting hired is a challenge, staying hired can be equally challenging. As Box 16.1 shows, staying hired depends on your expertise and your ability to communicate it, your initiative, and actively soliciting feedback about your job performance.

Life after college holds several ongoing options for operating in groups. You may choose to focus your energy on your career,

Box 16.1

Staying Hired: Expertise, Communication Skills, Initiative, and Feedback

Julie learned that her job in customer service was soon to be eliminated because of cutbacks. She looked around her company and identified an area that could use her people-helping skills. Although no formal opening existed in that department, Julie began volunteering her time in that area and soon was seen as a valued contributor. It was no surprise, therefore, when she presented her boss with a proposal to hire her in a position in that area. She was so persuasive that he accepted it! Julie's clear knowledge of what she does well, coupled with her ability to communicate it and her initiative, did much to ensure her staying hired.

Actively soliciting feedback on your job performance is another way to strengthen job security. In many ways, it is no different from checking in with a professor to see how you are doing academically. John worked for a company that had a reputation for putting off performance evaluation interviews. Because he was new to the organization and anxious to know how he was doing, John actively solicited the feedback he needed and was pleased to find that for the most part, he was meeting performance expectations. Remember, feedback is the corrective factor (pp. 329–330). It helps us see ourselves as others see us.

Although there are no guarantees of staying hired, bringing "polished" communication skills to the job market will clearly give you an edge.

The person with solid communication skills will also be able to manage other challenges produced by the changing workplace. In *Working Scared: Achieving Success in Trying Times* (1993), consultants Kenneth Wexley and Stanley Siverman describe several challenges contemporary workers must meet in order to keep their jobs. Those challenges include

- handling heavier workloads with less supervision in downsized organizations
- performing your job responsibilities, not as an individual, but as a member of a team, and subsequently being paid for what the team produces
- continually increasing the quality of your work
- operating in an international environment
- functioning in an increasingly diverse workforce

Each challenge requires the ability to communicate effectively with others in a work environment. In short, communication skills, along with critical-thinking skills and knowledge, are *imperative* to success.

marriage, or civic involvement. Whatever your choice or combination of choices, you will be involved in relationships where you have *continual* need for practicing the communication skills described above.

Active listening is as important when responding to the complaints of an employee as it is when resolving a squabble between two children.

I-messages are as valuable when dealing with a friend who let you down as they are in an exchange with a salesperson who shortchanged you. Feedback skills are as important in job performance evaluations as they are when communicating with your spouse about household responsibilities.

Life is about relationships. Daily you engage in interpersonal communications as they were represented in the communications model. Whether you are the sender or the receiver, you have the opportunity to speak and listen in all relationship-oriented situations you enter. Your skills in speaking and listening determine your success and satisfaction in these interactions. The French proverb that opened this chapter is true: "The spoken word belongs half to the one who speaks and half to the one who hears."

Action-Oriented Thought Starters

1. Choose a partner from one of the groups you belong to. Sit back to back. Designate one person as the speaker and the other as the listener.

   a. As speaker, choose an issue or concern of importance to you. Share that topic with the listener for about 5 minutes. As listener, attempt to listen actively to the speaker using the guidelines for responding found in the active-listening section.

   b. After the 5-minute period ends, face your partner and describe how it felt to listen without being able to see facial expressions or posture. Which nonverbal cues did you miss the most?

   c. Switch roles as speaker and listener and repeat the process.

2. Choose one of the groups you belong to and observe the use of *you*-messages and *I*-messages.

   a. If possible, count the frequency of both kinds of messages and calculate the proportion (percentage) of each. For example, if

20 messages were communicated during a half-hour period, 14 *you*-messages and 6 *I*-messages, the percentages of each type of message would be 70% and 30%, respectively.

b. What effect did each type of message have on the group discussion?

c. Share your observations with the group and solicit their feedback.

3. This chapter identified two contrasting styles of listening: active listening and defensive listening. Write entries in a journal for one or two weeks that describe which styles are used most and by whom in your interpersonal relationships.

a. To what extent are the listening styles influenced by the person or persons involved, the subject discussed, or your mood?

b. What were the consequences of using defensive listening?

c. What were the consequences of using active listening?

Suggested Answers to "Changing *You*-Messages to *I*-Messages"

1. "You never listen to me!"

I feel ignored when you read the newspaper while I talk to you, because I wonder if I'm important to you.

2. "Why can't you ever meet me on time?"

When you don't show up on time, I feel annoyed because I've changed my schedule to make sure I meet you at the time I thought we agreed to.

3. "You're acting like a baby."

I feel frustrated when you are unwilling to try any of my suggestions, because I'm running out of ideas.

4. "You drive me crazy!"

When you say one thing one moment and something different the next, I feel really frustrated because I'm not sure what you actually mean.

5. "All you think about is yourself."

   I feel angry when you rarely ask how I feel, because I thought I was important to you.

6. "You make me so angry!"

   When you argue with me about everything, I feel angry because I thought and hoped we could work something out.

References and Recommended Readings

Adler, R. B., & Towne, N. (1987). *Looking out/looking in* (5th ed.). New York: Holt, Rinehart, and Winston.

Baird, J. E., & Schubert, A. (1974). Nonverbal behavior and leadership emergence in task-oriented and informal group discussion. Paper presented at the meeting of the International Communications Association, New Orleans, LA.

Egan, G. (1977). *You and me: The skills of communicating and relating to others.* Pacific Grove, CA: Brooks/Cole.

Gabor, D. (1994). *Speaking your mind in 101 difficult situations.* New York: Simon & Schuster.

Hanna, M. S., Hantz, A. M., & Wilson, G. L. (1989). *Interpersonal growth through communication* (2nd ed.). Dubuque, IA: Wm. C. Brown.

Hanna, M. S., & Wilson, G. L. (1990). *Groups in context: Leadership and participation in small groups* (2nd ed.). New York: McGraw-Hill.

Leathers, D. G. (1976). *Nonverbal communication systems.* Boston: Allyn and Bacon.

Phelps, S., & Austin, N. (1987). *The assertive woman: A new look.* San Luis Obispo, CA: Impact Publishers.

Wexley, K. N., & Silverman, S. P. (1993). *Working scared: Achieving success in trying times.* San Francisco, CA: Jossey-Bass.

CHAPTER 17

Learning in Class and Study Groups

Friendly Reminders

❏ As you read this chapter, think about the increasing role that peers have in your cognitive development.

❏ Apply concepts of interpersonal communication to being a participant in small groups.

❏ *You* choose a friendly reminder.

"No man is an island entire of itself; every man is a piece of the continent."
—John Donne (1572–1631),
English poet

The previous chapter demonstrated that learning strategies for college and career include not only self-management (Part One of this book) and study skills (Part Two) but also the ability to communicate. No one is an island—especially in college. Unless you are among those whose postsecondary education is obtained primarily through television courses or correspondence, you are a member of at least one interacting group—the classroom group. Your introductory knowledge of interpersonal communication skills has prepared you for concepts that you can use in your class and study groups, the two situations discussed in this chapter. Chapter 18 will focus on other group settings such as campus organizations, the workplace, your residence situation, and the college as a whole. Knowing how to function effectively in these groups builds knowledge, confidence, and skills that make life easier for you now and in your career.

The Class Group

If you are asked what you learn in class, you are likely to name such disciplines as anthropology, biology, chemistry, and (onward through the academic alphabet) zoology. But there is more happening in class than a teacher imparting information about anthropology or zoology. Whether courses are lively or dull, the classroom is a *dynamic* situation. That is, classes reflect a continuing intellectual, social, and emotional interaction among a group of individuals who agree to spend about 50 hours together during a 3- to 4-month period. A 4-year education may be viewed as a collection of *40 to 50 group experiences;* each course is a miniature education, a microcosm of diverse, interacting individuals.

Two dimensions of the interaction contribute significantly to how much you learn and your attitudes toward learning: communication patterns and your learning orientation. Communication patterns are controlled primarily by the instructor; the learning orientation is a characteristic of the student.

Patterns of Classroom Communication

Each of your courses has a characteristic pattern of communication between instructor and students. The pattern falls within a range represented in Figure 17.1, with teacher-centered communication at one end, student-centered communication at the other end, and combinations of the two patterns in between.

❑ Teacher-centered Communication

To borrow an analogy from Brazilian educator Paulo Freire, teacher-centered communication is like banking: The instructor deposits knowledge in the student's mind bank, and the student's role is to receive and save the knowledge for future use (Belenky, Clinchy, Goldberger, & Tarule, 1986). Teacher-centered communication occurs in courses where instructors must present very difficult or technical material, in large classes where interaction with students is difficult, and in situations where instructors believe that student input will not facilitate learning. Figure 17.1(a) depicts this pattern as one-way, from teacher to student. An extreme example of teacher-centered communication is a course in which the instructor lectures for the duration of the class, asks perfunctorily (go ahead, look up the definition) if there are questions (there are none), then leaves; students have no input. Teacher-centered communication enables the instructor to

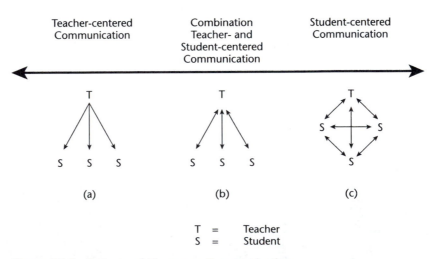

Figure 17.1   Patterns of Classroom Communication

present a considerable amount of information efficiently, but many students (and teachers) dislike the absence of student input and interaction.

❏ Student-centered Communication

Figure 17.1(c) shows that student-centered is opposite teacher-centered communication. This pattern occurs in classes where students are highly motivated and well prepared, understand the material in advance of class, and are encouraged by instructors to interact. In essence, student-teacher interaction is the primary *tool* for communicating subject matter. Seminars and honors courses, especially at the advanced level, are examples of the student-centered pattern. The pattern promotes a high amount of discussion, student expression, and satisfaction, although it usually results in covering less material.

❏ Combined Teacher- and Student-centered Communication

Between teacher- and student-centered communication patterns is a combination that reflects student collaboration or cooperation in the learning process. Figure 17.1(b) symbolizes two-way communication between student and teacher. Other examples where teacher- and student-centered communications are combined include

- After a teacher lectures on a specific topic for several minutes, he or she encourages students to comment or raise questions or forms small groups to discuss the material.

- The instructor presents a topic with continuous interaction by asking questions or eliciting student comments throughout class time.

- A lecture is followed by a problem-solving, laboratory, or demonstration period that involves students.

- The instructor lectures but gives assignments that require students to present reports to the class.

The combination patterns permit instructors to present the necessary information, and they enable students to participate during portions of class. Research indicates that students generally learn, remember, and enjoy class more in courses where they regularly contribute to the class meetings.

So, you say to yourself smugly, "If more teachers spent less time lecturing and more time letting me talk I would be a better student."

NOT NECESSARILY!

It's not that simple! Yes, professors are responsible for designing courses so students learn the content in a manner that stimulates their interest. Many instructors would argue persuasively that well-organized lectures are the best way to communicate knowledge and maintain student interest. Others would strongly argue that student-centered, collaborative learning is highly effective. The particular communication pattern a teacher chooses depends on several factors, including

- the material (some topics lend themselves to student involvement on a regular basis; others do not)

- the students' prior knowledge and preparation (you cannot discuss or apply what you do not understand)

- the instructor's teaching skills and style (most college teachers are not taught how to teach; they learn from experience and feedback)

- the amount and quality of *student participation* and collaboration

❏ Student Responsibility in the Teaching-learning Process

To what extent are students responsible for contributing to that group experience known as the college course? Consider the following situation. Professor Johnson designed her sophomore-level social-science course so that students would learn important concepts, theories, and research studies. Additionally, she planned for teacher-student interaction through question/answer sessions, small-group discussion, and assignments that enabled students to apply what they learn. Students would have to work hard in the course, but the professor designed it to cover the material, stimulate interest, *and* provide opportunities for students to become collaborators in the teaching-learning process.

Reading Assignment

On the first day of class, Professor Johnson asks her 30 students to perform a general reading of the material before each class so that they are prepared to ask and answer questions, participate in discussion, and relate the material to their experiences. She indicates clearly that student participation benefits the whole class, that participation is part of the final grade, and that tests will be based on the class meetings.

During the next two weeks, she observes that about ten students ask and answer questions, share experiences, or offer comments and ideas; she praises them appropriately for their contributions. To involve the remaining students, Professor Johnson announces in advance that she will choose students who have not spoken and solicit their opinions or ask questions that they should be able to answer. A few students respond well to her questions; many decline to participate. When she divides the class into small groups to discuss particular topics, some students make helpful comments; others say nothing or try to change the subject. Sometimes the classroom environment supports a high level of trust and deeper levels of self-disclosure; often it does not. Occasionally there is the sense of a group frame of reference emerging.

As the course progresses to midterm, the class begins to develop its "personality." Some students remain regular and thoughtful participants who *give* to the teaching-learning process. Others sit *passively* waiting to *receive* whatever it is they are supposed to know for an exam. Many students seem to be at the absolute level in Marcia Baxter Magolda's model of cognitive development. Some silent members of the class occasionally communicate hostility nonverbally to those who participate. Some regular participants become sensitive to the unfriendly stares or posture of persons who never contribute. Small-group discussions become productive only for students who prepare assignments and subsequently work together.

Although Professor Johnson tries to stimulate the silent students while acknowledging those who participate, the quality of the student-centered classroom activities is lowered by those who do not get involved. Toward the end of the term, a few of the active students have become so self-conscious about their participation (and high test grades), they become silent. Frustrated by the mixed success of her attempts to involve students, Professor Johnson spends more time lecturing and less time in student-centered activities. She has lost some of her enthusiasm. She realizes that it is much easier to lecture than to work collaboratively with students.

Does this situation sound familiar? It may. It characterizes too many college classrooms.

Do those students who contributed little or nothing to class share responsibility for the problems described? Most teachers and many students would quickly answer yes. Each term conscientious teachers design their courses to increase student involvement. Each term "take-charge" students work to become *active* learners. Each term *passive*

Box 17.1

How Students and Teachers Irritate Each Other

It seems inevitable that people who interact regularly will sooner or later annoy each other. Psychologist Drew Appleby investigated how students and teachers irritate each other in a small college (Appleby, 1990).

What Irritates Teachers?

Sixty-three faculty members were asked by students to identify student behaviors that irritate teachers. Of the 30 different behaviors mentioned, 9 accounted for 77% of the faculty's responses. The 9 behaviors, classified as immature or inattentive, are shown below; the numbers in parentheses indicate how many times each behavior was mentioned.

Immature Behaviors
talking during class (35)
chewing gum, eating, or drinking noisily (17)
being late (16)
creating disturbances (10)

Inattentive Behaviors
sleeping during class (18)
cutting class (16)
acting bored or apathetic (16)
not paying attention (15)
being unprepared (13)

Appleby's study does not indicate the extent to which teachers communicate to students their exasperation with these bad habits. Remember, though, forewarned is forearmed! Many instructors do not express their irritation openly, so think twice before you shove that gum in your mouth as you enter the classroom.

What Irritates Students?

Turnabout is fair play. When 215 students in the same college were asked by other students to name three irritating teacher behaviors, 91% of their responses fell into the two categories below; the 9 most frequently mentioned behaviors are listed.

Communication Problems
presenting poor lectures (for example, being unprepared, speaking in a monotone, digressing, speaking too fast, rambling, repeating too often, being unorganized) (147)
not explaining concepts (14)

Unresponsiveness to Student Needs
keeping class beyond end of period (52)
arriving late for class (37)
showing partiality to favorite students (18)
demonstrating a condescending attitude toward students (17)
acting as if their class is the only one that students are taking (17)
indicating that their point of view is always correct (16)
embarrassing students in class (16)

Appleby observed that several annoying behaviors were often mentioned by both groups. For example, both teachers and students are irritated by late arrivals. Teachers don't want students to pack up their materials before class is over, and students don't want teachers to continue lecturing after the period ends. Neither teachers nor students are tolerant of the other cutting class, and neither appreciates the sight or sound of gum chewing, eating, or drinking noisily. Appleby believes that mutually irritating behaviors may reflect a causal relationship. That is, irritating student behaviors may lead to irritating teacher behaviors and vice versa. This study lends support to the idea that a college course is a group experience in which all participants share responsibility for its success.

students damage the quality of a group learning experience that was designed to enrich the teaching-learning process for everyone. Some students are quick to name familiar reasons for remaining quiet. Yes, there are uninspiring instructors who do not know how to teach effectively. Yes, there are obnoxious students who sometimes dominate classroom discussions with trivial or attention-getting comments. But you will encounter dull and obnoxious people throughout life. The truth is that *college students share with an instructor the responsibility for classroom learning in courses where student participation is expected.*

What keeps students from becoming active members (collaborators) in class?

First, most of us grow up conditioned by previous educational experiences and a dominating electronic mass media to be passive receivers of information. Shedding the protective cloak of passivity is a difficult and gradual process. Yet it can occur in courses where teachers attempt to involve students in the teaching-learning process.

Second, some college teachers (also conditioned by their earlier experiences) do not know how or do not try to teach collaboratively.

When the opportunity arises, what can you do to make a class an interactive group experience?

1. Recognize that each course is one of the 40 to 50 *group* experiences that constitute your formal academic instruction (the overt curriculum). You *can* learn far more than anthropology or zoology; you can learn the lifelong skill of how people function in groups. You will need that skill in today's team-oriented workplace.

2. Use the resources of group members. Your instructors are highly trained individuals with considerable knowledge and experience that goes well beyond the classroom and the campus. What you learn in class is often the tip of their iceberg of expertise. Try to understand *how* they think, value, feel, evaluate, interact, and use their knowledge. Similarly, listen carefully to peers. The diversity in cultural, racial, educational, socioeconomic, religious, and age backgrounds represented by your classmates may be a microcosm of global human experience. College classrooms may be the best or only exposure you get in life to such diversity. You do not have to agree with the views of your instructors and fellow students. However, to the extent that you listen to and try to understand their perspectives, you are better prepared to understand your world after college.

3. Provide thoughtful feedback. Although the instructor is the group leader who controls the class activities, students can influence

the teaching-learning process. Students are senders as well as receivers of information. If there are specific ways that students can participate more in class, discuss their potential with peers, then diplomatically solicit the opinion of your instructor outside of class. Good teachers are open to feedback.

Although end-of-course evaluation forms are administered too late to permit changes that affect you, your feedback may contribute to improvements in subsequent courses.

4. Participate. Prepare for class. Overcome shyness about speaking in public. Be willing to take the risk of asking and answering questions, sharing observations and experiences, and of being wrong sometimes. Be able to rebound when you are criticized. Resist the negative influence of apathetic classmates. Become an active learner.

5. Remember that passivity cannot direct you to your goals. The diploma you receive on graduation day is a piece of paper. It has no magic power to transform you from a passive student into an active, take-charge individual who seeks professional and personal success. Passivity is not a marketable trait!

Learning Orientation

The communication pattern is an important but not the only factor that influences the quality of your classroom experiences. Your orientation to learning is another important determinant.

Throughout life you have learned to become effective by following certain rules and strategies. Some strategies produce success and others do not. You approach new situations using methods that have worked in the past.

David Kolb (1984) believes that learning occurs in a four-stage cycle of experiential learning as diagrammed in Figure 17.2. As you read about this process, recall a specific task or idea that you recently learned, such as a new computer program, driving a stick-shift automobile, or understanding your college's registration regulations. Determine the role each of Kolb's four stages played in mastering the new information or skill. According to Kolb, learning begins with direct, *concrete experience* of the task or idea to be learned (e.g., executing a computer command, driving a stick-shift car, reading the handbook of academic regulations).

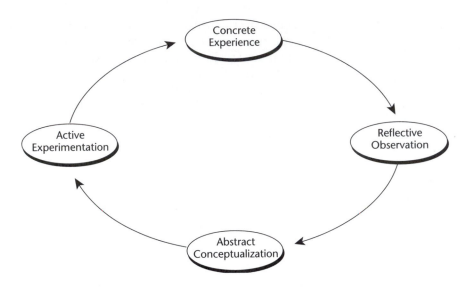

Figure 17.2 David Kolb's Experiential Learning Cycle

In the second stage you stop and think about what you are doing, especially if the action did not accomplish its purpose. For example, if you tried unsuccessfully to save the computer file, if moving the gear shift didn't cause the car to go in reverse, or if the regulation about dropping a class isn't clear, you are likely to stop and reflect (*reflective observation*) on your actions.

Next, you attempt to understand your actions in terms of a general principle (*abstract conceptualization*) that you can apply to similar situations. For instance, the principle underlying "Save" is that it is a "File" category of commands. Getting the car in reverse in a stick-shift automobile requires depressing the clutch pedal as you must do to shift into any gear. Completing a form is required to drop a class because the college must have all class changes (dropping and adding) in writing for record-keeping purposes.

Finally, you act (*active experimentation*) on the general principle (abstract conceptualization) you derived from thinking about (reflective observation) your original action (concrete experience). You click the "File" window to save the information you wrote, depress the clutch to shift into reverse, or complete the drop/add form to officially drop the class. The cycle of learning for that specific experience has been completed. You repeat the cycle with each new experience.

Kolb regards the four components of the experiential learning cycle as *modes* or *orientations* to learning. Your *learning orientation* refers to the ideas, strategies, and rules you use to deal with everyday problems such as the examples above, although you are seldom aware of your orientations. As a result of your past successes and failures, you tend to develop preferences (strengths) for some orientations and ignore others. Kolb believes that your preferences for and against particular orientations significantly affect how you learn.

What do Kolb's learning orientations have to do with classroom learning? Have you wondered why some courses or teachers are easier or more difficult than others? Are the differences due solely to subject matter or the personal characteristics of the instructor? Sometimes. However, *think about* (that's my reflective observation and abstract conceptualization taking charge!) the role that the differences and similarities in your learning orientations could play. If you thoroughly enjoy the hands-on, case study approach of your marketing course but get bored with the apparently unending discussions in your history course, your learning orientation, the teachers' learning orientations, and the assignments in each course could be very different. You may *want* to learn history as much as you *want to* learn marketing, but your orientation for marketing (active experimentation) may be much stronger than your orientation to discussing history (reflective observation).

How do the four learning orientations differ? The brief descriptions below distinguish among the four orientations.

Orientation 1: Concrete Experience

Persons preferring the concrete experience mode of learning tend to rely on their feelings, intuitions, hunches, and experiences (as opposed to reasoning and analysis) when they approach new situations. They are more concerned about the uniqueness of their present experience than about theories or abstract notions of how reality might be. They have an artistic, open-minded approach to life; they work well in unstructured situations. Finally, they are people oriented: They like, accept, work with, and learn from other people.

Orientation 2: Reflective Observation

Persons who prefer the reflective observation mode learn best by trying to understand or comprehend the subject. They are patient, impartial, thoughtful, and detached observers who usually see things from several perspectives. They rely on their own thoughts and opinions to form judgments.

Orientation 3: Abstract Conceptualization

The abstract conceptualization mode describes individuals who prefer to use logic, analysis, and reasoning instead of feeling or intuition. They like the planned, precise, and rigorous approach to problem solving that characterizes science.

Orientation 4: Active Experimentation

As the name suggests, individuals for whom the active experimentation mode dominates are practical, hardworking "doers" who have little time for reflection. They are willing to take risks, but they want to see the results of their work. Reflective observation is opposite of active experimentation, and concrete experience is opposite of abstract conceptualization.

Kolb's research combines the four orientations into various learning styles, the complexity of which is beyond the scope of this chapter. The descriptions of the four learning orientations are short and general; avoid making inferences beyond what you read. However, try to identify your preferred mode or modes of learning and how they may influence your ability to learn in each of your courses.

For instance, in which mode or modes are you the strongest? The weakest? Or is your preferred orientation a balance among the four modes? Could your success (or failure) in some courses be due in part to the match or mismatch between your learning orientation and that of the instructor? If you like the rigors of abstract thinking, precision, and analysis, you may perform well in courses where the teacher emphasizes these modes of thinking, whether the course is philosophy, physics, or literature. Similarly, if you are a strong "concrete thinker," your feeling, intuitive, and people-oriented modes could be liabilities in a science or math course.

Returning adult students may be especially affected by their learning orientations. If past experiences at home, on the job, or with pastimes have promoted development of one orientation at the expense of others, returning students may wish to choose courses that reinforce existing orientations or courses that shift their thinking to other orientations.

You will naturally seek courses and instructors that nurture your preferred learning orientations; such courses could be the anchor to your career. However, because life's experiences require continual change and adaptation, you should become competent in each orientation so that you can shift from one mode of learning to another when it becomes necessary. According to Marialla Svinicki and Nancy Dixon (1987), teachers use a variety of instructional activities, such as the following, to support the four learning orientations.

Concrete experience: fieldwork, simulations, data collection, observations, laboratory experiences, interviews, examples, reading primary sources, and problem sets.

Reflective observation: journals, logs, brainstorming, discussion, thought questions, and rhetorical questions.

Abstract conceptualization: lectures, analogies, papers, projects, and model building.

Active experimentation: homework, fieldwork, projects, simulations, case studies, and laboratory experiences.

In short, view these learning activities as *opportunities* to develop skills in their respective orientations.

Study Groups

Although most chapters in this book emphasize the development of individual self-management and study strategies, learning often occurs best in small group settings. Some instructors use small groups to generate discussion, solve problems, discuss cases, conduct research, or perform projects. Students often form groups to prepare for class, complete assignments, or study for exams. The next section offers insight and practical advice for learning in study groups.

Advantages and Disadvantages of Group Study

If properly conducted, study groups can have several advantages. Group study *can*

- enhance the motivation of its members through mutual support, encouragement, and monitoring

- encourage the sharing of different ideas, perspectives, and problem-solving approaches

- become an occasion for review and recitation of course material in preparation for tests

- become a forum for practicing group skills and serving as a member of a team

However, if study groups are not properly conducted, group study can degenerate into gossip, griping, or bull sessions. If members are poorly prepared, have inaccurate or incomplete information, avoid difficult topics, or discuss material superficially, group study creates the *illusion* of learning. Finally, excessive use of group study may foster a dependency relationship and a clique mentality.

How to Succeed in Group Study

The following guidelines enable you to structure your group study sessions for success. Follow them carefully but not rigidly. Be concerned about completing your task, but be sensitive to the members of your group. Your knowledge of the communication model and skills described in the previous chapter gives you an edge for conducting effective study sessions.

1. Consider carefully those with whom you are going to study. Before you agree to join or form a study group, try to determine your peers' academic proficiency and their attitudes toward attending class, taking notes, and preparing for tests. In short, ask yourself how much you are likely to learn from these individuals. Do not invite the "leech" (whether friend or roommate) who never studies but seeks to exploit the group's resources. Besides, a student who *hears* peers discuss material that is unfamiliar learns little or nothing.

2. Limit the size of your group to five or fewer members. Larger groups discourage participation by everyone; quiet members may contribute minimally. If several more peers want to join a study group, suggest that two groups be formed.

3. Discuss these guidelines before you begin the first meeting of your group. They offer a structure within which successful collaboration is possible.

4. Agree in advance that each member comes prepared to contribute. Research indicates that the overall quality of a group's efforts is the *average* of its individual contributions. In short, do not lower group productivity by coming unprepared.

5. Begin each meeting by clarifying the group's goals and agenda. For example, what is the specific purpose of the session? How long will it last? Approximately when will you take a break and for how long? What specific material will you discuss? Agreeing on goals and an agenda reduces misunderstandings and discourages digressions.

6. If the group agrees that a *leader* is desirable, elect a peer who is respected, has solid communication skills, and can monitor time, discourage digressions, follow the agenda, and still participate in the discussion.

7. Often, an "expert" emerges from a study group, someone who knows most or certain topics better than the other members. If an expert emerges, remember three points. First, an expert can quickly transform the role of "equal participants" to "teacher" and "students." Do you want that to occur very often? Having a peer serve as occasional tutor on certain topics can benefit the group. But when that peer assumes the role of teacher or tutor often, the equality of group members is reduced and the goals of group study change.

Second, ensure that the expert is truly expert. The adage of the blind leading the lame readily applies to group study. Be willing to question each other; ask for the source of the information that seems unclear or questionable. Finally, consider the motive of the expert. Is it based on altruism or self-aggrandizement (go ahead, look up the definition)?

8. Assign each person the role of critical thinker. It is easy for a cohesive group of individuals to become passive, complacent, and uncritical to maintain a friendly atmosphere. Recall from the previous chapter that a group framework emerges when individuals share similar perceptions and experiences. Sometimes a group framework can be harmful: Half-truths are willingly accepted and interpretations of key concepts go unquestioned.

Members can provide constructive criticism by directing comments to the person's statements, not to the person. Use active-listening responses such as "If I understand you correctly . . ." or "What you seem to be saying is . . . ." Use *I*-messages to communicate your feelings about specific remarks or behaviors that are not appropriate. Conversely, praise group members for insightful remarks.

9. Obtain feedback about the immediate and long-range effectiveness of the session. Immediate feedback involves spending the last few minutes of each session summarizing main points and gaining closure on your activities. How productive was the session? Was the time allotted sufficient? Was there a sense of equal participation? Are there topics that need further study either individually or by the group?

Good feelings after a study session do not necessarily translate into good grades. To evaluate the long-range impact of your group study, schedule a debriefing session soon after the instructor returns your exam or project. What did you do correctly and incorrectly? Reflect on past group sessions to ascertain the strengths and weaknesses of each. How could the group be more effective in the future? Compare grades. If all or most of you performed well, the value of group study speaks for itself. If the best of you obtained a mediocre grade, in comparison with students not in your group, you need to reevaluate the efforts of your study group. If you have difficulty making a study group succeed, consult staff in the learning assistance center or your teacher.

In summary, this chapter has extended the concept of interactive communication to classroom communication patterns, learning orientations, and group study. In Chapter 18 you will encounter additional group settings that can generate insights for learning in groups.

Connecting Groups to Your Career

By now you know that this section of the chapter will connect the relevance of learning in groups to careers. The three subjects described in this chapter are no exception.

First, classroom communication patterns are analogous to those observed in the marketplace. In some job settings the nature of the job, the supervision required, and the communications permitted are one way: from supervisor to employee. Your job is to perform your assigned responsibilities as instructed; your input is seldom sought. Such jobs may offer structure, security, and some freedom from stressful responsibilities, but your personal satisfaction is likely to be limited. Sometimes you can influence the way supervisors treat you.

You are likely to encounter jobs and supervisors that encourage or require regular two-way communication. You are expected to demonstrate initiative, listen actively, interact effectively, and respond appropriately. In an increasing number of challenging and rewarding positions, you work as part of a team where members and supervisor interact continuously as equals. In fact, many corporate recruiters seek evidence of teamwork abilities in applicants (Needham, 1991). Will *you* be prepared to function interactively as a member of a team?

Kolb's four learning orientations have implications for careers. The following lists career fields and the learning orientations associated with each. That is, individuals who are strong in these particular combinations of learning modes *tend* to enter the career fields named.

- *Concrete experience and active experimentation:* business, marketing, educational administration, and certain health fields

- *Concrete experience and reflective observation:* social work or personnel

- *Abstract conceptualization and active experimentation:* engineering, accounting, or medicine

- *Abstract conceptualization and reflective observation:* research fields (Kolb, 1984)

Be aware that these statements are based on research studies. They do not specify the relationship between your particular orientation and a specific career. To obtain further information about a short self-description questionnaire that David Kolb devised to measure learning styles (the *Learning Style Inventory*), consult the counseling or learning assistance department of your institution. Many counselors are familiar with Kolb's inventory.

Finally, your experiences in productive study groups are opportunities to practice interpersonal communication skills while performing a task that is evaluated and graded. In essence, study groups give you practice for teamwork activities required in several occupations. When Marcia Baxter Magolda (Chapter 14) observed significant increases in independent and contextual knowing in her sample 2 years after they completed college, she concluded that a contributing factor was collaboration. In school, peers were not usually seen as sources of knowledge, and group work was usually limited. However, in many work settings an employee's ability to succeed was directly related to his or her ability to collaborate with peers on a continual basis

(Baxter Magolda, 1994). The results of Baxter Magolda's research suggest that you should welcome opportunities inside and outside the classroom to work with and learn from your fellow students.

Action-Oriented Thought Starters

1. Reread the scenario describing Professor Johnson's attempts to involve students in the social-science class.

   a. Recalling what you learned about communication patterns, learning orientations, and group study, what advice would you give to students in Professor Johnson's class, including those who did and did not participate?

   b. What would you tell Professor Johnson?

2. Identify the most and least favorite courses in which you are currently enrolled.

   a. For each course try to determine the learning orientations (if any dominate) that characterize the instructor and the assignments through which the material must be learned.

   b. For each course connect the particular learning orientations that seem to characterize the teacher or course to your preferred orientations. In what ways are they similar or different? How do these differences facilitate or hinder your performance, attitudes, and feelings about each course?

3. Think about your most and least successful group-study experiences. What factors could have accounted for the outcomes?

References and Recommended Readings

Appleby, D. C. (1990). Faculty and student perceptions of irritating behaviors in the college classroom. *The Journal of Staff, Program, & Organization Development, 8*(1), 41–46.

Baxter Magolda, M. (1994). Post-college experiences and epistemology. *The Review of Higher Education, 18*(1), 25–44.

Belenky, M. F., Clinchy, B. M., Goldberger, N. R., & Tarule, J. M. (1986). *Women's Ways of Knowing.* New York: Basic Books.

Grasha, A. F. (1987). *Practical applications of psychology* (3rd ed.). Glenview, IL: Scott, Foresman.

Kolb, D. A. (1984). *Experiential learning: Experience as the source of learning and development.* Englewood Cliffs, NJ: Prentice-Hall.

Needham, R. H. (1991). First job survival guide. *Managing Your Career,* Spring, 4–7.

Svinicki, M. D., & Dixon, N. M. (1987). The Kolb model modified for classroom activities. *College Teaching, 35*(4), 141–146.

Learning from Campus Organizations, Residence Groups, the Workplace, and the College Climate

CHAPTER 18

Friendly Reminders

❏ Preview Chapter 18 using the Preview Checklist on page 11, follow the Deep strategies on page 9, and interact with the material by taking notes, marking, and reviewing.

❏ You *can learn* from your peer groups.

❏ *You* choose a reminder.

"If you judge by the homework they assign, some professors act as if their course is the only subject to be learned."

—unknown student

"Make your friends your teachers and mingle the pleasures of conversation with the advantages of instruction."

—Baltasar Gracian (1601–1658),
Spanish author

Each chapter in this book has begun with a thought-provoking quotation. While neither the exact source nor the precise words can be verified, at least one unknown student has uttered the first statement above within earshot of the instructor.

The student is correct! Sometimes we teachers "work" students as if our class is your only learning experience. In fact, what you learn outside of class from other people, including your friends, sometimes exceeds what you acquire from a course. The words of the unknown student and Baltasar Gracian provide a framework for discussing four "classrooms" that have the potential for expanding your knowledge of learning from groups: campus organizations, residence groups, the workplace, and the college as an organization.

Campus Organizations

Traditionally, educators viewed student involvement in campus organizations or student groups as a "nice-but-not-necessary" *cocurricular* activity; course work came first. Although family, course work, and job are the top priorities, cocurricular activities are a highly desirable component of contemporary education. In fact, student groups can provide so many opportunities that they could be viewed as an essential component of the covert curriculum.

Spend a couple minutes now and list below several organizations that operate on your campus.

_____   _____

_____   _____

_____   _____

_____   _____

Your list probably contains cocurricular activities such as student government, campus publications, sports groups, religious and ethnic organizations, music and arts groups, volunteer or service clubs, academic groups, sororities, and fraternities. Research has shown that students, especially commuters, who participate in campus activities tend to be more satisfied with their college experiences than students who do not get involved with campus life.

Why Join a Campus Organization?

Several reasons for belonging to student groups are

1. to develop social relationships and support networks

2. to have fun

3. to gain knowledge

4. to develop new, or strengthen existing, interests

5. to provide change from the routines of academic and work activities

6. to practice communication skills

7. to develop leadership skills

Each reason reflects one aspect of a healthy, well-rounded college experience. Collectively, they represent activities that could have a major influence on your personality, social development, and career advancement.

Easing into a Campus Organization

When students arrive on campus, they are quickly confronted with a menu of tantalizing cocurricular activities. Take your time before you make your selection from the menu.

First, settle in and deal with your priorities: courses, schedule, personal affairs, job, and family responsibilities. You have plenty of time to get involved. If you ignore priorities, your college experience may end in one or two terms.

Next, determine how much time remains after your priorities are established. How many hours a week can you afford to give a campus organization? To be safe, should you wait a semester before you join any groups?

Third, become a reflective observer and shop the organization marketplace before you commit yourself to a particular group. Attend a few meetings, observe, and try to answer these questions.

- How do leaders and members interact with each other? Is the atmosphere formal or informal, friendly or hostile? Do members seem to trust each other?

- What has the group accomplished in the past? What are its goals for this year?

- How much input do members appear to have in the decisions?

- Is the workload spread across the whole group, or do a few people do all of the work? What is the balance of work and fun, and what is accomplished?

- Are there opportunities for leadership positions?

- Is the organization respected on campus?

- Will you enjoy being part of this group?

Remember the following *don't*s.

- Don't expect to receive clear or quick answers to these questions.

- Don't expect student organizations to always function smoothly, especially when a new school year begins.

- Don't volunteer for an activity that you cannot complete.

- Don't volunteer for leadership positions your first year. In fact, be apprehensive if a newcomer is asked to accept high-level responsibilities. Try to envision how you could work your way into a leadership position in one or two years.

The Importance of Leadership Roles

A student who serves in a leadership position in an active campus organization functions like a manager in a company. Consider the activities that a student leader may be expected to perform.

- Work cooperatively for, and respond to, the needs of group members.

- Plan and conduct meetings.

Box 18.1

Bob and Beth, Balance and Breadth

Consider Bob and Beth, two college graduates who were hired within a 4-month period by a large company that operated a training development and applied research department.

Beth was a B– student in college. She had the intellectual ability to perform at the A or A– level, but as a full-time student, she held a part-time job (department assistant) and participated in cocurricular activities. She was president of the school's Social-Sciences Club and held a position in student government. Beth was hired for the research position because of the psychology research courses she completed and her ability to work with others.

During her first month on the job, Beth demonstrated that she could handle several responsibilities. She was highly organized, managed time well, learned new tasks quickly, and felt comfortable relating to peers, her immediate supervisor, and the company vice president. Beth worked effectively with employees in related departments and soon became the departmental liaison. When clients visited the unit during her second month, Beth briefed them on the status of the research projects.

Beth was not brilliant, but her critical-thinking skills were invaluable when problems developed with projects. Her strong interpersonal and job-related skills made her a highly respected employee.

When a position similar to Beth's became available a few months later, one of the applicants was Bob. Bob graduated from college with a degree in social-sciences and an A average. He had not participated in college activities or developed strong relationships with peers or teachers. He dedicated himself almost completely to his studies. Against the recommendations of the supervisor, the company vice president insisted that Bob be hired because of his brilliant mind and enviable academic record.

- Coordinate schedules and events.

- Work with an organization sponsor and administrators (directors, assistant deans, deans).

- Perform public relations.

- Work with college offices, vendors, and other services.

- Work with persons of diverse cultural, social, and academic backgrounds.

Bob was very successful in resolving technical issues, but that was the extent of his effectiveness. His lack of social skills made it difficult for coworkers to relate to him socially or on the job. In meetings he seldom spoke and when he did, the remarks were often inappropriate. His relationship with his peers and supervisor were strained. When clients visited the department, Bob was assigned tasks that kept him in his office.

About a year later the national economic situation led to the closing of the research department. Beth and Bob were forced to seek employment elsewhere. Who do you think was more employable, Bob or Beth?

Certainly Bob does not represent all A students, nor Beth all B– students. Nor does student involvement in campus organizations sharply determine the futures of most students. Basic personality traits existing prior to college account for some differences between Beth's and Bob's choices in college and their job behaviors. Bob maintained an A average, but he paid a price for his high grades: He neglected to develop the social, interpersonal, and job-related skills required for most occupations. Beth did not graduate with academic honors, but she had skills and experiences in college that made her a valued employee.

Campus activities are a great opportunity to achieve balance in your intellectual and social development. Some colleges acknowledge the importance of cocurricular activities by creating a Student Development Transcript, a formal written record that documents the learning that students gain beyond the classroom (Hofmann, Pelc, and Rosenlof, 1987). Such a record helps you translate your experiences with campus organizations into eye-catching entries on your job resumé.

- Work under considerable pressure while carrying a full load of courses, working part-time, and managing personal responsibilities.

Leadership experience in campus groups helps you develop a wide range of skills and attitudes that will facilitate your advancement in other organizations you join. Recall from Box 18.1 that Beth's leadership roles in college gave her experience in communicating, planning, organizing, and working with people. It is no surprise that she quickly became an asset to her department.

Finally, student leaders contribute to the overall quality of student life in an institution. Colleges that have productive campus organizations enrich the education of their students.

Leadership skills are developed gradually through training, experience, and the application of basic concepts. Let's examine two issues of particular importance: how to conduct meetings and four fundamental principles of leadership.

How to Conduct Meetings Effectively

Meetings can make or break an organization and its leadership. In his classic book *The Time Trap,* Alec MacKenzie (1972) identified 21 rules for conducting meetings; they are condensed here to 9 guidelines.

1. Before calling a meeting, clearly define its purpose to yourself and the members of your group.

2. Carefully choose the time and place in consultation with those you want to attend.

3. Distribute an agenda at least one day in advance to help others prepare. Place the most important items at the top of the agenda.

4. Start the meeting on time, no more than one or two minutes after it was scheduled to begin. Meetings that start late punish those who arrive early and reward those who arrive late.

5. Ask someone to record minutes and help you monitor time.

6. Stick to the agenda and control digressions, but be flexible.

7. Devote a few minutes at the end to summarize the group's accomplishments, clarify assignments, and establish the time and date for the next meeting.

8. Respect the commitments of those who agreed to attend by ending the meeting on time.

9. Follow up on decisions, assignments, and agreements made during the meeting.

Although MacKenzie omitted it from his list, a tenth guideline is to thank everyone who attends and publicly acknowledge members who perform special assignments.

Four Principles of Leadership

In his book *Practical Applications of Psychology,* Anthony Grasha (1987) defines leadership as "a process of providing guidance and direction to a group" (p. 358). Conducting meetings is one form of guidance. Grasha describes four aspects of leadership that are pertinent to campus organizations.

1. Leadership is the use of one's interpersonal *influence* to help members reach the goals your organization established. A leader can influence people by exercising different types of power, including

   - *legitimate power* (power given as the elected head of the group)

   - *reward* and *coercive power* (rewards and punishments)

   - *expert power* (power acquired through your knowledge and skills)

   - *referent power* (power acquired through the respect and admiration of others for what you have done)

   If you were the leader of a group, which types of power would you prefer to use? Which type would you avoid using?

2. Contrary to our stereotypes, leaders and followers do not differ significantly on the *personal* characteristics they possess. You can assume that you have as much potential for becoming a leader as anyone else in your group. Generally, communication skills are more important for leadership than particular personality traits.

3. The *assumptions* that a leader forms about followers strongly influence the leader's attitudes. For instance, if you assume that most of your peers are apathetic, dull, or need to be coerced into action, then you will treat them accordingly. In turn they will behave as you expect them to. However, if you assume that most members are self-motivated, capable, and willing to work, you will treat them as mature individuals, and they will respond maturely. In short, be sensitive to the assumptions you make about your peers.

4. A leader's *style* should reflect concerns for accomplishing the group's tasks and goals while developing and maintaining strong interpersonal relationships among group members. Some leaders are mainly concerned with the tasks that must be done, even if

relationships are strained (*task-oriented* leaders). Other leaders are primarily concerned with strengthening relationships, even if the task is not completed (*relationship-oriented* leaders). Which approach is correct? It depends. Some situations call for task-oriented leadership, others for relationship-oriented leadership, and still other situations demand a combination. As you become experienced with student groups, you may recognize circumstances that call for either or both styles of leadership.

On most campuses opportunities exist for participating in leadership training. When you are able, take advantage of workshops or seminars that teach leadership concepts and activities; consult the student affairs office on your campus. One familiar means of obtaining leadership experience is to become a resident assistant in a college dormitory. Not only do leadership experiences build skills, they create valuable components of your job resumé.

Residence Groups

Your living arrangement is likely to be the most intense group experience you encounter in college because you spend at least half of each day in close contact with others with whom you live. The most common residence situations include

- sharing a room or occupying a private room in one of your institution's residence halls

- living at home with parents and siblings

- living with spouse or children, or both

- sharing an apartment off campus

Each situation shares common elements with the others; each differs from the others.

The stresses that arise from living with others are most prominent for freshmen, but they continue throughout college. Consider the challenges of living with others in the following situations.

- moving from home into a residence hall and sharing a room with a stranger, while simultaneously learning to manage money, time, personal belongings, and the stresses that accompany such transitions

- feeling isolated as a commuter student, believing that you will miss important campus experiences

- adding the responsibilities of student to those of spouse, parent, and employee

- wanting to become part of your group, but feeling their pressures to change your attitudes toward drinking, drugs, sex, or school-work to conform to their views

- experiencing low self-esteem, depression, or concern with physical attractiveness that affects how others treat you and how you treat yourself

- experiencing competition in class, relationships, and with family members

- facing a lack of privacy, time for your studies, and time for yourself

- performing more than your share of responsibilities, while others fail to do their share of the work

- lacking time or money to have as much fun as others in your group

- learning to compromise with your roommate regarding study times, sleeping, room furnishings, space, room temperature, and visitors

- experiencing the pressures of being a new student, an ethnic minority, an older student (or all of these)

- feeling guilty about going back to school because it takes money from the family budget and time from family activities

Who said that college would be mostly fun!

Applying Learning Skills to Residence Life

Every situation that creates stress is an opportunity (another classroom) for learning, another minicourse in the covert curriculum that connects college to career. What strategies can you use to learn from your residence situation? A few were suggested earlier.

- Ideas and suggestions presented in Chapter 8, "Passing the Stress Test," can help you understand and deal with stress.

- Recommendations presented in Chapter 6, "G.O.: Get Organized," and in Chapter 7, "Getting Around," show you how to organize your work environment and use campus resources to your advantage.

- Concepts presented in Chapter 16, "A Primer on Interpersonal Skills," help you learn to communicate and get along with people.

- On several occasions, we have emphasized the importance of obtaining and using feedback to guide your attitudes and behavior.

- Enroll in courses, workshops, or support groups that provide instruction in communication, interpersonal skills, assertiveness management, and stress management. Education is achieved, not received.

- Recognize that you are not alone. Discuss these issues with counselors, family, or close friends. Many of your peers share your experiences and feelings.

- Any list of strategies could end with the simple advice to be open-minded, open to feedback, flexible, resilient, and persistent.

Finally, recognize that most of these remarks have been directed to the *downside,* the challenges of living in a group. Don't forget about the fun, camaraderie, sharing, and satisfaction that is part of group living. Learning how to get along with people is among life's greatest challenges and its greatest rewards.

The Workplace

Chapter 1, "A Guide to the Learning Skills," emphasized that learning involves W-O-R-K. W-O-R-K is one of life's best teachers, and for most persons it is life's main event. Although students such as Warren (Box 4.2: Coffee, Capitalism, and the Covert Curriculum) recognize the links between their job and the classroom, others fail to make the connection.

For some students, work and course work dovetail perfectly. For the business person, health-service provider, or technician who works during the day, evening or weekend classes may deal directly with workplace issues.

However, many students hold jobs that appear to have little or nothing to do with their long-range goals. For example, what does serving food in the college cafeteria have to do with becoming a manager? (Read on for one answer.) The purpose of this section is to persuade you that all or most jobs contain *some* opportunities for acquiring knowledge, skills, and attitudes that transfer to future positions. Consider a few of the on-campus and off-campus jobs students hold:

- working the desk or shelving books in the college library

- peer tutor

- child care

- resident assistant

- clerk in an admissions, student affairs, sports, or financial assistance office

- assembly-line worker

- service station attendant

- retail sales clerk

- checkout clerk at a grocery store

What can you transfer from these seemingly irrelevant jobs to your future positions? Much more than you might believe.

What Jobs Can Teach You

❏ Jobs Involve Relationships

No matter what you do, employment places you in a supervisor-subordinate relationship, similar to the teacher-student relationship you experience in the classroom. At work, as in the classroom,

- you are responsible to a higher authority for performing certain tasks on time

- you communicate interactively with people around you according to certain patterns or procedures

- you can observe how others, especially your supervisor, exhibit attitudes and behaviors that you may wish to imitate or avoid

- you learn how to get along with others

From this perspective, is any job, even the most boring and mundane, totally irrelevant to college and career?

❏ Jobs Force You to Examine Your Attitudes and Behaviors

Regardless of what you do, the habits and attitudes you establish can transfer, consciously or unconsciously, to subsequent jobs. It is important, then, to understand your ideas and preferences regarding work.

How many of the following questions are relevant to your current work setting?

1. Do you prefer to work alone or in the presence of others?

2. Are you punctual, dependable, and reliable? (Would your supervisor agree with your answer?)

3. Are you willing to start work early and work beyond closing time, or do you follow the clock precisely? Why?

4. Do you feel comfortable supervising others?

5. Do you like new responsibilities?

6. Are you willing to acquire new information and skills that are unrelated to your career plans?

7. How do you feel about working with people of different racial, gender, ethnic, or age groups?

8. Do you prefer hands-on work to analysis and problem solving?

9. Do you need your work environment to be highly organized and predictable?

10. Are you able to maintain a positive attitude toward work even when the job is boring?

11. Do you have the stamina to work long hours and remain alert?

Whether your job is simple or complex, dull or lively, such questions should help you reflect on your attitudes and behaviors. Chances are that you will encounter some of these issues in your first postcollege job interview.

A final comment pertains to that first postcollege job. If your college degree is in high demand, if you are exceptionally skilled (academically and socially), or if you have good connections, you may be among those privileged college graduates who step immediately into a high-paying, prestigious position. However, thousands of new college graduates have no alternative but to accept low-paying and uninspiring entry-level positions, jobs that burst the bubble of their career expectations and prevent them from paying back student loans in a timely manner. Chances are that you will be better able to survive such jobs if you have been inoculated by hard work, varied job experiences, a positive mental attitude, and the capacity to be flexible and resilient, as Matt was (see Box 18.2).

❑ Your Job May Connect Course Work to Your Career

Sometimes, the work you perform to support yourself through college can lead to a career. The case of Carmen, sketched in Chapter 2, described how she integrated her clerical responsibilities with her course work and subsequently advanced through the ranks. Box 18.3 tells about another student.

Although students generally start planning their career during the second semester of their senior year, most regret their delay. Freshmen will benefit from browsing through materials at the career and job-placement center on their campus. For example, the *Wall Street Journal* publishes semiannually *Managing Your Career,* the college edition of the *National Business Employment Weekly.* This periodical contains several short articles on careers and job search tactics. Also look for publications such as *The Black Collegian, Careers and the Disabled, Career Woman, Hispanic, Journal of Career Planning and Employment,* and *Working Woman.*

In conclusion, your job during college is not simply a source of income. It is an opportunity to learn about the nature of work, working relationships, and your attitudes and behaviors. It could be the starting point of a career.

Your College Climate

Your school is, itself, a group of individuals who comprise a formal organization and reflect a particular culture or climate. Its members occupy certain roles (for example, student, faculty, staff, administrator) within a

From Pilot to Painter—
an Attitude Adjustment

Since his junior year of high school, Matt had wanted to fly planes. He obtained his degree and commercial pilot's license from a university with an excellent flying program. Unfortunately, Matt graduated at a time when an oversupply of pilots was searching for a diminishing number of jobs in a shaky economy. During the next year, Matt conducted an exhaustive search but could not find work as a pilot; opportunities went to experienced pilots. Often he was depressed. Sometimes he expressed disappointment and anger about his college education. However, Matt had learned from his family, his part-time jobs, and his college experience to *adapt, persist, be flexible, and maintain a positive attitude.*

During the next two years, Matt worked in three unsatisfying sales jobs. He still wanted to fly, but the only positions available were part-time and required a cross-country move. He chose to stay near home. On a few occasions, Matt assisted an acquaintance who was a painting contractor. Matt learned the work quickly and tolerated long hours and paint spatters in order to pay his bills. He developed a positive attitude toward the work and grew to enjoy it, becoming a good painter. Finally, Matt started his own painting service. Within a year, Matt's business grew into a successful full-time operation, and he hired unemployed college graduates to help him.

Matt continues to make a satisfactory living as a painting contractor. He still wants to fly but his desire is not as strong as it was a few years ago. Will he remain a painting contractor? Perhaps. Will he ever fly commercially? Perhaps.

There are thousands of college graduates like Matt who dream, plan, and work to achieve specific goals but are subsequently thwarted. And like Matt, most will be able to apply much of what they learned in college to their situations in life: how to adapt and change (as Carl Rogers advised), how to use most of the intellectual skills and some of the knowledge acquired, and how to readjust their attitudes towards life's many obstacles. As indicated earlier in *Learning Skills for College and Career,* your college education is not primarily the attainment of grades or the accumulation of facts, many of which become obsolete or go unused. You learn from college's covert curriculum: *how* to change and adapt, *how* to set and adjust goals, *how* to use feedback, *how* to manage stress, and *how* to think independently. And life goes on. And you can enjoy it.

From Busing to Business

Kim began working her sophomore year in the college cafeteria clearing dishes and serving food. As a business major, she had hoped she could get a part-time job in retail sales or in a corporate setting, but none was available. Although cafeteria work was boring and somewhat demeaning, Kim accepted it with a healthy attitude and worked conscientiously. Her supervisor showed her appreciation of Kim's work by raising her hourly salary each semester.

Kim accepted the offer to work the following year with more responsibilities and a higher hourly wage. She expressed interest in cafeteria operations and continued to increase her knowledge and skills. Some of the concepts Kim learned in her business courses helped her understand the food-service operations.

At the beginning of her senior year, Kim was appointed assistant cafeteria manager and assigned a broad range of responsibilities for the whole operation. Two months before she graduated, Kim was offered a manager's position in another college cafeteria the food-service company operated.

When Kim began her humble, low-paying job she never expected that it would lead to a manager's position by graduation. Not all jobs have the promotion potential that Kim's did, but her case is not rare. Many people remain with the same employer after completing their education and advance. Be open to the possibility that even mundane part-time jobs like Kim's could lead to long-term employment. As scientist Charles Kettering once remarked, "Where there is an open mind, there will always be a frontier."

hierarchy of power, each interacting with others through his or her frame of reference. Members of the school organization use formal and informal channels of communication at varying levels of trust and self-disclosure, adhering to guidelines specified in handbooks, in personnel policies, and by custom. Collectively, the members of this large group create an atmosphere, *an organizational climate,* that exerts considerable influence (consciously or unconsciously) on your attitudes and feelings toward the institution, its members, and yourself.

How much are you benefiting from your membership in this group? What are your sources of satisfaction and dissatisfaction? As you answer the Student Satisfaction Scale on the following page, try to separate personal issues affecting you from your perceptions of the college's organizational climate so that you can more clearly understand your responses to the scale.

Student Satisfaction Scale

For each question circle the response that best describes your level of satisfaction.

To what extent am I satisfied with:	Very much			Somewhat		Not at all	
a. my courses?	7	6	5	4	3	2	1
b. my teachers?	7	6	5	4	3	2	1
c. my relationship with my advisor?	7	6	5	4	3	2	1
d. my relationship with peers?	7	6	5	4	3	2	1
e. my relationship with staff/administrators?	7	6	5	4	3	2	1
f. campus events and activities?	7	6	5	4	3	2	1
g. the school's attitude toward issues of personal choice?	7	6	5	4	3	2	1
h. campus housing?	7	6	5	4	3	2	1
i. campus services (library, security, food services, etc.)?	7	6	5	4	3	2	1
j. campus facilities?	7	6	5	4	3	2	1
k. the school's attitudes toward students?	7	6	5	4	3	2	1
l. the school's policies about personal safety?	7	6	5	4	3	2	1
m. the resources for help when I need it?	7	6	5	4	3	2	1
n. its resources for helping me reach my goals?	7	6	5	4	3	2	1
o. my personal development?	7	6	5	4	3	2	1
p. the match between my values and those of my school?	7	6	5	4	3	2	1

Your responses to these items reflect your current *perceptions* of your environment, the college's organizational climate as you experience it. The actual environment may be similar to or different from your experiences. Check your perceptions with people you trust and respect.

In general, if most of your responses are 6s or 7s, be pleased with the good match between you and your "group." Your interactions with others seem satisfying; your expectations are being met.

If your responses are scattered throughout the scale, be pleased with the favorable responses and search for the roots of your dissatisfaction.

If most of your responses are 1s and 2s, again search for the causes of your unhappiness. Your widespread dissatisfaction is probably affecting your performance in the classroom and your relationships. Dissatisfaction with certain aspects of college life can generalize to other experiences and produce negative attitudes. For example,

- problems with a roommate may create a negative attitude toward all aspects of residence life

- your failure to get higher than a C in a course can create dislike for other courses in that discipline

- students who add too many night courses to a schedule that includes family responsibilities and a full-time job can grow bitter about their education, family, and college

- students who are dissatisfied with certain school policies can easily find fault with everything

The feelings that students experience in such cases may or may not be justified. Left unresolved, however, problems usually have deleterious (go ahead, look up the definition) effects on one's frame of reference, level of trust, and willingness to remain a member of that group.

If you experience dissatisfaction with particular aspects of college life, resolve to deal with the issues soon, directly, honestly, and rationally. Use all resources available whether they are the communication skills you learned in Chapter 16 or the campus resources presented in Chapter 7. Perhaps transferring to another institution is the best solution; perhaps you can resolve the issues to your satisfaction and remain where you are.

Periodically retake the Student Satisfaction Scale and study your responses. Sometimes the climate of an organization can change, for better or for worse, just as the membership of a group changes. When changes occur in a group, you are likely to be affected.

In summary, opportunities exist outside the classroom for learning in groups. They include campus organizations, your residence situation, and your job. View them as classrooms and the people you interact with as potential sources of learning. Finally, recognize that your experiences with specific aspects of college life can create attitudes that affect how you think and feel toward the institution itself.

Connecting These Groups to Your Career

The connections between campus organizations and career were made explicit. Learning to live and work with others is a lifelong process. Use your living and workplace situations in college as opportunities for personal and professional development. Finally, think about the larger organization of which you are a member. Obtain and use feedback about the way you function in the group and its influences on your feelings, attitudes, and behaviors. You are likely to encounter similar issues in any organization you join. Your job may depend on your ability to respond, as Box 18.4 explains.

Action-Oriented Thought Starters

1. Become acquainted with a student leader whom you respect.

   a. Use Grasha's leadership concepts and observe how the leader exercises power (reward, coercive, expert, legitimate), emphasizes task or relationship styles of leadership, and treats peers.

   b. If you were in the leader's position, what attitudes and behaviors would you want to imitate? Which ones would you avoid?

2. Talk with staff in the financial assistance office or the job placement office on your campus. Ask about campus-based jobs that have potential for

   • learning to handle responsibility

   • learning career-related skills

   • advancement

   • working with other students

Box 18.4

Succeeding on the Job and in College: Common Themes

At the end of *Working Scared: Achieving Success in Trying Times,* consultants Kenneth Wexley and Stanley Silverman (1993) identify several keys to surviving in a company when jobs are threatened. Their recommendations to employees (the first part of each statement below) are adapted to a college setting. As you read the authors' conclusions, ask how each relates to your "job" as a student, your success in the organization that is your college and, where relevant, to the job that helps pay your college bills.

1. *Adaptability.* Whether the changes you encounter at work are good or bad, change (like death, taxes, and tests) is a certainty of life. Successful employees not only continually adapt to change, but also champion change.

Recall Carl Rogers's belief that true education is learning how to learn and how to change, and Hans Selye's observation that adaptability is the basis for homeostasis and resistance to change. The ability to change is one key to success in school and on the job.

2. *Continual learning.* Employees and employers must commit themselves to lifelong learning, which is the continual learning of new skills, knowledge, information, and jobs.

Recall the remarks in Chapter 1 emphasizing that learning how to learn is just as important as learning what to learn, especially as information is continually becoming obsolete. Education does not end when you graduate; it continues for life.

3. *Continual improvement* is best expressed on the job as "Whatever you are doing today, you can do a little better tomorrow." Employees can make themselves more successful if they continually and gradually improve everything they do at work.

Similarly, when students gradually (semester by semester) increase (at a realistic level) demands on themselves for improvement, they are likely to reach, and possibly surpass, their short-term and intermediate goals.

4. *Empowerment.* Successful employees understand the extent to which they have the responsibility and authority to take action to help others in their organization.

As students develop intrinsic motivation and progress through the stages described by Marcia Baxter Magolda, their intellectual and emotional maturity empowers them to achieve their personal and professional goals.

(continued on next page)

Box 18.4 (continued)

5. *Self-understanding.* If employees are to deal successfully with other individuals, they must understand how their own values and attitudes influence the ways they perceive, think, and act.

Your education (inside and outside the classroom) is, in many respects, a 4- or 5-year program in self-understanding with input provided by your courses, teachers, peers, and others. "Know thyself" may be the most important reason for attending college.

In summary, Wexley and Silverman's recommendations for achieving success in the workplace during trying times should not surprise the perceptive college student. The same themes are the keys to success in college.

3. In Chapter 14, "Becoming an Independent Thinker," Marcia Baxter Magolda asserted that higher levels of knowing include an increased attention to the views of peers. Often, we can learn important insights from our peers. Boxes 18.1, 18.2, and 18.3 are true-life examples that are instructive.

   a. Summarize the most significant insight you gained from each example.

   b. What characteristics do Beth, Matt, and Kim share in common?

   c. Describe someone you know who is like Beth, Bob, Matt, or Kim.

   d. Not everything a classmate says or does is worth thinking about. However, identify one or two instances when a classmate made a point you thought was insightful.

   e. Identify a belief, insight, or experience you think would be valuable for your classmates to know.

References and Recommended Readings

Grasha, A. F. (1987). *Practical applications of psychology* (3rd ed.). Glenview, IL: Scott, Foresman.

Hofmann, K., Pelc, S., & Rosenlof, J. (1987). Beyond the classroom . . . *Journal of Career Planning and Employment, 48*(1), 66–71.

Kaye, E., & Gardner, J. (1988). *College bound: The student's handbook for getting ready, moving in, and succeeding on campus.* New York: College Entrance Examination Board.

MacKenzie, R. A. (1972). *The time trap.* New York: McGraw-Hill.

Wexley, K. N., & Silverman, S. B. (1993). *Working scared: Achieving success in trying times.* San Francisco, CA: Jossey-Bass.

Epilogue

"I find the great thing in this world is not so much where we stand, as in what direction we are moving: To reach the port of heaven, we must sail sometimes with the wind and sometimes against it—but we must sail, and not drift, nor lie at anchor."

—Oliver Wendell Holmes, Sr. (1809–1894),
American poet, novelist, physician

Where have we been? Where are *you* going?

Six major currents of thought have guided your reading.

1. Learning *how* to learn is as important as learning *what* to learn. According to Carl Rogers, the educated person learns how to learn, how to adapt, and how to change. So as you progress through your course work, work equally hard on the covert curriculum. Together they connect college to your personal and career development.

2. Positive change is produced by self-awareness and self-control. Becoming aware of yourself (who you are, how you think and feel), others, and your environment is an essential step to maturity. Self-control transforms (taking charge) awareness into positive action.

3. Goals are essential. Set realistic and specific goals for your daily activities; start developing long-range goals. Life *is* a journey. If you intend to enjoy it, you will need a compass.

4. Learning is an active process that requires energy, W-O-R-K, and persistence. Counteract passivity promoted by earlier experiences by taking charge of yourself and what you learn. Remember the words of America's first woman secretary of state, Madeleine Albright: "I do not believe that things happen accidentally, I believe you earn them." (Gibbs, 1997).

5. Use all resources available, including other people, information, and financial means, but especially your inner resources.

6. Growth proceeds from feedback. Develop skills for obtaining feedback and the courage to use it. (I would appreciate receiving your feedback about what you have learned and the strengths and weaknesses of this book. Please send your comments on the postage-paid form on the last page of this book.)

For each of us, life is a continuous journey that is accomplished by constant attention to its many maps. Educators Arthur Chickering (Chickering, 1969) and Linda Reisser (Chickering & Reisser, 1993) believe that a student's psychosocial development is a *journey of increasing complexity.* During development, seven maps (vectors) are provided that "describe major highways for journeying toward individuation— the discovery and refinement of one's unique way of being—and also toward communion with other individuals and groups, including the larger national and global society" (p. 35). *Students journey differently through the vectors at different rates, but always they move from a lower to a higher level of complexity in the vector.* In short, your path from freshman to graduation is a journey from the psychosocially simple to the psychosocially complex.

1. In the first vector, *developing competence,* students move from lower to higher levels of intellectual, interpersonal, and physical competence. Intellectual competence, the skills you develop in using your mind, includes mastering course content; building skills in comprehension, analysis, and synthesis; and developing your intellectual and aesthetic sophistication. Intellectual competence is the map that characterizes the major focus of your college course work, and consequently, the focus of most chapters of *Learning Skills for College and Career.* Interpersonal competence includes listening, cooperating, communicating, and tuning and responding to other people in one-on-one or group settings (Chapter 16, "A Primer on Interpersonal Skills"). Physical and manual competence cover a range of skills including artistic, constructing objects, self-discipline, and athletic. You increase your competence in these three areas by learning to trust your abilities, by obtaining accurate feedback about your performance, and by integrating your skills with a sense of self-assurance.

2. In the vector of *managing emotions,* you progress from lower to higher levels of control over (a) potentially disruptive emotions (e.g., fear, anger, anxiety, desire, aggression, guilt, depression, shame), (b) your feelings, and (c) your ability to integrate your feelings with

action. This control is accomplished as you learn to develop awareness of your feelings, find socially acceptable forms of emotional release, and learn to substitute self-regulation for the repression of your emotions. You also learn awareness of your positive emotions such as sympathy, rapture, relief, worship, yearning, and awe. Chapter 8, "Passing the Stress Test," presented concepts and techniques for managing your emotions.

3. *Moving through autonomy toward interdependence* requires students to learn self-sufficiency, accept responsibility for pursuing self-chosen goals, and become less influenced by others. This vector involves changing from (a) emotional dependence to freedom from continual reassurance and approval, (b) poor self-direction to instrumental independence (i.e., self-organized and self-directed activities and problem-solving situations, mobility), and (c) independence to the recognition and valuing of interdependence. Part One, "Taking Charge," introduced you to several dimensions of this map.

4. When you use the map *developing mature interpersonal relationships,* you journey from lower to higher levels of interpersonal and intercultural tolerance of differences, and from having nonexistent, short-term or unhealthy intimate relationships to a higher capacity for intimacy, in-depth sharing, tolerance of flaws, and commitment. You learn to treat others as they are, rather than as stereotypes. Also, you shift from excessive dependency or dominance toward an interdependence among equals. Chapter 16, "A Primer on Interpersonal Skills," primed you to consider this aspect of your journey.

5. Identity, introduced in Chapter 2, "Where Are You Going? Why? Motives for College," is an important map in Chickering and Reisser's journey to maturity. Identity formation is somewhat dependent on the four vectors previously mentioned. The vector *establishing identity* is a journey from discomfort to comfort with your (a) body and appearance, (b) gender and sexual orientation, (c) sense of self in your social, cultural, and historical contexts, (d) self-concept in relation to your roles and lifestyle, (e) sense of self in response to feedback from others, (f) levels of self-esteem and self-acceptance, and (9) personal stability.

6. *Developing purpose* enables you to articulate your interests, goals, and plans clearly with respect to your vocation, personal interests, and commitments to relationships. You used this map in Chapters 2, "Where Are You Going? Why? Motives for College," 3, "Setting

and Monitoring Goals," 4, "The Covert Curriculum: Connecting College to Career," and 5, "Take Charge of Your Time."

7. *Developing integrity* is closely related to the two previous vectors (developing purpose, establishing identity). In reaching maturity, your values are transformed from dualistic, rigid, and self-centered to values that are humanizing (considering other people's interests and views), personalizing (affirming your core values while respecting those of others), and congruent (matching your personal values with socially responsible behaviors). Some aspects of this vector were addressed by Marcia Baxter Magolda's stages of cognitive development in Chapter 14, "Becoming an Independent Thinker."

Chickering and Reisser contend that the developmental process of journeying to infinite complexity applies to students of virtually all ages. They also believe that the major themes contained in their model are compatible with specific research studies they cite of women, nonwhite students, and gay/lesbian/bisexual students. In addition, Chickering and Reisser warn that "Institutions that emphasize intellectual development to the exclusion of other strengths and skills reinforce society's tendency to see some aspects of its citizens and not others" (p. 41). In other words, college's overt curriculum may be the primary but not the sole focus of your short-term and intermediate goals. Your education must include travel through all available vectors during your journey if you are to gain an understanding of yourself and those who sail for their ports along side of you.

May the themes and ideas we presented in *Learning Skills for College and Career* enable you to reach your ports safely and happily.

References and Recommended Reading

Chickering, A. (1969). *Education and identity*. San Francisco, CA: Jossey-Bass.

Chickering, A., & Reisser, L. (1993). *Education and identity* (2nd ed.). San Francisco, CA: Jossey-Bass.

Gibbs, N. (1997, February 17). The many lives of Madeleine. *TIME*, pp. 52–58, 60–61.

Glossary

absolute knowing The first of Baxter Magolda's four stages of cognitive development characterized by reliance on authorities, the absence of personal voice, and the construction of the world in simple, dichotomous terms. (Chapter 14)

abstract conceptualization Kolb's orientation or preference for approaching new learning situations with a reliance on logic, analysis, and reasoning. (Chapter 17)

active experimentation Kolb's orientation or preference for approaching new learning situations characterized by practicality, diligence, and doing ("hands-on"), as opposed to reflective observation. (Chapter 17)

active listening A technique in effective communication in which the receiver reflects or summarizes the sender's feelings and content to the sender. (Chapter 16)

affective strategies Techniques that promote remembering by practicing mental and physical activities such as goal setting, stress management, exercise, rest, nutritious eating, concentration, and time management. (Chapter 12)

analysis The fourth level of the Bloom taxonomy where learning occurs through breaking down ideas and concepts into smaller components. (Chapters 13, 14)

application The third level of the Bloom taxonomy where learning occurs by transferring knowledge or skills to different situations. (Chapter 14)

blaming In this style of distorted thinking, individuals hold others responsible for their own pain and misfortune, or they hold themselves responsible for every problem. (Chapter 8)

catastrophizing A style of distorted thinking in which a person expects and waits for the worst to happen, and good events are only a temporary interruption from life's crises. (Chapter 8)

coercive power A form of power that is derived from one's ability to punish others. (Chapter 18)

column format A method of notetaking in which main ideas are noted on the left third of a page in a critical-concept column and the supporting information is recorded in the remaining space under a content column. (Chapter 10)

comprehension The second level of the Bloom's taxonomy in which learning is accomplished by understanding (versus memorizing) facts and ideas. (Chapters 13, 14)

comprehension-monitoring strategies Techniques that promote remembering by reflecting on one's thought processes, questioning one's motivation, and remaining conscious of one's mental activities. (Chapter 12)

concentration The ability to direct and maintain your attention to the act of learning; it is a skill and power that fuels your motivation and actions. (Chapter 6)

concrete experience Kolb's orientation or preference for learning in new situations that is characterized by a reliance on feelings, intuitions, and experiences. (Chapter 17)

contextual knowing The fourth and highest of Baxter Magolda's stages of cognitive development; Contextual Knowers recognize the complexity and uncertainty of knowledge and form their judgments based on particular contexts. (Chapter 14)

covert curriculum Those numerous, routine, skill-related activities, behaviors, and attitudes that are transacted inside and outside of the classroom that collectively reflect a student's overall work orientation and habits and include the learning skills presented in this text. (Chapter 4)

daily DO-list A sheet used to record nonroutine tasks to be completed on a day. (Chapter 5)

deep strategy An effective approach to learning characterized by the tendency to understand and interact with material, search for principles, and attempt connections with prior learning. (Chapter 1)

distortion theory The belief that forgetting occurs because information has been misconstrued or twisted. (Chapter 12)

distress A damaging, painful side effect to the body produced by situations to which we respond. (Chapter 8)

elaboration strategies Techniques that promote remembering by making connections among facts, concepts, and ideas to make material meaningful. Examples include visual imagery, mnemonics, summarizing, and questioning. (Chapter 12)

emotional barriers Obstacles in the message component of listening that occur when the listener becomes emotionally aroused by ideas communicated by the speaker. (Chapter 9)

emotional reasoning In this style of distorted thinking the person believes that if he or she feels something is true, then it is true. (Chapter 8)

error analysis The process of analyzing errors made on tests and classifying them according to attitudinal, learning, or test-taking factors. (Chapter 13)

expert power A form of power that is derived from one's knowledge and skills. (Chapter 18)

extrinsic motivation A condition in which the forces that arouse and direct one's behavior originate outside the person in the external world. (Chapter 2)

evaluation The sixth and highest level of the Bloom taxonomy where learning involves forming judgments about ideas using relevant criteria. (Chapters 13, 14)

fading theory A theory of forgetting that states that information is lost due to lack of use. (Chapter 12)

feedback Information provided to regulate or modify some aspect of behavior. (Chapters 3, 16)

foreclosure An immature status in identity development when a person appears to be committed to particular beliefs and goals, often to please adults, but has not carefully examined those commitments. (Chapter 2)

forgetting The failure to recall something previously learned or experienced. (Chapter 12)

frame of reference Selective perceptions, background, and recent experiences that serve to filter the meaning of a message in the communication process. (Chapter 16)

generativity The middle adult stage of development reflecting the mature adult's concern for leaving a legacy to the next generation. (Chapter 2)

goal A result or milestone that a motivated person strives to reach. (Chapter 3)

half life The length of time following graduation in which the knowledge acquired in a particular area becomes obsolete. (Chapter 1)

hearing A passive, generally involuntary process in which the brain receives and interprets sounds from the external environment. (Chapter 9)

identity achievement A mature status in identity development that follows years of exploring, questioning, and clarifying one's values, beliefs, and career alternatives. (Chapter 2)

identity diffusion An immature status in identity development characterized by a sense of incompleteness, self-consciousness, conflict, and a poor sense of self-identity. (Chapter 2)

I-messages A technique of effective communication consisting of the sender's statements of feelings, what has happened, and how that behavior affects the sender. (Chapter 16)

independent knowing The third of Baxter Magolda's stages of cognitive development characterized by the development of a distinctive point of view but one that lacks critical judgment. (Chapter 14)

intellectual barriers Obstacles created in the message component of listening that are due to the use of complex or unfamiliar words by the speaker. (Chapter 9)

interacting A method for improving reading comprehension in which the reader summarizes, marks, and critically reads the material. (Chapter 11)

interference theory The belief that forgetting is due to previously or subsequently learned information that inhibits our ability to recall. (Chapter 12)

intermediate goals Specific, realistic objectives required to reach long-range goals that can be accomplished between 1 and 4 years. (Chapter 3)

intrinsic motivation A condition in which the forces that arouse and direct one's behavior originate inside the person, not from the outside world. (Chapter 2)

knowledge (memorization) level The lowest level of the Bloom taxonomy in which learning consists of storing and retrieving information. (Chapters 13, 14)

legitimate power Power that is based on one's elected or appointed position within an organization. (Chapter 18)

listening An active, voluntary process in which the listener deliberately attends to, interprets the meaning of, and responds to a message. (Chapter 9)

learning orientation The particular strategies, rules, and ideas a person uses to deal with everyday problems, according to Kolb. (Chapter 17)

locus of control The extent to which a person believes that his or her actions are determined primarily by his or her own behavior (internal locus of control) or by outside forces (external locus of control). (Chapter 2)

long-range goals Realistic objectives that can be achieved in a 5- to 10-year period. (Chapter 3)

long-term memory The third component of the memory system, which receives and stores vast amounts of information from short-term memory. (Chapter 12)

memory The capacity to store, retain, and retrieve information. (Chapter 12)

message The component of the general model of communication that consists of the information being transmitted between the speaker or sender and the receiver. (Chapters 9, 16)

mind reading A style of distorted thinking in which a person seems to know how others behave and what others think about him or her without ever talking with them. (Chapter 8)

moratorium The "time-out" status of identity development in which individuals question and experiment with their beliefs but do not commit to them. (Chapter 2)

motive A process that energizes behavior and directs it to a particular goal. (Chapter 2)

myth of change A style of distorted thinking in which a person believes that the power of his or her will or love is sufficient to change someone. (Chapter 8)

myth of fairness A style of distorted thinking in which the person sets a standard for fairness and expects everyone else to follow it. (Chapter 8)

negative identity An immature status of identity development where the individual maintains values opposite those of parents or other adults. (Chapter 2)

nonverbal communication Factors involved in communicating, such as appearance, posture, and facial expressions that are not expressed in words. (Chapter 16)

notetaking The process of selecting and recording information contained in a spoken or written message. (Chapter 10)

organizational climate The social or cultural atmosphere or mood that characterizes an organization and is the collective product of its members. (Chapter 18)

organizational strategies Techniques that organize information into a hierarchy to promote remembering. Tree diagrams, concept maps, and concept circles are examples. (Chapter 12)

outline format A method of taking notes in which topics are organized and categorized hierarchically into major headings and subheadings. (Chapter 10)

overgeneralization In this style of distorted thinking, a person reaches a global conclusion based on a single instance or piece of evidence. (Chapter 8)

overt curriculum The curriculum or program of official educational offerings described in the college catalog and course schedule. (Chapter 4)

perfectionism In this style of distorted thinking, individuals do not tolerate their own mistakes and expect to achieve at the optimum level. (Chapter 8)

physical environment A factor in listening and concentration that consists of all elements outside the individual such as lighting, sounds, room, and other people. (Chapter 9)

polarized thinking A style of distorted thinking in which the individual views events and people in dichotomous terms (i.e., good/bad, right/wrong) and allows no middle ground. (Chapter 8)

poor-retrieval theory The belief that forgetting occurs not because of decay, distortion, repression, or inhibition, but simply because information is not accessible at the moment it is needed. (Chapter 12)

positive self-control The acceptance of responsibility for the things a person can control while developing learning skills; it increases the chances for personal and professional success. (Chapter 2)

posttest debriefing A procedure followed after an exam in which the student compares the contents of the exam to several factors, including preparation, notes, readings, and preparation for future tests. (Chapter 13)

previewing A procedure for preparing to read in which the reader pages through a chapter, reads paragraph headings and their first sentences, asks questions, attends to illustrations, and reads the summary/conclusions. (Chapter 11)

qualifiers Qualifying words that modify the meaning of a statement and include words such as always, never, and sometimes. (Chapter 11)

receiver The person in the general communication model accepting the message from the speaker or sender. (Chapters 9, 16)

reciting A strategy for improving reading comprehension in which the reader reads aloud or recites the material in his or her own words. (Chapter 11)

recognition tests Examinations, such as multiple-choice, true/false, and matching, in which the student must recognize and choose the correct answer from a selection of answers. (Chapter 13)

referent power A source of power that is acquired through the respect and admiration by others for what you have done so far. (Chapter 18)

reflective observation Kolb's orientation or preference to approaching new problems that is characterized by the reliance on patient, thoughtful, and impartial observation from several perspectives. (Chapter 17)

rehearsal strategies Techniques that promote remembering by copying, repeating, reciting, taking notes, and underlining material. (Chapter 12)

remembering The active process of recalling something that has already been learned or experienced. (Chapter 12)

rereading A strategy for improving reading comprehension that is often combined with questioning to increase effectiveness. (Chapter 11)

retrieval tests A form of examination, such as the essay, in which the student must recall, reconstruct, and communicate the correct answer. (Chapter 13)

reviewing A process of summarizing reading material or notes to strengthen reading comprehension and remembering. (Chapter 11)

reward power   Power that derives from a person's ability to reward other persons. (Chapter 18)

self-contracting   A behavior-modification technique for providing feedback composed of a written agreement with yourself to perform specific actions and in return, receive specific rewards. (Chapter 6)

self-disclosure   A condition for developing interpersonal communications in which the sender and receiver reveal themselves to each other according to different levels such as facts, opinions, and feelings. (Chapter 16)

sender   In the general communication model, the sender or speaker transmits the message to the receiver. (Chapter 16)

sensory memory   The first component of the memory system in which information is received through the senses but remains for a fraction of a second before it is transferred to short-term memory or dropped out of memory. (Chapter 12)

short-term goals   Specific and realistic objectives that can be accomplished within a year. (Chapter 3)

short-term memory   The second component of the memory system, which receives information from the sensory system and stores about seven pieces of information for up to 30 seconds before transferring it to long-term memory or letting it drop out of memory. (Chapter 12)

shoulds   In this style of distorted thinking, individuals follow a list of absolute ideas to govern their own and others' behavior. (Chapter 8)

speaker   The speaker component of the general communication model is the person who transmits the message to the receiver. (Chapter 9)

stress   A straining force or side effect produced by any situation to which we respond. (Chapter 8)

student-centered communication   A pattern of classroom expression in which motivated and prepared students interact with each other and the teacher. (Chapter 17)

study habit   The habit of studying at regular times in the same places in order to associate the act of studying with a particular time and place. (Chapter 6)

surface strategy   An ineffective approach to learning characterized by the tendency to react to material passively, memorize, ignore principles or patterns, and ignore connections with prior learning. (Chapter 1)

synthesis level   The fifth level of the Bloom taxonomy characterized by the combining of ideas to form a new idea or concept. (Chapters 13, 14)

teacher-centered communication   A pattern of classroom expression in which the teacher communicates to students, but discourages communication from or among students. (Chapter 17)

term schedule   A form blocked for seven days that records the weekly routine of activities during an academic term. (Chapter 5)

transitional knowing   The second of Baxter Magolda's stages of cognitive development characterized by the recognition of multiple perspectives of uncertain knowledge. (Chapter 14)

TPI (Time Per Item)   The amount of time, on the average, allocated to complete a test question after deducting time for surveying, editing, and proofreading an exam. (Chapter 13)

trust   A condition for developing interpersonal communication in which the sender and receiver develop confidence in each other's honesty and integrity. (Chapter 16)

victim of circumstances   A style of distorted thinking in which individuals believe they have no control over events in their life and are helpless to do anything. (Chapter 8)

weekly work list   A form blocked so as to record each course assignment, due date, resources needed, and estimated and actual times to complete each task for a week. (Chapter 5)

Name Index

Adams, H., 283
Adelman, P. B., 205
Adler, R. B., 343
Adler, T., 250, 256
Agnes, M., 259, 280
Albright, M., 386
Alexander, D. K., 118, 130
Alighieri, D., 184
Andreas, B., 138, 159
Andretti, M., 36
Appleby, D. C., 295–296, 305, 350–351, 362
Aristotle, 319
Austin, N., 343

Bahrick, H., 250
Baird, J. E., 327, 343
Barker, L. L., 167–168, 182
Baron, A. 118, 130
Baron, R. A., 20, 22, 32, 34, 38, 49
Baxter Magolda, M. B., 284, 289–295, 303, 305, 361–362, 384, 389
Beebe, S., 319
Beebe, S., 319 [different from above]
Beirne-Smith, 188, 203
Belenky, M. F., 346, 363
Benson, H., 147, 159
Benton, S. L., 184, 204
Best, J. B., 274, 281
Black, C., 159
Blane, J. P., 29, 32
Bloom, B. S., 284–288, 293–296, 303, 305
Burley-Allen, M., 173, 181

Camus, A., 46
Carnevale, A. P., 56, 62
Chickering, A., 387–389
Christian, D., 197, 204
Churchill, W., 51, 58
Clinchy, B. M., 346, 363
Collins, M., 57, 62
Combs, P., 130
Costner, N., 167, 179, 181
Covey, S. R., 65, 82, 106

David, M., 159
DaVinci, L., 236
Davis, M., 163
DeMille, C. B., 34, 46
Disraeli, B., 96
Dixon, N. M., 357, 363
Donne, J., 345
DuBois, N. F., 197, 204
Duffy, G. G., 219, 228

Egan, G., 343
Englehart, M. D., 284, 305
Entwistle, N., 9, 12
Erickson, B. L., 3, 12
Erikson, E. H., 14, 16, 32
Estell, D., 228
Evans, M., 7

Fanning, P., 163
Flatley, J. K., 42, 49
Ford, H., 302
Franklin, B., 64
Fuller, T., 234
Furst, E. J., 284, 305

Gabor, D., 343
Gainer, L. J., 56, 62
Gardner, J., 130, 385
Gibbs, N. 386, 389
Goldberger, N. R., 346, 363
Gowin, D. B., 239, 240, 257
Gracian, B., 365
Grasha, A. F., 363, 371–372, 382, 384
Greenberg, J., 20, 22, 32, 34, 38, 49
Guterman, M. S., 159

Halonen, J., 282–283, 305
Halpern, D., 305
Hamachek, D., 235, 237, 256
Hamilton, C., 177, 182
Hanna, M. S., 343
Hanson, C., 93, 106
Hantz, A. M., 343

395

Subject Index

To the owner of this book:

I enjoyed writing *Learning Skills for College and Career,* Second Edition, and I hope you have enjoyed reading it. So that this book can be improved in a future edition, would you take the time to complete this sheet and return it? Thank you.

School _____

Instructor's name (optional) _____

1. What did you like *most* about the book? _____

   _____

   _____

   _____

   _____

2. What did you like *least* about this book? _____

   _____

   _____

   _____

   _____

3. In what course did you use this book? _____

   _____

4. In the space below or on a separate sheet of paper, please write specific suggestions for improving this book and anything else you'd care to share about your experience in using the book. _____

   _____

   _____

   _____

   _____

   _____

   _____

Optional:

Your name: _____ Date: _____

May Brooks/Cole quote you, either in promotion for *Learning Skills for College and Career*, Second Edition, or in future publishing ventures?

Yes: _____ No: _____

Sincerely,

Paul Hettich